Modern Concurrency in Java
Virtual Threads, Structured Concurrency, and Beyond

A N M Bazlur Rahman

O'REILLY®

Modern Concurrency in Java

by A N M Bazlur Rahman

Copyright © 2025 A N M Bazlur Rahman. All rights reserved.

Published by O'Reilly Media, Inc., 141 Stony Circle, Suite 195, Santa Rosa, CA 95401.

O'Reilly books may be purchased for educational, business, or sales promotional use. Online editions are also available for most titles (*https://oreilly.com*). For more information, contact our corporate/institutional sales department: 800-998-9938 or *corporate@oreilly.com*.

Acquisitions Editor: Louise Corrigan
Development Editor: Angela Rufino
Production Editor: Jonathon Owen
Copyeditor: Audrey Doyle
Proofreader: Miah Sandvik

Indexer: nSight, Inc.
Cover Designer: Karen Montgomery
Cover Illustrator: José Marzan Jr.
Interior Designer: David Futato
Interior Illustrator: Kate Dullea

September 2025: First Edition

Revision History for the First Edition
2025-09-16: First Release

See *https://oreilly.com/catalog/errata.csp?isbn=9781098165413* for release details.

The O'Reilly logo is a registered trademark of O'Reilly Media, Inc. *Modern Concurrency in Java*, the cover image, and related trade dress are trademarks of O'Reilly Media, Inc.

The views expressed in this work are those of the author and do not represent the publisher's views. While the publisher and the author have used good faith efforts to ensure that the information and instructions contained in this work are accurate, the publisher and the author disclaim all responsibility for errors or omissions, including without limitation responsibility for damages resulting from the use of or reliance on this work. Use of the information and instructions contained in this work is at your own risk. If any code samples or other technology this work contains or describes is subject to open source licenses or the intellectual property rights of others, it is your responsibility to ensure that your use thereof complies with such licenses and/or rights.

978-1-098-16541-3

[LSI]

To my daughter, Rushda, whose love, growth, and boundless curiosity inspired the pages of this book. The sound of your laughter and your playful interruptions motivated every word I wrote.

To my beloved wife, Tabassum, for your unwavering support and for creating the loving space that allowed me to complete this journey.

Table of Contents

Preface. ix

1. Introduction. 1
    A Brief History of Threads in Java   1
        Java Is Made of Threads   2
        Threads: The Backbone of the Java Platform   4
    The Genesis of Java 1.0 Threads   6
        Starting Threads   8
    Understanding the Hidden Costs of Threads   9
        How Many Threads Can You Create?   10
    Resource Efficiency in High-Scale Applications   11
        The Parallel Execution Strategy   13
        Introducing the Executor Framework   18
        Remaining Challenges   19
    Beyond Basic Thread Pools   21
        Cache Affinity and Task Distribution   21
        Work-Stealing Algorithm   21
        Bringing Composability into Play with CompletableFuture   23
    A Different Paradigm for Asynchronous Programming   25
        Drawbacks of Using Reactive Frameworks   26
    Revolutionizing Concurrency in Java   28
        The Promise of Virtual Threads   28
        Seamless Integration with Existing Codebases   29
        Virtual Threads and Platform Threads   29
        Intelligent Handling of Blocking Operations   29
        Benefits of Embracing Virtual Threads   30
    In Closing   30

2. Understanding Virtual Threads... 31
What Is a Virtual Thread? 31
   The Two Kinds of Threads in Java 32
   Key Differences from Platform Threads 33
Setting Up Your Environment for Virtual Threads 34
   Creating Virtual Threads in Java 36
Adapting to Virtual Threads 37
Demonstrating Virtual Thread Creation in Java 40
   Throughput and Scalability 41
   The Fundamental Principle Behind Virtual Threads' Scalability 42
   The Practical Implications 45
How Virtual Threads Work Under the Hood 46
   Stack Frames and Memory Management 46
   Carrier Threads and OS Involvement 46
   Handling Blocking Operations 46
   Transparency and Invisibility 47
   Simplifying Asynchronous Operations 47
   The Promise of Structured Concurrency 50
Managing Resource Constraints with Rate Limiting 51
   Understanding Semaphores in Java 54
   Why Use a Semaphore? 59
Limitations of Virtual Threads 61
   Pinning 62
   Addressing the Pinning Problem with ReentrantLock 64
   Native Method Invocation and Pinning 68
The Conundrum of ThreadLocal Variables in Virtual Threads 71
   Challenges with Virtual Threads 72
Monitoring 74
   Monitoring ThreadLocals 75
   Monitoring Pinning 76
   Viewing Virtual Threads in jcmd Thread Dumps 81
Generating Thread Dumps with HotSpotDiagnosticsMXBean 86
Practical Tips for Migrating to Virtual Threads 86
   Reaffirming the Benefits of Virtual Threads 87
   It's About Scalability 88
In Closing 89

3. The Mechanics of Modern Concurrency in Java........................... 91
Thread Pool 91
   Why Do We Need a Thread Pool? 92
   Building a Simple Thread Pool in Java 92

The Executor Framework	96
Callable and Future: Handling Task Results	101
The ForkJoinPool	103
Why ForkJoinPool for Virtual Threads?	108
Continuation	113
Building Our Own Virtual Threads from Scratch	117
Virtual Threads and I/O Polling	122
In Closing	123

4. Structured Concurrency... 125
The Challenge of Unstructured Concurrency	126
The Promise of Structured Concurrency	132
Understanding the API	133
StructuredTaskScope	133
Scopes and Subtasks: Relationship and Lifecycle	138
Joining Policies with Joiner	139
Common Joining Policies	140
Exception Handling in StructuredTaskScope	166
Configuration	179
Custom Joiners	185
Memory Consistency Effects	202
Nested Scopes	205
Observability	209
In Closing	214

5. Scoped Values... 217
The Burden of Passing Context	217
Parameter Pollution	220
Interface Brittleness	220
Coupling and Testability	220
Introducing ThreadLocal	220
Limitations of ThreadLocal Variables	222
Toward Lightweight Sharing	225
Core Components of ScopedValue	225
Running ScopedValue	228
ScopedValue and Structured Concurrency	235
Performance Considerations	236
Usability and API Design	236
Migrating to Scoped Values	237
In Closing	245

6. **The Relevance of Reactive Java in Light of Virtual Threads.............. 247**
    Understanding Reactive Programming in Java   248
        Blocking Versus Non-blocking I/O   249
        Event-Driven Architecture   272
        Asynchronous APIs   276
    Reactive Programming in Java   279
        Understanding Reactive Streams   279
        Backpressure   286
        Benefits and Downsides of Reactive Programming   292
    In Closing   294

7. **Modern Frameworks Utilizing Virtual Threads............................... 297**
    Spring Boot   297
        Manual Configuration   300
    Quarkus   302
        Jakarta EE   306
    In Closing   309

8. **Conclusion and Takeaways... 311**

Index.. 313

Preface

Why I Wrote This Book

Concurrency has long been one of the most challenging aspects of Java development. It has consistently evolved to meet the demands of modern software development while maintaining a strong commitment to backward compatibility. Among all the advancements Java has introduced over the years, Project Loom's introduction of virtual threads marks a fundamental shift in the world of concurrency.

Concurrency is inherently challenging, and this difficulty has only increased with the rise in performance demands. Even for seasoned developers, managing it effectively remains a complex task. Today, modern applications are primarily I/O-driven, as they interact with numerous other systems, especially within the microservices architecture that dominates recent software development to meet the growing demands of scalability.

I/O operations often take a significant amount of time. When a thread makes an I/O call, it typically has to wait for the operation to complete, which has been the traditional approach. While modern operating systems can manage millions of open sockets, the number of available threads remains limited. As a result, meeting the growing demand for higher throughput with traditional threads has become increasingly complex.

In response to this limitation, various techniques and alternative concurrency models have been devised, but each comes with its own set of trade-offs. Virtual threads represent a promising solution by leveraging lightweight, user-mode threads that can be multiplexed onto a smaller number of kernel threads. This approach enables more efficient use of system resources. It enhances scalability, marking a notable improvement in the world of concurrency.

When I first encountered virtual threads, I was immediately intrigued. They felt like a long-awaited breakthrough that could fundamentally change how we write concurrent programs on the JVM, offering a simple and elegant solution where Java previously lacked one.

I began experimenting with virtual threads, documenting my findings on my blog, and speaking at conferences. The enthusiastic response from the developer community reaffirmed that virtual threads were not just another enhancement but a fundamental shift in the approach to concurrency.

As I continued to explore, I discovered a wealth of resources emerging around virtual threads—official documentation, insightful blog posts, GitHub repositories with real-world examples, and excellent conference sessions. While these resources were individually valuable, each focused on different aspects of the topic. Some addressed technical implementations, while others discussed migration strategies and specific use cases.

Through continuous writing, speaking, and hands-on work, I gained a clearer and more comprehensive understanding of the subject. This exploration provided a comprehensive understanding of the motivations behind project Loom, its integration with Java's existing concurrency model, and its implications for building scalable and maintainable systems. My respect for Java's ability to adapt to change while maintaining backward compatibility has only intensified throughout this journey.

Eventually, I realized there was an opportunity to consolidate all this understanding into a single, practical resource. This book is not just a theoretical exploration but a practical, hands-on guide that gathers all the necessary concepts, examples, and best practices into a single, comprehensive resource.

Who This Book Is For

This book is designed for Java developers who already possess a foundational understanding of concurrency and multithreading. It is not a beginner's guide to these topics. Instead, it targets those who have experience writing concurrent programs using traditional tools, such as `Thread`, `ExecutorService`, synchronization, and collection utilities like `ReentrantLock` and `Semaphore`, and are looking to deepen their understanding of the modern concurrency features introduced in recent Java releases, particularly virtual threads, structured concurrency, and scoped values. If you're looking to learn the fundamentals of concurrency, *Java Concurrency in Practice* by Brian Goetz (Addison-Wesley Professional) is still the recommended book.

If you've ever encountered challenges with thread exhaustion, blocking I/O, thread pool tuning, or managing complex lifecycle and cancellation logic, this book will help you rethink these issues in light of Java's evolving concurrency model. It is particularly beneficial for:

- Mid- to senior-level developers aiming to modernize their concurrent code
- Architects designing scalable systems
- Performance-oriented engineers interested in building robust concurrent applications
- Team leads assessing new technologies
- Anyone curious about the future of Java concurrency

Junior developers with a basic understanding of Java will also find this book useful for an overview of modern concurrency. However, a prior or concurrent study of foundational topics such as synchronization, race conditions, and data publishing is highly recommended for a complete understanding. These fundamentals are vital for effectively writing concurrent code in your applications. While some modern frameworks hide these details from everyday developers, things become critical when encountering a serious bug. Fundamental knowledge is always essential for understanding the subject, and concurrency is no exception.

What This Book Offers

This book consolidates everything I've learned about Project Loom and virtual threads into one comprehensive resource. Inside, you will find:

- An exploration of Java's concurrency evolution, from platform threads and the Executor framework to CompletableFuture and reactive programming
- A deep dive into the mechanics of virtual threads, structured concurrency, and scoped values
- Practical, real-world examples that demonstrate how to apply these new features effectively
- Extensive coverage of not only virtual threads but also structured concurrency and scoped values
- Guidance on how modern frameworks like Spring Boot, Quarkus, and Jakarta EE are integrating virtual threads

Whether you are new to virtual threads or have been following Project Loom from its inception, you will discover valuable insights and practical knowledge.

The examples and concepts in this book require at least JDK 21, as that is when virtual threads became officially available. However, some chapters discuss features that are still in preview or have been recently finalized. Therefore, having access to a newer JDK version, such as 24 or even 25, will enable you to make the most of all the examples and discussions.

How This Book Is Organized

This book is structured to take you on a journey from understanding the importance of virtual threads to mastering their use in production applications. Here's what you can expect in each chapter:

Chapter 1, "Introduction"
We begin by exploring the evolution of concurrency in Java, tracing its development from platform threads through the Executor framework, Fork/Join, and CompletableFuture, with a brief introduction to reactive programming. This historical context helps you appreciate why virtual threads are a game changer. You'll discover the trade-offs we've made over the years and understand why Project Loom takes a fundamentally different approach.

Chapter 2, "Understanding Virtual Threads"
In this chapter, we introduce virtual threads in a hands-on manner. You'll learn what they are, how they differ from platform threads, and how to create them. We explore throughput improvements, scalability benefits, and practical examples. Key topics include rate limiting with Semaphores and important limitations such as pinning and ThreadLocal considerations.

Chapter 3, "The Mechanics of Modern Concurrency in Java"
This chapter dives deep into the mechanics of concurrency. We investigate thread pools, the Executor framework, and the ForkJoinPool that powers virtual threads. A key highlight is building our own virtual thread implementation from scratch using continuations. By creating NanoThreads, you'll gain a profound understanding of how virtual threads operate under the hood.

Chapter 4, "Structured Concurrency"
Here, we discuss one of Project Loom's most significant innovations: StructuredTaskScope. You'll learn how it addresses the problems of unstructured concurrency, master different joining policies, handle exceptions gracefully, and build robust concurrent applications. The chapter covers everything from basic usage to custom joiners and nested scopes. Please note that at the time of writing, structured concurrency is still in preview. I hope this preview version remains largely unchanged, but if there are updates, I will address them in subsequent editions.

Chapter 5, "Scoped Values"
Context propagation in highly concurrent applications has always posed challenges. This chapter demonstrates how scoped values provide a superior alternative to ThreadLocal for virtual threads. You'll learn the API, see practical examples in the context of structured concurrency, and understand when and how to transition from ThreadLocal.

Chapter 6, *"The Relevance of Reactive Java in Light of Virtual Threads"*
In this chapter, we aim to understand the differences in approaching concurrency between virtual threads and reactive programming. We examine the differences between blocking and nonblocking I/O, event-driven architecture, and the trade-offs associated with each approach. This chapter will help you make informed choices about when to utilize virtual threads versus reactive frameworks.

Chapter 7, *"Modern Frameworks Utilizing Virtual Threads"*
Explore how major frameworks are embracing virtual threads. We cover Spring Boot, Quarkus, and Jakarta EE, providing practical configuration examples and best practices. This chapter bridges the gap between learning about virtual threads and applying them in production environments.

Chapter 8, *"Conclusion and Takeaways"*
We conclude with key insights and a look at the future of concurrent programming in Java.

How to Read This Book

This book is designed to be read sequentially, as each chapter builds on concepts from the previous ones. However, if you are already familiar with certain topics, feel free to jump ahead to the chapters that interest you the most.

For beginners to virtual threads
Start with Chapter 1 to understand the historical context, then proceed through each chapter in order.

For experienced developers
If you prefer, you may skim Chapter 1 and proceed directly to Chapter 2 for hands-on experience with virtual threads. Don't skip Chapter 3; building virtual threads from scratch provides invaluable insights.

For architects and team leads
Pay special attention to Chapters 4–5, which cover structured concurrency and scoped values, as well as Chapter 6, which compares these concepts with reactive programming. This will aid in making informed architectural decisions.

A Hands-On Approach

Each chapter includes plenty of code examples, and I expect that as you read, you'll have your IDE open to try out the code examples one by one. Don't just read the code; run it, modify it, break it, and fix it. There's no better way to internalize these concepts than through experimentation.

For your convenience, all source code is available at *https://github.com/Modern-Concurrency-in-Java*. Each chapter comes with its own package containing fully runnable examples. I strongly encourage you to write the code yourself while reading the book. However, if you prefer to skim and experiment with the code, feel free to clone the repository before you begin reading.

If you have a technical question or a problem using the code examples, please send an email to *support@oreilly.com*.

This book is here to help you get your job done. In general, if example code is offered with this book, you may use it in your programs and documentation. You do not need to contact us for permission unless you're reproducing a significant portion of the code. For example, writing a program that uses several chunks of code from this book does not require permission. Selling or distributing examples from O'Reilly books does require permission. Answering a question by citing this book and quoting example code does not require permission. Incorporating a significant amount of example code from this book into your product's documentation does require permission.

We appreciate, but generally do not require, attribution. An attribution usually includes the title, author, publisher, and ISBN. For example: "*Modern Concurrency in Java* by A N M Bazlur Rahman (O'Reilly). Copyright 2025 A N M Bazlur Rahman, 978-1-098-16541-3."

If you feel your use of code examples falls outside fair use or the permission given above, feel free to contact us at *permissions@oreilly.com*.

Conventions Used in This Book

The following typographical conventions are used in this book:

Italic
    Indicates new terms, URLs, email addresses, filenames, and file extensions.

`Constant width`
    Used for program listings, as well as within paragraphs to refer to program elements such as variable or function names, databases, data types, environment variables, statements, and keywords.

`Constant width bold`
    Shows commands or other text that should be typed literally by the user.

`Constant width italic`
    Shows text that should be replaced with user-supplied values or by values determined by context.

This element signifies a tip or suggestion.

This element signifies a general note.

This element indicates a warning or caution.

O'Reilly Online Learning

For more than 40 years, *O'Reilly Media* has provided technology and business training, knowledge, and insight to help companies succeed.

Our unique network of experts and innovators share their knowledge and expertise through books, articles, and our online learning platform. O'Reilly's online learning platform gives you on-demand access to live training courses, in-depth learning paths, interactive coding environments, and a vast collection of text and video from O'Reilly and 200+ other publishers. For more information, visit *https://oreilly.com*.

How to Contact Us

Please address comments and questions concerning this book to the publisher:

O'Reilly Media, Inc.
141 Stony Circle, Suite 195
Santa Rosa, CA 95401
800-889-8969 (in the United States or Canada)
707-827-7019 (international or local)
707-829-0104 (fax)
support@oreilly.com
https://oreilly.com/about/contact.html

We have a web page for this book, where we list errata and any additional information. You can access this page at *htttps://oreil.ly/modern-concurrency-java*.

For news and information about our books and courses, visit *htttps://oreilly.com*.

Find us on LinkedIn: *https://linkedin.com/company/oreilly-media*

Watch us on YouTube: *https://youtube.com/oreillymedia*

Acknowledgments

First and foremost, I am deeply grateful to Allah (glory be to Him, the Exalted) for granting me the strength, patience, and opportunity to complete this book. Without His help, this journey would not have been possible.

I extend my heartfelt thanks to my wife and daughter, who made the greatest sacrifice by allowing me the time to write, time we could have spent together. Their support, patience, and love carried me through the many long nights and weekends dedicated to this project. This book is as much theirs as it is mine, and I am deeply grateful for their understanding and unwavering support.

I would also like to thank my parents, whose pride in my work continues to inspire me. Witnessing their joy with each book I write is one of my greatest rewards and motivates me to continue pushing the boundaries of my writing. Additionally, I am grateful to my father-in-law and mother-in-law for their enthusiasm and encouragement regarding my work. Their warm support and genuine excitement are absolutely invaluable to me.

I would like to express my appreciation to the reviewers, editors, and the entire production team at O'Reilly. Thank you for your trust and tireless efforts in shaping this book. To the Java community, your ideas, discussions, and contributions surrounding Project Loom and modern concurrency have been invaluable. Your role in helping me write a book that is both practical and forward-looking cannot be overstated.

Finally, to you, the reader: thank you for taking the time to pick up this book. I hope it empowers you to write better, safer, and more modern concurrent Java code. I look forward to hearing about your experiences with the book and its impact on your work.

CHAPTER 1
Introduction

> *Concurrency is about dealing with lots of things at once. Parallelism is about doing lots of things at once.*
> —Rob Pike

To truly appreciate something, it is crucial to know how it came to be, especially if we can discern the steps taken and the challenges overcome along the way. This understanding not only highlights ongoing progress but also helps us understand its relevance. Similarly, Java concurrency has come a long way since its inception. It took a long time to evolve to its current state. But if we want to understand recent advancements, such as virtual threads and structured concurrency in modern Java, we must first delve into its evolution. In this chapter, we will give you an initial view of Java concurrency and then briefly discuss how it has developed over time.

A Brief History of Threads in Java

Java was designed with concurrency in mind; it was one of the first languages to provide built-in support for multithreading. Over the years, Java's concurrency capabilities have been improved and refined, leaving behind some potholes and lessons along the way.

Java concurrency began with basic synchronization and thread management. Then came the introduction of the java.util.concurrent (*https://oreil.ly/5e8s1*) package in Java 5, which brought important new capabilities such as the Executor framework (*https://oreil.ly/lDFVL*), locks, and concurrent collections. Next, with the introduction of the Fork/Join framework in Java 7, Java engaged the concurrency performance of multicore processors. And most recently, with Project Loom (*https://oreil.ly/gcaYC*), Java addressed the complexity and limitations of traditional thread-based concurrency, with lightweight, user-mode threads and structured concurrency, ultimately aiming to make concurrent development simpler and more efficient.

Why does this evolution matter so much? As we uncover how Java's concurrency story unfolds, we discover a relentless pursuit of greater efficiency and simplified programming in the face of ever-growing complexity. This narrative extends beyond just Java; it reflects the trajectory of software development and Java's continued aspirations.

Let's dive deeper into understanding this evolution and appreciate the strides made in Java concurrency.

Java Is Made of Threads

Concurrency was an explicit design goal of Java, a language that was released with built-in thread capability and a threading feature that was a key differentiator of the language. It removed developers' dependency on operating-system-specific features to achieve concurrency.

In Java, a thread is the smallest unit of execution. It is an independent path of execution running within a program. Threads share the same address space, meaning they have access to the same variables and data structures of the program. However, each thread maintains its own program counter, stack, and local variables, enabling it to operate independently. This design also facilitates interaction among threads when necessary.

However, Java's threading model relies on the underlying operating system to schedule and execute threads. The operating system allocates CPU time to each thread, managing the transition between threads to ensure efficient execution. By distributing threads across multiple CPUs, the system can achieve true parallelism, enhancing the performance of concurrent applications (Figure 1-1).

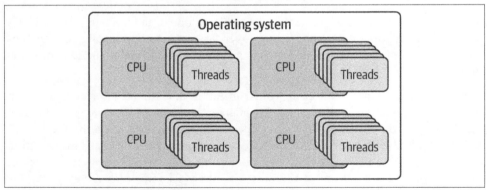

Figure 1-1. Execution of threads by different CPUs

The more threads we can have in a Java program, the more execution environment we effectively create. This gives us the ability to execute several operations simultaneously. This is particularly beneficial for applications that require high levels of parallelism or concurrency, such as web servers, data processing pipelines, and real-time systems. By leveraging multiple threads, these applications can perform multiple tasks simultaneously, thereby improving throughput and responsiveness.

Parallelism Versus Concurrency

The terms *parallelism* and *concurrency* are often used interchangeably. However, they mean two different things. Parallelism entails doing more than one thing simultaneously, so multiple processing units, such as two or more CPU cores, are needed. Concurrency is about designing programs where portions of their operation can overlap—even if not always simultaneously. Think of parallelism as multiple workers building a house side-by-side, while concurrency is like a single chef juggling multiple dishes in the kitchen. Now, if we add more chefs to the kitchen, the overall output improves, but it is not necessarily parallel; one chef might be chopping onions while another is putting a dish in the oven. The end goal remains preparing the meal—perhaps even multiple meals.

The notion of threads forms the very fabric of how the entire Java ecosystem is implemented and how it functions. It's the bedrock on which lots of powerful features and tools are based, and functions that many programmers take for granted simply wouldn't be possible without it. Whether it's the garbage collection system, which tackles the problem of memory management in Java, or the process of executing the simple output of a "Hello, World!" program in Java, threads are working away in the background.

Here's an example. Anyone who has written a Java program, even for the first time, will be familiar with the line most programming books start out with. It may seem like a single-threaded operation; however, the Java Virtual Machine (JVM) actually executes this code in a thread, commonly referred to as the *main thread*:

```
public class HelloWorld {
  public static void main(String[] args) {
    System.out.println("Hello, World!");
        // Displaying the thread that's executing the main method
    System.out.println("Executed by thread: "
        + Thread.currentThread().getName());
  }
}
```

When we run this program, the output would include the name of the thread executing the main method, which is typically `main`:

```
Hello, World!
Executed by thread: main
```

This example shows that even the most basic Java programs are already fundamentally threaded. The implication is profound: we, as Java developers, are harnessing the power of threads, whether we realize it or not, in virtually every part of our job, from running the most straightforward programs to using even the most advanced techniques, such as garbage collection.

And so, threads are a required element of Java—they're part of what makes Java a language that can scale up to handle large databases and massive distributed systems.

Threads: The Backbone of the Java Platform

Java threads are integral to all layers of the Java platform, playing a crucial role in various aspects beyond just executing code. For instance, they're the basis of exception handling, debugging, and profiling Java applications.

Exceptions and threads

In Java, every thread has its own separate call stack that records all method call invocations done during the thread's lifetime. When an exception is raised, that thread's call stack becomes a vital part of the diagnostic history; it shows the sequence of method invocations that led to the exception, helping developers trace the root cause of an issue. Here's that same example again:

```
import java.sql.SQLException;

public class CallStackDemo {
  public static void main(String[] args) throws InterruptedException {
    Thread thread = new Thread(CallStackDemo::processOrder);
    thread.setName("mcj-thread");
    thread.start();
    thread.join();
  }

  static void processOrder() {
    validateOrderDetails();
  }

  static void validateOrderDetails() {
    checkInventory();
  }

  static void checkInventory() {
    updateDatabase();
  }

  static void updateDatabase() {
    try {
```

```
          throw new SQLException("Database connection error");
      } catch (SQLException e) {
        throw new InventoryUpdateException("Database Error: " +
            "Unable to update inventory", e);
      }
    }
  }
}

class InventoryUpdateException extends RuntimeException {
  public InventoryUpdateException(String message, Throwable cause) {
    super(message, cause);
  }
}
```

In this scenario, the database update operation fails, which propagates back up the call stack. The main thread starts calling processOrder, which calls validateOrderDetails, which calls checkInventory, which calls updateDatabase, which then throws the exception. We now will get the following output in the console:

```
Exception in thread "mcj-thread" ca.bazlur.mcj.chap1.InventoryUpdateException:
Database Error: Unable to update inventory
    at ca.bazlur.mcj.chap1.CallStackDemo.updateDatabase(CallStackDemo.java:33)
    at ca.bazlur.mcj.chap1.CallStackDemo.checkInventory(CallStackDemo.java:26)
    at ca.bazlur.mcj.chap1.CallStackDemo.
    validateOrderDetails(CallStackDemo.java:22)
    at ca.bazlur.mcj.chap1.CallStackDemo.processOrder(CallStackDemo.java:18)
    at java.base/java.lang.Thread.run(Thread.java:1583)
Caused by: java.sql.SQLException: Database connection error
    at ca.bazlur.mcj.chap1.CallStackDemo.updateDatabase(CallStackDemo.java:31)
    ... 4 more
```

This trace allows developers to inspect the call stack within a specific thread context (i.e., the context of the mcj-thread thread where the exception occurred). This granularity is highly beneficial in the JVM, especially for debugging multithreaded applications where several threads may run concurrently on the same or different tasks. This detail helps us pinpoint issues faster, making debugging more focused and efficient, and leading to a quicker resolution.

Debugger and threads

How does the Java debugger figure out where exactly to pause the execution of a running application? The answer again is threading. By attaching itself to the various threads in the application, the debugger can select which of these individual threads to examine or even change their state while debugging an active application. This is fundamental to your ability to find and fix bugs in applications where several threads might be simultaneously executing at different stages, and where different threads might be interacting in ways that need to be understood.

Each action can be "stepped into," "stepped over," or "stepped out of" with respect to a thread. One or more independent call stacks for the active threads may be inspected in a debugging session. The call stack tells you what happened before, such as what caused a thread to be at a given point in a program. Understanding how a thread got to a certain state is invaluable when you're trying to figure out the cause of an unexpected exception or an erroneous data manipulation.

Profiler and threads

Threads are equally vital to understanding Java's operational dynamics, and they play a crucial role in profiling. Just as threading facilitates pinpoint precision in debugging, its utility extends to offering a granular perspective in profiling practices. In fact, threads are the backbone of performance analysis in Java. Profiling tools rely on threads to give you a detailed look at how your application is running. They use thread information to pinpoint slowdowns, troubleshoot tricky timing issues in multithreaded code, and help you find ways to make your application run faster. In short, threads are the key to understanding and improving the performance of your multithreaded Java applications.

Java threads play a significant role in many operations, such as diagnosis, debugging, and profiling, by providing detailed insight into the execution of individual thread-level programs. Despite not being directly used by developers, they keep operating underneath and augment the benefits of Java applications as well. Examples of this are garbage collection threads used for the management of memory; compiler threads in the just-in-time (JIT) system for performance enhancement; signal dispatcher, finalizer, and reference handler threads for smooth execution of JVM; and virtual machine (VM) and service threads for the core JVM tasks and diagnostics. Hence, it is easy to say that Java threads are one of the most essential layers of the Java platform, and a Java developer needs to understand them.

The Genesis of Java 1.0 Threads

Java 1.0 was released in 1996 and came with built-in support for threads. This defining feature set it apart from many languages at that time. In the early days, you could create threads by either extending the `Thread` class or implementing the `Runnable` interface. For example:

```
public class ThreadCreationDemo {
  public static void main(String[] args) {
    // Extending Thread class
    Thread t1 = new ThreadByExtension("Worker-1"); ❶
    t1.start();
    // Implementing Runnable (classic)
    Thread t2 = new Thread(
        new RunnableImplementation(), "Worker-2"); ❷
    t2.start();
```

```java
    // Anonymous inner class (Java 1.1)
    Thread t3 = new Thread(new Runnable() { ❸
      @Override
      public void run() {
        System.out.println("Anonymous: " +
            Thread.currentThread().getName());
      }
    }, "Worker-3");
    t3.start();
    // Lambda expression (Java 8)
    Thread t4 = new Thread(() -> ❹
        System.out.println("Lambda: " +
            Thread.currentThread().getName()),
        "Worker-4");
    t4.start();
  }
}

class ThreadByExtension extends Thread {
  public ThreadByExtension(String name) {
    super(name);
  }
  @Override
  public void run() {
    System.out.println("Extended Thread: " + getName());
  }
}

class RunnableImplementation implements Runnable {
  @Override
  public void run() {
    System.out.println("Runnable: " +
        Thread.currentThread().getName());
  }
}
```

Key design considerations from the start:

❶ Thread extension offers direct access to thread methods but uses up your single inheritance slot.

❷ The `Runnable` implementation became the preferred approach, separating task definition from thread management and preserving inheritance flexibility.

❸ Anonymous inner classes (Java 1.1) reduced boilerplate for one-off tasks before lambdas existed.

❹ Lambda expressions (Java 8) made the `Runnable` implementation even more concise, since it's a functional interface.

This foundational API has remained unchanged for nearly three decades, demonstrating its robust design. While Java has added countless concurrency enhancements, from `java.util.concurrent` to virtual threads, these original building blocks remain the foundation of Java's threading model.

Starting Threads

Whichever method we choose for creating a thread begins by invoking the `start` method on the `Thread` object. This is an essential step because calling `start` does more than just execute the `run` method; it also performs setup tasks like allocating system resources. The `start` method subsequently calls the `run` method in a new thread of execution.

It's crucial not to call the `run` method directly. Doing so will execute the `run` method in the calling thread, not in a new thread.

However, in modern Java applications, using the Executor framework is more efficient than manually creating threads through constructors. Executors abstract the process of thread management by maintaining a thread pool—a group of pre-created threads ready for executing tasks. This method significantly reduces the overhead associated with creating new threads.

When a task is submitted to an executor, it's placed in a queue. A thread from the pool then picks up the task from the queue and executes it. This setup simplifies concurrent programming and optimizes resource utilization by reusing threads.

Here's a simple example demonstrating how to use an executor to manage a thread pool:

```java
import java.util.concurrent.ExecutorService;
import java.util.concurrent.Executors;

public class ExecutorExample {
    public static void main(String[] args) {
        try (ExecutorService executor = Executors.newFixedThreadPool(5)) {
            for (int i = 0; i < 10; i++) {
                final int taskId = i;
                executor.submit(() -> {
                    System.out.println("Executing task " + taskId
                            + " in thread " + Thread.currentThread().getName());
                });
            }
        }
    }
}
```

Understanding the Hidden Costs of Threads

Many of today's web applications run on a thread-per-request model, where a thread is assigned to each request—the thread manages the whole request/response lifecycle. For instance, let's consider the lifecycle of a request on a typical web application running under a servlet container (Apache Tomcat, Jetty, or any Java EE web server). A *servlet container* is software responsible for processing requests coming to the web application. When a request arrives at the servlet container, the container assigns the request to one of the threads in its thread pool to process the request. That thread fires up, in effect saying, "Hey, I got this request coming from the user. It's mine now; I'll take care of it." The thread essentially takes responsibility for processing the whole request/response lifecycle (Figure 1-2).

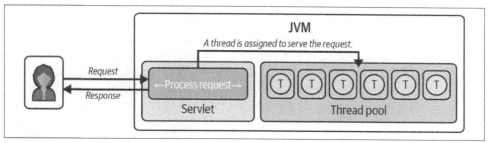

Figure 1-2. Thread pool handling servlet requests

This is particularly helpful when we have large numbers of simultaneous connections because increasing concurrency, in turn, increases the throughput of the web application. In fact, this is a key feature of the thread-per-request model, which allows modern web applications to scale in order to serve a growing volume of requests efficiently.

Amazingly, most modern operating systems can handle millions of concurrent connections, so it would seem reasonable to create yet more threads in order to improve throughput. More threads in the thread pool should indeed equate to more throughput, according to Little's Law.[1] However, even though that assumption appeared to be accurate, it turns out that this line of reasoning is a bit slippery—and will not always produce the expected results.

---

1 Little's Law is a key principle in queuing systems, including multithreaded applications. It relates latency, concurrency, and throughput, which are crucial for computing performance. In the next chapter, we'll discuss this in detail and demonstrate how higher concurrency leads to higher throughput.

Throughput in web applications is the rate at which requests are processed and the server delivers responses, typically measured in requests per second (RPS) or transactions per second (TPS). It indicates the application's capacity to handle load, serving as a critical metric for performance, scalability, and resource utilization. Throughput can be calculated as

$$\text{Throughput} = \frac{\text{Total Request Processed}}{\text{Total Time}}$$

This serves as a guide for benchmarking performance, scalability, and demand planning, and it paves the way for the optimal use of resources that ensure a quality user experience.

An important detail to bear in mind is the memory footprint of each thread: about 2 MiB[2] of memory (outside the heap per thread). This can quickly become a lot, especially in large-scale applications running thousands of concurrent connections—the aggregate memory footprint of the threads can make a world of difference in the actual number of connections you can run. Additionally, suppose your application uses all physical memory. In that case, you'll find yourself paging to disk, a significantly slower operation than even accessing RAM: the time-to-read difference when reading from disk versus RAM is a factor of 1,000. This alone can heavily impact performance.

Also, it is essential to understand that Java threads are actually a thin wrapper around the native threads provided by the host operating system. This means that the maximum number of threads you can create for any application is effectively limited by the native thread creation limit provided by the host operating system. Almost all operating systems have an upper limit on the number of threads that can be spawned. So an application's scalability potential is limited by this bottleneck.

Besides, there is the expense of context switching. Thread creation isn't just a memory overhead. It's also a CPU overhead. When you switch between threads, that's a context switch. The context of the current thread needs to be stored, and the context of the new thread needs to be brought back. All that context switching costs CPU cycles, and, on systems under high load, this overhead can make a huge difference in performance. This is another underappreciated source of weight in your application.

How Many Threads Can You Create?

Now that we have discussed the costs associated with threads, let's examine how to measure the limitation of thread creation in your environment. By running a simple

---

2 This is the default size in most Linux environments, but it depends on the operating system and can be tweaked.

test program, you can determine the maximum number of threads your system can handle before experiencing issues. Here's a skeleton code snippet to start:

```java
import java.util.concurrent.atomic.AtomicInteger;
import java.util.concurrent.locks.LockSupport;

public class ThreadLimitTest {
    public static void main(String[] args) {
        var threadCount = new AtomicInteger(0);
        try {
            while (true) {
                var thread = new Thread(() -> {
                    threadCount.incrementAndGet();
                    LockSupport.park();
                });
                thread.start();
            }
        } catch (OutOfMemoryError error) {
            System.out.println("Reached thread limit: " + threadCount);
            error.printStackTrace();
        }
    }
}
```

Let's execute this program to see how many threads can be created before running out of memory or hitting other system limitations:

```
Reached thread limit: 16363
java.lang.OutOfMemoryError: unable to create native thread: possibly out of
memory or process/resource limits reached
    at java.base/java.lang.Thread.start0(Native Method)
    at java.base/java.lang.Thread.start(Thread.java:1526)
    at ca.bazlur.chapter0.ThreadLimitTest.main(ThreadLimitTest.java:15)
```

On my machine, I encountered an `OutOfMemoryError` (*https://oreil.ly/vD03r*) after successfully creating 16,363 threads. This experiment highlights the point that there's a finite limit to the number of threads one can create, a constraint that is largely dictated by the underlying operating system and the hardware. Hence, the limit can be different on your machine.

As you can see, while threads provide substantial benefits in web application scalability, they do come with associated costs. These costs, though sometimes less obvious, should be carefully considered to ensure optimal performance.

Resource Efficiency in High-Scale Applications

Today's software applications are often expected to process large amounts of data and handle high volumes of incoming traffic simultaneously. These dynamics create a significant challenge for staying fiscally sound, especially when the cloud has become the default environment in which many businesses operate. Even the slightest degree of resource inefficiency can quickly turn into escalating costs. Since we have only a finite number of threads, it's essential to use them carefully. But threads get blocked in practice, so they're often not used effectively.

Consider the following example, where a method calculates a person's credit score based on various factors:

```
public Credit calculateCredit(Long personId) {
    var person = getPerson(personId);              // Database call - blocks thread
    var assets = getAssets(person);                // API call - blocks thread
    var liabilities = getLiabilities(person);      // Database call - blocks thread
    importantWork();                               // CPU-intensive work
    return calculateCredits(assets, liabilities);
}
```

The preceding code snippet shows a sequence of five method invocations, each happening one after the other. Suppose each would typically take 200 milliseconds to complete. Then the time it takes for the `calculateCredit()` method to execute would be about 1 second—roughly five times as long (1,000 milliseconds = 200 milliseconds × 5).

The real inefficiency here isn't that the thread is idle, but rather that it's blocked during input/output (I/O) operations. When the thread executes `getPerson(personId)`, it makes a database call and must wait for the network response. During this waiting period, the thread cannot be reassigned to handle other requests or perform other work. The same blocking occurs during the `getAssets()` and `getLiabilities()` calls. While the thread is technically "busy" executing these methods, it's spending most of its time blocked on I/O operations rather than doing productive computational work.

This blocking behavior represents a significant inefficiency: expensive thread resources are tied up waiting for external systems to respond, when they could potentially be serving other requests. In high-throughput applications, this can severely limit scalability since each blocked thread represents one fewer thread available to handle incoming requests.

Dealing with the key challenge of achieving high thread efficiency, in particular, trying to minimize the time that threads spend blocked on I/O operations, has driven many of Java's evolutions over time. This includes support for various paradigms such as asynchronous method invocations (allowing methods to run independently while I/O operations complete), thread pooling (reusing a fixed number of threads to perform tasks), and, more recently, modern reactive programming models (emphasizing non-blocking, event-driven interactions).

Let's start by introducing the classical methods of threading, such as manually creating and managing individual threads, and gradually move into what modern offerings provide.

The Parallel Execution Strategy

Looking at our preceding code snippet, we can see that there are some method invocations, namely, `getAssets()`, `getLiabilities()`, and `importantWork()`, that do not have interdependencies, so these methods can actually be dispatched to run in parallel. This approach to parallel execution will reduce the duration for which our main thread is blocked, even though we haven't totally eliminated blocking.

Our parallel execution strategy effectively allows the main thread to diminish idle time. This essentially means that, since the main thread is less idle, once this `calculateCredit()` method is done executing, it can quickly be free to do other work.

Let's start by creating the basic data structures we'll need for our credit calculation system:

```
// Credit calculation models
record Credit(double score) {}
record Person(Long id, String name) {}
record Asset(String type, double value) {}
record Liability(String type, double amount) {}
```

Now, let's implement our parallel execution approach:

```
import java.util.List;
import java.util.concurrent.Callable;
import java.util.concurrent.atomic.AtomicReference;

Credit calculateCreditWithUnboundedThreads(Long personId)
                                    throws InterruptedException {

    var person = getPerson(personId);

    var assetsRef = new AtomicReference<List<Asset>>();  ❶
    var t1 = new Thread(() -> {
        var assets = getAssets(person);
        assetsRef.set(assets);  ❷
    });

    var liabilitiesRef = new AtomicReference<List<Liability>>();
    Thread t2 = new Thread(() -> {
        var liabilities = getLiabilities(person);
        liabilitiesRef.set(liabilities);
    });

    var t3 = new Thread(() -> importantWork());  ❸

    t1.start();  ❹
    t2.start();
    t3.start();

    t1.join();  ❺
    t2.join();
```

```
        var credit = calculateCredits(assetsRef.get(), liabilitiesRef.get()); ❻

        t3.join(); ❼

        return credit;
}
```

Let's see how the preceding code works:

❶ Uses `AtomicReference` (*https://oreil.ly/zmP1k*) to safely share data between threads.

❷ Thread-safe assignment of results that can be accessed from the main thread.

❸ Independent work that can run in parallel without affecting the credit calculation.

❹ All three threads start executing concurrently, reducing overall execution time.

❺ Waits for assets and liabilities threads to complete before proceeding with credit calculation.

❻ Calculates credit using the results from parallel operations.

❼ Ensures the independent work completes before method returns.

We've used `AtomicReference` from the standard Java concurrency package—a thread-safe data structure that contains a reference to a single object. Since we are dealing with multiple threads, it is essential that we use it.

> Use `AtomicReference` when you need to share object references safely between threads. For primitive values, consider using `Atomic Integer` (*https://oreil.ly/0m6-z*), `AtomicLong` (*https://oreil.ly/bwxw6*), or other atomic primitives.

To complete our credit calculation service, we need to implement the supporting methods. Each method simulates real-world operations like database queries and API calls:

```java
// Simulated methods with 200ms delay each
private Person getPerson(Long personId) {
    simulateDelay(200);
    return new Person(personId, "John Doe");
}

private List<Asset> getAssets(Person person) {
    simulateDelay(200);
    return List.of(
        new Asset("House", 300000),
        new Asset("Car", 25000)
    );
}

private List<Liability> getLiabilities(Person person) {
    simulateDelay(200);
    return List.of(
        new Liability("Mortgage", 200000),
        new Liability("Credit Card", 5000)
    );
}

private void importantWork() {
    simulateDelay(200);
    System.out.println("Important work completed");
}

private Credit calculateCredits(List<Asset> assets,
                                List<Liability> liabilities) {
    simulateDelay(200);
    double totalAssets = assets.stream().mapToDouble(Asset::value).sum();
    double totalLiabilities = liabilities.stream()
        .mapToDouble(Liability::amount)
        .sum();
    double creditScore = (totalAssets - totalLiabilities) / 1000;
    return new Credit(creditScore);
}


private void simulateDelay(int milliseconds) {
    try {
        Thread.sleep(milliseconds);
    } catch (InterruptedException e) {
        Thread.currentThread().interrupt();
        throw new RuntimeException(e);
    }
}
```

Handling InterruptedException Correctly

When dealing with `InterruptedException` in Java, it's crucial to preserve the thread's interrupted status. The pattern shown demonstrates the proper way to handle this exception:

```
catch (InterruptedException e) {
    Thread.currentThread().interrupt();
    throw new RuntimeException(e);
}
```

When a thread is interrupted via `Thread.interrupt()` sets an internal flag, causing blocking methods (such as `sleep()`, `wait()`, or blocking I/O operations) to throw `InterruptedException`. However, catching this exception clears the interrupted flag, which can cause problems for code higher up the call stack that needs to know about the interruption.

`Thread.currentThread().interrupt()` resets the interrupted flag on the current thread. This ensures that any calling code checking `Thread.interrupted()` or `Thread.currentThread().isInterrupted()` will correctly see that an interruption occurred.

We can wrap the `InterruptedException` in a `RuntimeException`, which then allows us the interruption to propagate up the call stack even through methods that don't declare `InterruptedException` in their throws clause. This is particularly useful in contexts where you cannot add checked exceptions to method signatures (such as when implementing interfaces that don't declare them).

For comparison, we will also keep our original sequential version in the code:

```
// Sequential version (original)
public Credit calculateCredit(Long personId) {
// Method body available in the above.
}
```

To analyze performance improvements, it's helpful to measure the execution time of methods. Here's a utility class for this purpose:

```
import java.util.concurrent.Callable;

public class ExecutionTimer {
    public static <T> T measure(Callable<T> task) throws Exception {
        long startTime = System.nanoTime();
        try {
            return task.call();
        } finally {
            long endTime = System.nanoTime();
            // Convert to milliseconds
            long duration = (endTime - startTime) / 1_000_000;
            System.out.println("Execution time: " + duration + " milliseconds");
```

```
        }
      }
    }
```

This is a simplistic approach for understanding code execution. For robust benchmarking, consider using a microbenchmark harness (like JMH (*https://oreil.ly/w6Nsy*)) to account for factors like JVM warmup, dead-code elimination, and other optimizations.

Assuming that each method has a 200-millisecond execution time, we can determine how much time the preceding code will require for completion.

The `Thread.sleep(200)` method can be used to simulate this execution time. Now, let's create a demonstration that compares both approaches:

```
public class ParallelExecutionDemo {

    public static void main(String[] args) throws Exception {
        CreditCalculatorService service = new CreditCalculatorService();

        System.out.println("=== Sequential Execution ===");
        ExecutionTimer.measure(() -> service.calculateCredit(1L));

        System.out.println("\n=== Parallel Execution ===");
        ExecutionTimer.measure(() -> {
            try {
                return service.calculateCreditWithUnboundedThreads(1L);
            } catch (InterruptedException e) {
                Thread.currentThread().interrupt();
                throw new RuntimeException(e);
            }
        });
    }
}
```

If we execute the preceding code, it will print something like this:

```
=== Sequential Execution ===
Important work completed
Execution time: 1026 milliseconds
=== Parallel Execution ===
Important work completed
Execution time: 616 milliseconds
```

We've significantly improved the performance by refactoring the credit calculation and employing multiple threads. The new version runs 1.66 times faster than the old one (616 milliseconds compared to 1,026 milliseconds for the previous version), which is noticeably faster for the user.

Though parallelization enhances performance by mitigating or reducing the blocking time of the initiating thread, it comes with its own challenges, particularly concerning thread management and system resource utilization. The ad hoc creation of threads, as demonstrated, lacks a controlled mechanism for managing thread lifecycles and resource allocation. This can lead to an overproliferation of threads, which has the potential to exhaust system resources. Each thread, being a heavyweight resource, consumes memory and processing power. As a result, since threads are created on an ad hoc basis and there is insufficient control, threads will be created in abundance, leading to `java.lang.OutOfMemoryError` (*https://oreil.ly/vD03r*) exceptions, crashes, and other runtime bottlenecks.

Introducing the Executor Framework

To avoid the dangers of creating ad hoc threads, it's better to use one of the Java concurrency frameworks, such as the `ExecutorService`, that provides a more structured way of working with threads.

Furthermore, using an `ExecutorService` not only controls the number of concurrent running threads but also allows for efficient reuse of threads by managing their lifecycle for us, thus overcoming the overhead brought by the thread lifecycle.

Let's refactor the previous code and use `ExecutorService`:

```
public Credit calculateCreditWithExecutor(Long personId)
    throws ExecutionException, InterruptedException {

    try (ExecutorService executor = Executors.newFixedThreadPool(5)) { ❶
      var person = getPerson(personId);

      var assetsFuture = executor.submit(() -> getAssets(person)); ❷
      var liabilitiesFuture = executor.submit(() -> getLiabilities(person)); ❷
      executor.submit(() -> importantWork()); ❸

      return calculateCredits(assetsFuture.get(), liabilitiesFuture.get()); ❹
    }
}
```

Let's walk through what we have done here:

❶ Creates a thread pool that will be automatically shut down when the `try` block exits

❷ Submits both critical tasks that we need results from

❸ Submits additional work that doesn't need to block the main flow

❹ Waits for the critical tasks and processes their results

Now, let's measure the execution time of the code using `ExecutionTimer.measure()` and compare the results to the previous implementation:

```
public static void main(String[] args) throws Exception {
  System.out.println("\n=== Parallel Execution With Executors ===");
  ExecutionTimer.measure(() -> {
    try {
      return service.calculateCreditWithExecutor(1L);
    } catch (InterruptedException e) {
      Thread.currentThread().interrupt();
      throw new RuntimeException(e);
    }
  });
}
```

If we run the code, we will get output as follows:

```
=== Parallel Execution With Executors ===
Important work completed
Execution time: 630 milliseconds
```

Interestingly, the execution time remains very similar to the previous version. The executors provide useful facilities for managing concurrent work in Java applications —they make it easier to create and manage threads, they provide possible speedups for suitable workloads, and they make the code easier to organize and keep clean. Now, let's address the outstanding obstacles of the Executors package.

Remaining Challenges

The Executor framework brings significant improvements in resource management and asynchronous execution to Java applications. However, to maximize its benefits, it's crucial to be aware of its limitations.

Blocking on `Future.get()`
 Despite introducing asynchrony via `Future` objects, the `get()` method call still blocks execution. This means that while we've shifted the blocking from one place to another, we haven't completely eliminated it.

Potential for cache coherence overhead and false sharing
 When tasks are submitted to a thread pool, they are executed by threads that may run on different CPU cores than the main thread. This could lead to scenarios where the cache states of the two cores become inconsistent, creating the potential for performance degradation due to cache coherence protocols constantly invalidating and synchronizing cache lines across cores.

The idea is to improve data access speed so all modern CPUs have L-caches.[3] These caches store small chunks of data (size varies with hardware architecture) so that the next time the CPU needs that data, it can be retrieved from the cache instead of from slower main memory. This chunk of data is called a *cache line*, and its use significantly improves overall performance.

However, when multiple tasks run concurrently, there's a chance that data from two subsequent tasks might reside in the same cache line. If both tasks run on the same CPU, there's no need to look up the main memory again, as the data is already cached. That means the second operation will have been faster than the first, which is a small improvement. However, if the two tasks run on different CPUs, the second CPU has to invalidate its cache line if the first CPU modified any part of it, then reload the entire cache line from main memory or another core's cache.

This phenomenon, known as false sharing, occurs when different threads modify different variables that happen to share the same cache line. The frequent cache line invalidations and reloads may negatively impact overall performance in frameworks like the Executor framework, where tasks are distributed across CPUs.

Lack of composability
The Executor framework is still quite imperative in nature. There is nothing wrong with imperative-style code, but many developers find functional and declarative styles to be easier to read and maintain.

Cache Coherence Protocols

Modern CPUs use cache coherence protocols (e.g., MESI, MOESI) to ensure all cores see a consistent view of memory. When one core writes to a cache line, the protocol invalidates or updates that line in other cores' caches. This guarantees correctness but can introduce performance overhead due to frequent invalidations and data transfers across cores.

This leads back to our starting point: the natural question is "What now?" How do we solve these problems, and how can we use executors to write even more efficient and maintainable code in the future?

---

3 L-caches are the tiered levels of superfast memory (L1, L2, L3) within a CPU that store frequently used data for quick access.

Beyond Basic Thread Pools

The Executor framework is very helpful; however, scenarios like heavy cache contention or the need for complex task dependencies can be problematic, as I stated previously. Java's Fork/Join Pool addresses these challenges with a performance-focused design and specialized algorithms. This dedicated implementation of `Executor Service` delivers a more sophisticated thread-pooling mechanism, enhancing performance and resource efficiency through intelligent task scheduling. Let's explore further.

Cache Affinity and Task Distribution

Cache affinity refers to the concept of completing tasks in a way that leverages the locality of the CPU cache. If a task is executed on a particular CPU, its data gets loaded into the cache of that core. If other related tasks are executed on the same core, those other tasks can benefit from the data already cached there, reducing the memory access time and, thus, improving performance.

The Fork/Join pool encourages cache affinity because worker threads usually execute tasks from their own local queues. This is especially helpful if the tasks frequently access the same shared data. By maintaining cache affinity, the Fork/Join Pool minimizes cache misses, which occur when the data needed by a task is not present in the cache and must be fetched from the main memory—a significantly slower process.

Consider, for instance, a set of parallel tasks working on a large array. If these tasks are all processing different slices of that array, it pays to have them run on the same core; then, the data in those slices of an array can stay in the cache and be accessed quickly by the next task. Otherwise, we will have to continually reload this data into the cache. Cache affinity reduces the overhead associated with repeatedly loading data into the cache.

Work-Stealing Algorithm

The Fork/Join Pool also employs a dynamic work-stealing algorithm to efficiently balance the load among threads. Instead of a single shared task queue, each thread in a Fork/Join Pool has its own queue. When a thread runs out of work, it "steals" tasks from the tail of another thread's queue. This dynamic work-stealing algorithm maximizes CPU usage, ensuring that no thread sits idle while there are tasks to be done. Figure 1-3 illustrates the work-stealing algorithm used in the Fork/Join Pool. This method of dynamically redistributing tasks ensures that all threads remain productive, enhancing overall CPU utilization and minimizing idle time.

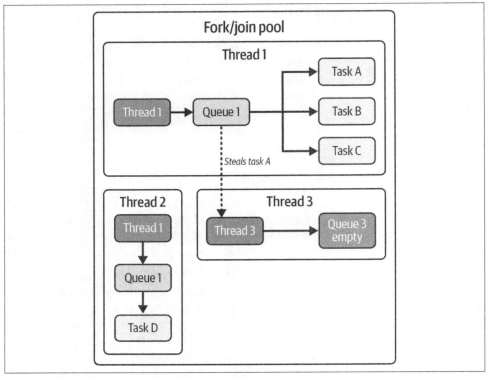

Figure 1-3. Work-stealing algorithm in Fork/Join Pool

Example of using a Fork/Join Pool

The Fork/Join Pool simplifies the process of sending tasks, and it automatically distributes the tasks efficiently without requiring additional management. Here's a basic example of how to use the Fork/Join Pool:

```
ForkJoinPool forkJoinPool = new ForkJoinPool();
forkJoinPool.submit(() -> {
    // your parallelized tasks here
}).join();
```

Notice how easy it is to submit tasks to a Fork/Join Pool. The framework automatically handles efficient work distribution, taking the burden of complex thread management off the developer.

Typically, the Fork/Join Pool is associated with the divide-and-conquer algorithm, using the `RecursiveAction` (*https://oreil.ly/JNpA4*) and `RecursiveTask` (*https://oreil.ly/4kYNM*) classes to break tasks into smaller pieces for the Fork/Join Pool. However, in this context, we are focusing on the Fork/Join Pool itself, not the divide-and-conquer strategies used to create these tasks.

I'll discuss the Fork/Join Pool in more detail in the following chapter.

Bringing Composability into Play with CompletableFuture

The Executor framework and the Fork/Join Pool offer performance improvements, but composing complex asynchronous workflows can still be cumbersome. To address this challenge, Java 8 introduced `CompletableFuture` (*https://oreil.ly/5VTeu*), a class designed to streamline asynchronous programming by focusing on composability and ease of use.

Let's look at how a composable and fluent API with `CompletableFuture` aligns with the earlier example.

Composable and fluent API

`CompletableFuture` transforms how we write asynchronous code, moving away from callback-heavy styles toward a declarative and functional approach. Its rich API empowers us to chain multiple asynchronous operations effortlessly, improving code readability and maintainability. Let's revisit the previous example:

```
import java.util.concurrent.CompletableFuture;
import java.util.concurrent.ExecutionException;
import static java.util.concurrent.CompletableFuture.*;

public Credit calculateCreditWithCompletableFuture(Long personId)
        throws InterruptedException, ExecutionException {
    return runAsync(() -> importantWork())  ❶
        .thenCompose(aVoid -> supplyAsync(() -> getPerson(personId)))  ❷
        .thenCombineAsync(supplyAsync(() -> getAssets(getPerson(personId))),  ❸
                (person, assets)
                    -> calculateCredits(assets, getLiabilities(person)))  ❹
        .get();  ❺
}
```

Let's examine how this `CompletableFuture` approach works:

❶ Starts the independent work asynchronously

❷ After important work completes, begins fetching `person` data asynchronously

❸ Combines the `person` data with `assets` fetched in parallel

❹ Calculates the final credit score using the combined results

❺ Blocks and waits for the final result to complete

This example demonstrates how `CompletableFuture` allows us to structure asynchronous workflows in a clear and concise manner. However, it is not without its disadvantages.

Let's explore the advantages and disadvantages of this API.

Advantages of using CompletableFuture

`CompletableFuture` transforms how you structure asynchronous code with its fluent API. Instead of tangled nested callbacks or sprawling class hierarchies of task objects, you define workflows as a series of transformations and intermediate computations. This improves readability and maintainability, reducing the likelihood of bugs in applications where asynchrony is central.

Under the hood, `CompletableFuture` builds on the Fork/Join framework, leveraging optimized work-stealing for efficient task distribution and better scalability under load. Built-in methods such as exceptionally, handle, and `whenComplete` give you explicit control over error handling. You can also supply custom executors to fine-tune thread management for specific workloads. Finally, while a blocking `get()` is sometimes required at boundaries, the majority of your pipeline can remain non-blocking, enabling highly responsive and resource-efficient code.

Disadvantages and limitations

Although `CompletableFuture` is a powerful feature in Java, it does require you to shift your mindset if you are already used to the imperative programming style. I would say that you may have to invest quite a bit to learn this rich API in order to use it in a meaningful way. You have to figure out the best places or value propagation techniques for the various methods it offers. This would be a considerable investment of time and practice, and with that comes the possibility of failing to use it correctly.

For example, the `get()` method is still a blocking method, which is necessary but can induce blocking in a flow that would otherwise undermine the use of asynchronous programming altogether if not used frugally. You also can have an issue in multichain `CompletableFuture` cases where you have more than one dependency and have to propagate and check the error in order to recover. This, if not designed correctly, can create a very big nightmare to debug. Finally, debugging code written in `Completable` `Future`'s chained style poses another challenge in flow control. If you are used to the default debugging tools available in various IDEs, stepping through the code, setting a breakpoint at a particular spot, and seeing the context of a statement by taking a step backward in the code is going to be highly challenging for you. This is because of the inverted and ambiguous execution flow of asynchronous code—it doesn't just get executed line by line.

While the benefits of asynchronous programming are clear, and `CompletableFuture` provides powerful features along with other alternatives like reactive frameworks, we must ask a critical question: Are we organizationally ready for this complexity?

Asynchronous programming fundamentally changes how we design, debug, and maintain applications. The gains in performance come with significant costs in cognitive overhead, debugging difficulty, and architectural complexity. Before adopting these patterns, consider whether your team has the experience to maintain clean code principles, handle complex error scenarios, and debug asynchronous call chains effectively.

This isn't merely a technical decision. It's an architectural commitment that affects every aspect of your application's lifecycle. Choose wisely based on your team's capabilities and your application's actual performance requirements.

A Different Paradigm for Asynchronous Programming

Although `CompletableFuture` provides powerful tools, changing one's mindset is not enough to address the remaining limitations (or to reach the higher levels of performance achievable in some cases). Reactive programming introduces a paradigm focused on data streams, asynchronous event processing, and non-blocking operations. Frameworks like RxJava, Akka, Eclipse Vert.x, Spring WebFlux, and others implement this paradigm in Java with rich toolsets.

For instance, let's reimagine our previous `calculateCredit()` example using Spring WebFlux. First, we need to add the necessary dependency and imports:

```
<dependency>
    <groupId>org.springframework</groupId>
    <artifactId>spring-webflux</artifactId>
    <version>6.0.0</version>
</dependency>
```

To test the reactive example, create a Maven project and add the `reactor-core` dependency, as shown in the preceding *pom.xml*.

Now we'll add the following method to our `CreditCalculatorService.java` class:

```
public Mono<Credit> calculateCreditReactive(Long personId) {
    Mono<Void> importantWorkMono = Mono.fromRunnable(() -> importantWork()); ❶
    Mono<Person> personMono = Mono.fromSupplier(() -> getPerson(personId)); ❷
    Mono<List<Asset>> assetsMono = personMono
        .map(person -> getAssets(person)); ❸
```

```
    Mono<List<Liability>> liabilitiesMono = personMono
        .map(person -> getLiabilities(person));  ❹

    return importantWorkMono.then(  ❺
        Mono.zip(assetsMono, liabilitiesMono)  ❻
            .map(tuple -> {
              List<Asset> assets = tuple.getT1();
              List<Liability> liabilities = tuple.getT2();
              return calculateCredits(assets, liabilities);  ❼
            })
    );
  }
```

Let's examine the reactive flow:

❶ Creates a `Mono` that executes important work asynchronously when subscribed

❷ Wraps the `person` lookup in a reactive stream

❸ Transforms the `person` stream to fetch assets asynchronously

❹ Transforms the `person` stream to fetch liabilities asynchronously

❺ Waits for important work to complete, then proceeds with credit calculation

❻ Combines `assets` and `liabilities` streams into a single stream containing both results

❼ Calculates the final credit score from the combined data

Looking at this code, you'll notice it's conceptually similar to the `CompletableFuture` approach but uses reactive streams terminology and operators. However, if you're unfamiliar with reactive programming, this approach can be puzzling and requires significant learning investment to understand concepts like Publishers, Subscribers, backpressure, and reactive operators.

I will not explain reactive programming in this book, as this is not the goal of this book, but you can explore other books written about the reactive stack.

Let's discuss some of the limitations we encountered in the reactive programming approach just to make sense of why we need something different or why we need virtual threads, which *is* the goal of this book.

Drawbacks of Using Reactive Frameworks

As the saying goes, "There's no such thing as a free lunch," and the same applies to reactive programming. Let's outline some of the key challenges it presents:

Steep learning curve

Grasping the fundamentals of the reactive programming paradigm requires a significant mental shift for developers who are already used to the imperative programming paradigm. Concepts like Observables (*https://oreil.ly/vboPE*), Observable operators (*https://oreil.ly/PEMon*), schedulers (*https://oreil.ly/5vIfH*), and backpressure (*https://oreil.ly/4koKP*), which are fundamental to reactive frameworks, require an investment of time and a potentially steep learning curve compared to other concurrency models.

Increased cognitive load

The functional programming style used in reactive frameworks can be too much for full-time developers with long tenures of imperative programming or object-oriented programming under their belts. Along with the heavy usage of lambdas, higher-order functions, and functional composition, chains of operators and transformations can make the code itself harder to grasp initially and, thus, more challenging to maintain (at least in the short term) among large projects or teams where not all the members have a similar amount of reactive programming experience.

Debugging difficulties

Traditional debugging tools and techniques don't always work so well with reactive systems on the fly. For instance, chained operators lead to asynchronous execution where, if an error does arise, the stack trace might provide insufficient context to find the root of the problem. You might miss the event that last occurred through event hopping between threads and operators. Specialized debugging tools, possibly provided as part of your reactive framework, might be required. This adds to the learning curve. For example, suppose a reactive pipeline fetches data from four different sources, transforms the four streams, and then combines the results. An error arising from the combine phase might result in a stack trace that points to the combine operator and makes it difficult to tell whether a particular upstream source or transformation is the root cause of the problem. Tracking the data flow throughout the reactive pipeline becomes tricky in complex pipelines with dozens of operators, tens of asynchronous operations, and so on. In the traditional threading model, debugging is relatively straightforward and comes at little cost.

Overcomplication risk

The composability possible through reactive frameworks' operator-based models, while very powerful, comes with the potential to create more complex products than are absolutely necessary for a given business requirement or user interface element. Just as one might be able to cook a chicken curry using every dish in a family's silver set, it is possible (and tempting) to solve every problem with something slightly more complicated than is really necessary. As such, reactive frameworks face the creative risk of allowing inexperienced programmers to overengineer their domain—a risk not unique to reactive frameworks themselves but one that occurs in any powerful abstraction or library when used by those who do not know when to stop.

Potential mismatch
Reactive programming frameworks are best suited for scenarios involving significant asynchronous operations, event-driven data flows, or high-throughput data streams. In other situations, some subset of reactive systems' or frameworks' capabilities might not be needed because there isn't much asynchronicity or the data flow isn't inherently event-oriented, or the effort to learn, abstract, and apply into the framework justifies the greater simplicity of a more basic synchronous or request-response approach.

Vendor lock-in
The essential ideas of reactive programming are undoubtedly transferable; however, each of the significant reactive frameworks has its own set of nuanced APIs. Picking one of them over the other means you will be locked into a specific framework, which naturally makes it harder to change libraries later, and potentially constrains flexibility somewhere down the line of the project's lifecycle. This lock-in can also have implications, such as difficulty in finding developers familiar with the chosen framework, potential for framework stagnation or lack of continued support, and challenges in migrating to a different framework if needed.

Having mentioned all of these challenges, there is absolutely no denying that reactive programming frameworks have the potential to enormously simplify the management of sophisticated asynchronous scenarios. However, we must examine their trade-offs in detail to understand if the benefits outweigh the costs for the project we're working on.

Revolutionizing Concurrency in Java

Java's traditional concurrency mechanisms have served us well, but as the application of concurrency has grown to more complex and additional use cases, various challenges have been presented along the way. That's why it is essential to explore new solutions.

The Promise of Virtual Threads

Now that we understand the shortcomings of our traditional approaches, we need to find a better way to fix those problems. This is precisely where Project Loom, a key step toward first-class modern concurrency in Java, comes into play. It introduced a new kind of thread called *virtual threads*, ushering in a new era of concurrency in Java. These are very lightweight threads and can be created on demand with next to no overhead compared to what is traditionally associated with thread creation. Virtual threads can be instantiated in the millions, unlocking new possibilities for highly concurrent and scalable applications.

Let's discuss some of the characteristics of virtual threads.

Seamless Integration with Existing Codebases

One of the key strengths of Project Loom lies in its seamless compatibility with existing Java codebases. For instance, if your application already uses the Executor framework, all you have to do to take advantage of virtual threads is pass an `Executors.newVirtualThreadPerTaskExecutor()` (*https://oreil.ly/K6hJ6*) to your existing `ExecutorService`:

```
Credit calculateCreditWithVirtualThread
    (Long personId) throws ExecutionException, InterruptedException {
  try (var executor = Executors.newVirtualThreadPerTaskExecutor()) { ❶
    var person = getPerson(personId);
    var assetsFuture = executor.submit(() -> getAssets(person));
    var liabilitiesFuture = executor.submit(() -> getLiabilities(person));
    executor.submit(this::importantWork);
    return calculateCredits(assetsFuture.get(), liabilitiesFuture.get());
  }
}
```

❶ Replace any traditional executor with `Executors.newVirtualThreadPerTaskExecutor()` to immediately gain the benefits of virtual threads.

This ease of integration ensures a smooth transition to the new concurrency model.

Virtual Threads and Platform Threads

Virtual threads ride on top of *platform threads*, also known as *classical threads*, which are also backed by the Fork/Join Pool, so they inherit the benefits of that more sophisticated thread pool. Thus, virtual and platform threads combine perfectly to produce the best resource utilization and scalability results.

Intelligent Handling of Blocking Operations

One of the most exciting aspects of virtual threads is their intelligent handling of blocking operations. When a virtual thread encounters a blocking operation—such as a sleep or network I/O—it automatically yields control back to the underlying platform thread. This allows the platform thread to continue executing other virtual threads, ensuring optimal utilization of available resources. Once the blocking operation is complete, the virtual thread can simply take up execution from where it left off, avoiding perceptible bottlenecks.

Benefits of Embracing Virtual Threads

Before diving into the nitty-gritty of virtual threads in the next chapter, let's take a quick look at how virtual threads revolutionize the way we handle concurrency in Java. Here are some of the key advantages:

Resource efficiency
    Virtual threads are lightweight, and we can spawn millions without exhausting resources, which permits highly concurrent, scalable applications.

Code simplicity
    With the ability to write blocking code without performance penalties, developers can now write and maintain a more straightforward, traditional imperative coding style. That means no additional learning curve and easier-to-maintain code.

Optimal utilization
    During blocking operations, virtual threads relinquish control, which ensures that platform threads remain utilized, increasing CPU and application performance.

One of the biggest concerns for developers using concurrency in Java is the specific information they must learn to use it correctly. Project Loom represents a huge step forward for the concurrent style Java developers create and use; it will let them write highly concurrent and efficient applications at scale while still using the patterns they are already familiar with.

In Closing

In this book, we will continue discussing virtual threads and explore more about this revolutionary technology in the next chapter.

As you dive deeper into virtual thread concepts, consider how they can transform your approach to designing concurrent applications. Virtual threads offer not just a new way to handle concurrency but also a more efficient, scalable, and intuitive method that aligns with modern computing demands.

CHAPTER 2
Understanding Virtual Threads

The price of reliability is the pursuit of the utmost simplicity. It is a price which the very rich find most hard to pay.
—Tony Hoare

Virtual threads are a groundbreaking addition to the Java concurrency toolkit that are fundamentally changing how developers write concurrent programs, making it practical to use threads as the primary unit of concurrency at massive scale. As we will discuss at length in this chapter, virtual threads differ significantly from the platform threads, or classical threads, that have served us over the years. In particular, while platform threads are managed by the underlying operating system or by thread libraries like those from POSIX, virtual threads are lightweight threads managed by the Java Virtual Machine (JVM) itself. This shift from OS-managed to JVM-managed threads represents more than just an implementation detail—it enables applications to create millions of threads without the memory and performance penalties that made such designs impractical with traditional threads. In this chapter, we'll take a deep dive into virtual threads by reviewing their architecture, discussing how they differ from platform threads, examining the motivation behind their creation for modern Java applications, and exploring how they simplify concurrent programming while delivering unprecedented scalability.

What Is a Virtual Thread?

Virtual threads are managed by the JVM, which allows them to operate more efficiently than traditional threads that rely on the operating system for scheduling and management. Virtual threads are executed on top of carrier threads, which are essentially threads from the Fork/Join Pool. This design allows virtual threads to inherit the benefits of advanced thread pooling mechanisms and efficient work-stealing algorithms.

It's important to note that the virtual thread scheduler implemented within the JVM is based on a work-stealing `ForkJoinPool`, operating in a First-In, First-Out (FIFO) mode. This `ForkJoinPool` serves as the foundation for scheduling virtual threads and is distinct from the common pool used for other purposes, such as the implementation of parallel streams, which operate in a Last-In, First-Out (LIFO) mode.

The parallelism of the virtual thread scheduler, which refers to the number of platform threads available for scheduling virtual threads, is a configurable parameter. By default, it is set to the number of available processors on the system, ensuring optimal utilization of hardware resources. However, developers can fine-tune this parameter using the `jdk.virtualThreadScheduler.parallelism` system property, allowing them to adjust the level of parallelism based on their specific application requirements and workload characteristics.

You can set system properties in Java using the `-D` command-line option when you start your Java application, like this:

```
java -Djdk.virtualThreadScheduler.parallelism=4 -jar yourApp.jar
```

In this example, the `jdk.virtualThreadScheduler.parallelism` system property is set to 4. Replace *yourApp.jar* with the actual name of your Java application.

In code, you can use the `System.setProperty(key, value)` (*https://oreil.ly/-goJu*) method:

```
System.setProperty("jdk.virtualThreadScheduler.parallelism", "4");
```

Please keep in mind that these settings need to be adjusted before they are used for the first time; this is typically done at the beginning of the main method or even before your Spring/Jakarta EE/Quarkus application context starts up.

The Two Kinds of Threads in Java

With the introduction of virtual threads, Java now features two distinct kinds of threads: platform threads and virtual threads (Figure 2-1).

Platform threads
: These are the threads native to Java since its inception, which explains why they're sometimes called *traditional* or *classical threads*. You might also encounter terms like *native threads* or *OS threads* in different contexts. In the Java Development Kit (JDK), they are officially called *platform threads*. A platform thread is a heavyweight thread that is executed through the underlying operating system, relying on the OS for thread scheduling and management. Platform threads maintain a one-to-one mapping between Java threads and kernel threads, which are managed by the operating system. These threads utilize the operating system's existing scheduling and context-switching mechanisms. Platform threads have been the foundation of Java's concurrent programming model since the language's inception.

Virtual threads

Virtual threads, sometimes called *user-mode threads* or *lightweight threads*, are a new addition to Java's concurrency model since JDK 21. Unlike platform threads, virtual threads are managed entirely by the JVM. Millions of virtual threads can be created without exhausting system resources. Virtual threads are not directly mapped to kernel threads. Instead, multiple virtual threads share a smaller pool of carrier threads (which are platform threads), allowing the JVM to efficiently multiplex many virtual threads onto relatively few OS resources.

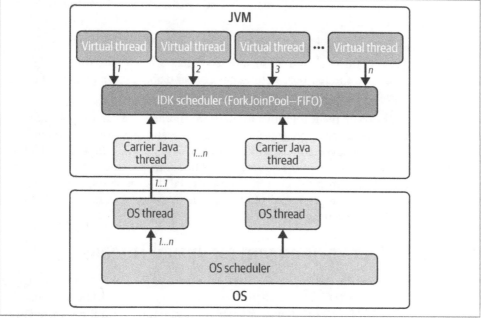

Figure 2-1. Internals of thread scheduling: virtual threads, carrier threads

Key Differences from Platform Threads

Now that we know there are two kinds of threads—platform threads and virtual threads—let's explore some of the key differences between them:

Lightweight
    Virtual threads use much less memory and fewer resources than platform threads, so you can create millions of virtual threads without exhausting machine resources.

Scheduling
>Virtual threads are scheduled by the JVM, not by the operating system, making better use of CPU cycles and bypassing any overhead incurred by an operating system thread scheduler.

Blocking tolerance
>Virtual threads don't come with a performance penalty when they need to do blocking operations, such as read from the console, read from a file or network connection, write to a file or network, or sleep. That's because when a virtual thread encounters a blocking operation, it yields control back to the carrier thread, allowing other virtual threads to continue executing efficiently.

Seamless integration
>Virtual threads are designed to seamlessly integrate with existing codebases. Developers can continue to use coding patterns and abstractions that are familiar to them, without having to adjust their workflows.

Given that we cannot fix the limitations of platform threads and can only do so much to scale them, virtual threads present a more scalable and performant concurrency model—one that we believe can and will transform how Java developers think about concurrent programming. Over the course of this book, in this and subsequent chapters, we will dive deeper into the details of how virtual threads work, look at how to use them in real-world projects, and offer example projects to help you get started with developing in this exciting new world.

Setting Up Your Environment for Virtual Threads

Project Loom's virtual threads are now a stable feature as of JDK 21. To start using them, ensure you have JDK 21 installed. For managing multiple JDK versions, we recommend SDKMAN (*https://sdkman.io*). This versatile tool streamlines installation and allows for easy switching between versions. Refer to the official SDKMAN website for installation instructions. Installing a JDK with SDKMAN enables developers to easily manage Java versions and dependencies on their systems, facilitating Java development tasks.

After installing SDKMAN, use the following command to list available JDK versions (see Figure 2-2 for the result):

```
sdk list java
```

```
===============================================================
Available Java Versions for macOS ARM 64bit
===============================================================
 Vendor        | Use | Version       | Dist     | Status    | Identifier
---------------------------------------------------------------
 Corretto      |     | 21.0.2        | amzn     |           | 21.0.2-amzn
               |     | 21.0.1        | amzn     |           | 21.0.1-amzn
               |     | 17.0.10       | amzn     |           | 17.0.10-amzn
               |     | 17.0.9        | amzn     |           | 17.0.9-amzn
               |     | 11.0.22       | amzn     |           | 11.0.22-amzn
               |     | 11.0.21       | amzn     |           | 11.0.21-amzn
               |     | 8.0.402       | amzn     |           | 8.0.402-amzn
               |     | 8.0.392       | amzn     |           | 8.0.392-amzn
 Gluon         |     | 22.1.0.1.r17  | gln      |           | 22.1.0.1.r17-gln
               |     | 22.1.0.1.r11  | gln      |           | 22.1.0.1.r11-gln
 GraalVM CE    |     | 21.0.2        | graalce  |           | 21.0.2-graalce
               |     | 21.0.1        | graalce  |           | 21.0.1-graalce
               |     | 17.0.9        | graalce  |           | 17.0.9-graalce
 GraalVM Oracle|     | 21.0.2        | graal    |           | 21.0.2-graal
               |     | 21.0.1        | graal    |           | 21.0.1-graal
               |     | 17.0.10       | graal    |           | 17.0.10-graal
               |     | 17.0.9        | graal    |           | 17.0.9-graal
 Java.net      |     | 23.ea.12      | open     |           | 23.ea.12-open
               |     | 23.ea.11      | open     |           | 23.ea.11-open
               |     | 23.ea.10      | open     |           | 23.ea.10-open
               |     | 23.ea.8       | open     | installed | 23.ea.8-open
               |     | 23.ea.7       | open     |           | 23.ea.7-open
               |     | 23.ea.6       | open     |           | 23.ea.6-open
               |     | 23.ea.5       | open     |           | 23.ea.5-open
               |     | 23.ea.4       | open     |           | 23.ea.4-open
               |     | 23.ea.3       | open     |           | 23.ea.3-open
               |     | 23.ea.2       | open     |           | 23.ea.2-open
               |     | 23.ea.1       | open     |           | 23.ea.1-open
               |     | 22.ea.36      | open     |           | 22.ea.36-open
               |     | 22.ea.35      | open     |           | 22.ea.35-open
               |     | 22.ea.34      | open     |           | 22.ea.34-open
```

Figure 2-2. SDKMAN list command output for available Java versions

To install JDK 21 (if you don't have it already), use:

sdk install java <YOUR_FAVORITE_JDK_DISTRIBUTION>

For example, if you use OpenJDK, then you'll use:

```
sdk install java 21.0.2-open
```

This chapter uses JDK 21, which remains the most widely adopted version for virtual threads in production environments. In subsequent chapters, we'll switch to the latest JDK versions to explore newer features such as:

- Scoped values
- Structured concurrency

Creating Virtual Threads in Java

Now that we have JDK 21 installed, let's explore ways to create virtual threads in Java.

For simple use cases, the `Thread.startVirtualThread()` (*https://oreil.ly/FIiZ3*) method offers a direct approach. It takes a `Runnable`, so we can pass a lambda expression, and whatever we pass through it will execute. For example:

```
Thread.startVirtualThread(() -> {
        System.out.println("Unleash massive parallelism with virtual
        threads! Here's a taste.");
    });
```

If you run the preceding code, you might expect to see a message on your console. However, nothing will be printed! Why? Virtual threads in Java are daemon threads by default. This means that when the main thread (the one that created the virtual thread) finishes, the JVM terminates any remaining daemon threads.

To ensure your virtual thread's task completes, you need to wait for it to finish:

```
public static void main(String[] args) throws InterruptedException {
    Thread vThread = Thread.startVirtualThread(() -> {
        System.out.println("Virtual threads make concurrency effortless!" +
            "See for yourself.");
    });
    vThread.join();
}
```

For more control over thread creation, you can use the Thread Builder API:

```
var startedThread = Thread.ofVirtual()
    .start(() -> System.out.println("Hello world!"));
startedThread.join();
```

To create a thread without starting it immediately, use this code:

```
var unstartedThread = Thread.ofVirtual()
    .unstarted(() -> System.out.println("Hello world!"));
// Start the thread later when needed
unstartedThread.start();
```

If your application already uses executors, you can smoothly transition to virtual threads:

```
try (var virtualExecutor = Executors.newVirtualThreadPerTaskExecutor()) {
    Future<String> future = virtualExecutor.submit(this::callService);
    // Process the future result
}
```

This is especially helpful in large projects where immediate refactoring for virtual threads might be impractical.

Having these different approaches allows us to seamlessly integrate virtual threads into our existing codebase, taking advantage of the improved performance, scalability, and resource efficiency offered by this new concurrency model while maintaining familiar coding patterns and abstractions.

Adapting to Virtual Threads

The introduction of virtual threads brought necessary changes to Java's Thread API, but in a way that optimizes for developer familiarity. A virtual thread in Java is essentially an instance of the Thread (*https://oreil.ly/miPlt*) class, and cancellation works the same way as it does for platform threads: by invoking the interrupt() (*https://oreil.ly/hcXDN*) method. The code running within the thread must either check the interrupted flag or call methods that handle interruption automatically (which most blocking methods do).

Let's see an example of thread interruption in platform and virtual threads.

Platform thread interruption:

```java
public class PlatformThreadInterruption {
    public static void main(String[] args) {
        Thread platformThread = Thread.ofPlatform().start(() -> { ❶
            try {
                System.out.println("Platform thread started...");
                for (int i = 0; i < 5; i++) {
                    System.out.println("Platform thread working: " + i);
                    Thread.sleep(1000); // Simulate work
                }
                System.out.println("Platform thread finished.");
            } catch (InterruptedException e) { ❷
                System.out.println("Platform thread interrupted!");
                // Handle cleanup if needed
            }
        });
        try {
            Thread.sleep(2500);   // Let the thread run for a bit ❸
        } catch (InterruptedException e) {}
        platformThread.interrupt(); ❹
    }
}
```

Virtual thread interruption:

```java
public class VirtualThreadInterruption {
    public static void main(String[] args) {
        Thread virtualThread = Thread.ofVirtual().start(() -> { ❶
            try {
                System.out.println("Virtual thread started...");
                for (int i = 0; i < 5; i++) {
                    System.out.println("Virtual thread working: " + i);
                    Thread.sleep(1000); // Automatically yields
                                        // to other virtual threads
                }
```

```
            System.out.println("Virtual thread finished.");
        } catch (InterruptedException e) { ❷
            System.out.println("Virtual thread interrupted!");
            // Handle cleanup if needed
        }
    });
    try {
        Thread.sleep(2500);   // Let the thread run for a bit ❸
    } catch (InterruptedException e) {}
    virtualThread.interrupt(); ❹
    }
}
```

Let's understand the interruption flow in both examples:

❶ Creates either a platform or virtual thread using the builder pattern.

❷ Catches `InterruptedException` when the thread is interrupted during a blocking operation.

❸ Main thread waits 2.5 seconds, allowing the worker thread to complete two to three iterations.

❹ Interrupts the worker thread, triggering the exception and cleanup.

If we run the above code, we will get following outputs:

```
java PlatformThreadInterruption.java
Platform thread started...
Platform thread working: 0
Platform thread working: 1
Platform thread working: 2
Platform thread interrupted!
```

and

```
java VirtualThreadInterruption.java

Virtual thread started...
Virtual thread working: 0
Virtual thread working: 1
Virtual thread working: 2
Virtual thread interrupted!
```

Both examples produce identical output, demonstrating that virtual threads maintain the same interruption semantics as platform threads. The key difference is that virtual-thread blocking operations (like `Thread.sleep()`) automatically yield the underlying carrier thread to other virtual threads.

While virtual threads maintain familiar APIs, they have some distinct characteristics that reflect their lightweight, managed nature, for example, thread groups.

All virtual threads belong to a single thread group; there is no API to create a virtual thread with a different thread group. If we create a virtual thread and invoke the `getThreadGroup()` method, we will always get instances of the same `ThreadGroup`. For example:

```
public class VirtualThreadGroupExample {
    public static void main(String[] args) throws InterruptedException {
        Set<ThreadGroup> threadGroups = new HashSet<>();

        for (int i = 0; i < 100; i++) { ❶
            Thread vThread = Thread.ofVirtual().start(() -> {
                try {
                    Thread.sleep(10);
                } catch (InterruptedException e) {
                    Thread.currentThread().interrupt();
                }
            });
            threadGroups.add(vThread.getThreadGroup()); ❷
        }
        Thread.sleep(1000); // Wait for threads to complete
        System.out.println("Unique thread groups: " + threadGroups.size());
        System.out.println("Thread group: " + threadGroups.iterator().next());
    }
}
```

In the preceding code, what we have done is:

❶ Create 100 virtual threads to test thread group assignment

❷ Collect thread groups from all virtual threads into a set

When we run the preceding code, we will get the following output:

```
Unique thread groups: 1
Thread group: java.lang.ThreadGroup[name=VirtualThreads,maxpri=10]
```

From the preceding output, we see virtual threads have several immutable characteristics that simplify their management:

Priority
 Virtual threads have a priority level set to `NORM_PRIORITY` (*https://oreil.ly/g1mpf*).

Daemon status
 All virtual threads are daemon threads by default. Any attempt to change this status using `setDaemon` (*https://oreil.ly/9VuRC*) has no effect.

Thread priority
 Calling `setPriority` (*https://oreil.ly/IRu_B*) on a virtual thread does not change its priority.

The Thread API has also been updated to include some new methods and deprecate others:

Is Virtual
  The `Thread::isVirtual` (*https://oreil.ly/OeLMn*) instance method helps you determine if a thread is virtual.

Duration-based methods
  Java 19 introduces `join(Duration)` (*https://oreil.ly/TgkJ9*) and `sleep(Duration)` (*https://oreil.ly/sIYV6*) instance methods, which are unrelated to virtual threads but add convenience.

Thread ID
  The nonfinal `getId()` (*https://oreil.ly/klDiG*) method is deprecated, and it is recommended to use the final `threadId()` (*https://oreil.ly/vq0IK*) method instead.

As for deprecated methods, since Java 20, the `stop()` (*https://oreil.ly/-V_Ao*), `suspend()` (*https://oreil.ly/hflbW*), `resume()` (*https://oreil.ly/SsQv5*), and `countStackFrames()` (*https://oreil.ly/fFdg8*) methods will throw an `UnsupportedOperationException` (*https://oreil.ly/UZ7zY*) for both platform and virtual threads, as they are inherently unsafe, as mentioned in the Java Documentation (*https://oreil.ly/lSBHU*). These methods have been deprecated since Java 1.2 and are scheduled for removal.

Virtual threads have some minor limitations, however. It's worth noting that the static `Thread::getAllStackTraces` (*https://oreil.ly/ZCVGV*) method only returns stack traces of platform threads, excluding virtual threads. Also, there is currently no way to find out which platform thread is executing a given virtual thread.

While virtual threads introduce some changes and limitations to the Thread API, the broad similarity to the existing API and threading concepts makes the transition to virtual threads largely invisible to developers. Using the new capabilities within the updated guidelines, developers can continue with their existing codebase but will now reap the reward of virtual-thread performance and scalability.

Demonstrating Virtual Thread Creation in Java

Virtual threads unleash the true scalability potential of Java applications. By using these virtual threads, you can make a Java application dramatically more scalable because you can have many more tasks running in parallel. It's crucial for modern server applications to handle thousands of concurrent requests. We'll now take a look at virtual threads in action.

Consider the following example where we submit 10,000 tasks using an executor that creates a new virtual thread for each task:

```
try (var executor = Executors.newVirtualThreadPerTaskExecutor()) {
    IntStream.range(0, 10_000).forEach(i -> {
        executor.submit(() -> {
            Thread.sleep(Duration.ofSeconds(1));
            return i;
        });
    });
}
```

The tasks are simple: each just sleeps for one second. This is easily achievable on modern hardware with 10,000 virtual threads running concurrently. What's impressive is that the JDK manages this with a minimal number of OS threads, potentially even just one.

By contrast, if we used `Executors.newCachedThreadPool()` (*https://oreil.ly/mzIbV*), which creates a new platform thread for each task, the program might crash due to the overhead of creating 10,000 OS threads. Similarly, using a fixed thread pool like `Executors.newFixedThreadPool(200)` (*https://oreil.ly/dttrO*) would drastically limit concurrency. With only 200 platform threads, many tasks would run sequentially, causing the program to take significantly longer to complete.

Throughput and Scalability

Virtual threads can achieve a throughput of about 10,000 tasks per second after sufficient warm-up. If you increase the number of tasks to 1,000,000, the program still runs smoothly, achieving a throughput of nearly 1,000,000 tasks per second.

It's important to clarify that virtual threads are not designed to be faster but to offer greater scalability. They follow Little's Law, providing higher throughput by enabling greater concurrency, not by executing tasks more quickly.

Under ideal circumstances, virtual threads can substantially enhance throughput in applications with the following characteristics:

High number of concurrent tasks
    Virtual threads can be a game-changer if your application has more than a few thousand concurrent tasks. This is ideal for high-volume web servers needing to handle thousands of requests simultaneously or for applications performing many I/O-bound operations in parallel.

Non-CPU-bound workload
    Virtual threads are particularly beneficial when tasks spend more time waiting (e.g., for I/O operations) than they do performing CPU-bound operations.

This is an important caveat: While virtual threads introduce a new level of scalability to Java applications, they are not a cure-all for concurrency. They're likely to be most effective when we have lots of concurrent tasks coupled with lightweight non-CPU-bound workloads. Compared with traditional multithreading, virtual threads can provide a new dimension of scalability to Java applications. This allows developers to build highly concurrent and scalable applications that can handle a vast number of requests without taxing our CPU cycles or memory.

The Fundamental Principle Behind Virtual Threads' Scalability

Little's Law is a fundamental principle that provides valuable insights into the performance of queuing systems, including multithreaded applications. It establishes a mathematical relationship between latency, concurrency, and throughput, three key elements that are intrinsically tied to the performance of any computing system.

The law is elegantly simple, stating that for a stable system, the throughput (λ) is given by:

$$\lambda = \frac{N}{d}$$

Let's delve into the components of Little's Law and learn about their significance:

Throughput (λ)
    The average number of items (e.g., tasks, requests) completed per unit of time

Concurrency (N)
    The average number of items being processed simultaneously

Response time (d)
    The average time it takes for a single item to be processed from start to finish

What's remarkable about Little's Law is its agnosticism toward the nature of the system it describes. It doesn't differentiate between time spent "doing work" versus "waiting," nor does it care about what constitutes the unit of concurrency—be it a thread, a CPU core, an ATM machine, or even a human bank teller. It simply offers a formula to scale up throughput.

Virtual threads and Little's Law

Traditional threading models often hit a wall due to OS-level limitations on the number of threads that can be spawned. When this happens, the system's throughput becomes constrained by Little's Law. The law shows us that if we can't increase N (concurrency), we're left with only one other variable to manipulate: d (latency). However, reducing latency is not always within a developer's control, especially in I/O-bound tasks.

This is where virtual threads come into the picture. They offer a way out of this limitation by allowing for a much higher N—that is, they enable higher concurrency without requiring a change in the programming model. This is a significant advantage because it directly leads to higher throughput, as indicated by Little's Law. Virtual threads offer a way to scale up *N* without proportionally scaling down *d*.

To illustrate this concept, let's craft a code example that allows us to measure and demonstrate how Little's Law's principle of throughput relates to virtual threads and their scalability benefits:

```
import java.time.Duration;
import java.time.Instant;
import java.util.concurrent.ExecutorService;
import java.util.concurrent.Executors;
import java.util.concurrent.atomic.AtomicLong;
import java.util.stream.IntStream;

public class LittleLawExample {
  public static void main(String[] args) {
    int numTasks = 10000;  ❶
    int avgResponseTimeMillis = 500; // Average task response time  ❷
    // Simulate adjustable I/O-bound work
    Runnable ioBoundTask = () -> {
      try {
        Thread.sleep(Duration.ofMillis(avgResponseTimeMillis));  ❸
      } catch (InterruptedException e) {
        Thread.currentThread().interrupt();
      }
    };

    System.out.println("=== Little's Law Throughput Comparison ===");
    System.out.println("Testing " + numTasks + " tasks with "
                       + avgResponseTimeMillis + "ms latency each\n");
    benchmark("Virtual Threads",
        Executors.newVirtualThreadPerTaskExecutor(), ioBoundTask, numTasks);
    benchmark("Fixed ThreadPool (100)",
        Executors.newFixedThreadPool(100), ioBoundTask, numTasks);
    benchmark("Fixed ThreadPool (500)",
        Executors.newFixedThreadPool(500), ioBoundTask, numTasks);
    benchmark("Fixed ThreadPool (1000)",
        Executors.newFixedThreadPool(1000), ioBoundTask, numTasks);
  }

  static void benchmark(String type, ExecutorService executor, Runnable task,
                       int numTasks) {
    Instant start = Instant.now();  ❹
    AtomicLong completedTasks = new AtomicLong();
    try (executor) {  ❺
      IntStream.range(0, numTasks)
          .forEach(i -> executor.submit(() -> {
            task.run();
            completedTasks.incrementAndGet();  ❻
          }));
    }  ❼
    Instant end = Instant.now();
```

```
        long duration = Duration.between(start, end).toMillis();
        // Tasks per second
        double throughput = (double) completedTasks.get() / duration * 1000;  ❽
        System.out.printf("%-25s - Time: %5dms, Throughput: %8.2f tasks/s%n",
            type, duration, throughput);
    }
}
```

Let's explore what we have accomplished in this program:

❶ Ten thousand tasks provide sufficient load to demonstrate throughput differences while keeping execution time manageable.

❷ A response time of 500ms simulates realistic I/O operations like database queries or API calls, representing the *d* (latency) component in Little's Law.

❸ `Thread.sleep()` mimics blocking I/O operations. With virtual threads, this automatically yields the carrier thread to other virtual threads.

❹ Measures total execution time from task submission start to completion of all tasks.

❺ `Try-with-resources` ensures proper executor shutdown and waits for all submitted tasks to complete.

❻ `AtomicLong` safely tracks completed tasks across all concurrent threads.

❼ When the `try` block exits, all submitted tasks have finished executing.

❽ Converts completed tasks per total time into tasks per second for easy comparison.

In this example, we simulate an I/O-bound task with an average response time of 500 milliseconds. We then benchmark the throughput achieved by virtual threads and compare it with fixed thread pools of varying sizes, which represent the traditional threading model.

When we execute the preceding code, we get results demonstrating virtual threads' dramatic advantage:

```
=== Little's Law Throughput Comparison ===
Testing 10000 tasks with 500ms latency each
Virtual Threads           - Time:   552ms, Throughput: 18115.94 tasks/s
Fixed ThreadPool (100)    - Time: 50381ms, Throughput:   198.49 tasks/s
Fixed ThreadPool (500)    - Time: 10106ms, Throughput:   989.51 tasks/s
Fixed ThreadPool (1000)   - Time:  5080ms, Throughput:  1968.50 tasks/s
```

As you can see from the results, virtual threads outperform traditional thread pools in terms of throughput for this I/O-bound scenario. Virtual threads can achieve a throughput of around 18115.94 tasks per second, while even a large fixed thread pool of 1,000 threads can only manage a throughput of around 1,968.50 tasks per second.

The previous example provides a basic demonstration of Little's Law with virtual threads. For more rigorous performance analysis in production environments, consider these enhancements:

- JVM warm-up runs to account for just-in-time compilation effects
- Multiple benchmark iterations with statistical analysis (mean, standard deviation)
- Memory usage monitoring to understand resource trade-offs
- Realistic I/O simulation with latency variance (±10–20%) to model real-world conditions
- Scalability testing across different task volumes to identify breaking points
- Timeout protection and proper error handling for robust measurements

These improvements help distinguish between genuine performance differences and measurement artifacts, providing more reliable insights for production decision-making. For critical performance evaluations, consider using established microbenchmarking frameworks like Java Microbenchmark Harness (JMH).

With platform threads, throughput can improve with larger thread pools, but there's a limit. Eventually, OS resources will be constrained, and thread management overhead becomes the bottleneck.

This example clearly demonstrates how virtual threads can leverage Little's Law by enabling a higher value of N (concurrency) without the need to scale down d (latency) proportionally. Virtual threads can achieve superior throughput by allowing for a significantly higher number of concurrent tasks, particularly in I/O-bound scenarios where reducing latency is not a viable option.

The Practical Implications

Virtual threads free developers from having to tweak or even fundamentally rethink their programming models to achieve more throughput. If an application has many mostly I/O-bound tasks that spend a lot of time waiting, then we can substantially increase throughput without having to change how those tasks are written.

By exploiting virtual threads, we can, in effect, increase N in Little's Law, which in turn increases concurrency and, therefore, throughput. This is particularly useful when the latency d is hard to reduce due to the nature of the work (e.g., network I/O or disk I/O).

It's important to note, however, that virtual threads are not a silver bullet for all performance issues. In situations where I/O is the bottleneck, virtual threads can offer dramatic improvements in throughput; however, virtual threads aren't going to help in situations where the bottleneck is not the number of concurrent tasks that are active but instead the amount of available computational throughput.

When developers grasp Little's Law and its implications for virtual threads, they'll have a better sense of when and how virtual threads can be used to make their applications more scalable and faster.

How Virtual Threads Work Under the Hood

Virtual threads offer a significant leap in Java's concurrency model. To understand their power, let's explore their core mechanisms.

Stack Frames and Memory Management

At the core of virtual threads is an alternative implementation of `java.lang.Thread` that stores its stack frames in Java's garbage-collected heap. In contrast, traditional threads store stack frames in monolithic memory blocks allocated by the operating system. This novel approach eliminates the need to estimate a thread's required stack size. A virtual thread's memory footprint starts from just a few hundred bytes, and it automatically adjusts as the call stack grows and shrinks. This dynamic memory management significantly improves resource efficiency.

Carrier Threads and OS Involvement

The operating system is unaware of virtual threads; it only recognizes platform threads, which remain the unit of OS-level scheduling. To execute code in a virtual thread, the Java runtime mounts it onto a platform thread, known as a *carrier thread*. These carrier threads are part of a specialized `ForkJoinPool`. This process involves temporarily copying the necessary stack frames from the heap to the carrier thread's stack. Essentially, the carrier thread is "borrowed" to run the virtual thread's code.

Handling Blocking Operations

One of the most consequential improvements is how virtual threads deal with blocking operations. When a virtual thread arrives at an operation that would typically block— perhaps it's waiting for I/O—it can be unmounted from its carrier thread. Its modified stack frames are copied back to the heap, and the carrier thread gets freed to go off and do other work. This functionality has been retrofitted to almost all blocking points in the JDK. It's what makes virtual threads highly efficient in resource utilization.

Transparency and Invisibility

The process of mounting and unmounting a virtual thread is transparent to the Java code. There is no way for the Java code to discern the identity of the current carrier thread. Even `ThreadLocal` (*https://oreil.ly/0TLqb*) values of the carrier thread are invisible to a virtual thread. This level of abstraction ensures that virtual threads can be used seamlessly without requiring changes to existing Java codebases.

The concept of virtual threads is reminiscent of virtual memory systems. In a virtual memory system, applications run under the illusion that they have access to effectively unlimited amounts of address space. This is enabled by a hardware-level mapping between which part of virtual memory is actually memory, and which part is disk. Similarly, virtual threads create the illusion of effectively unlimited multithreading, by sharing scarce and costly platform threads. Inactive virtual thread stacks are "paged out" to the heap, just as unused memory pages in a virtual memory system are "paged out" to disk.

More about how virtual threads work and their internals will be discussed in later chapters.

Simplifying Asynchronous Operations

With virtual threads, asynchronous operations and task aggregation become a breeze. In Java, the burden of blocking while waiting for the asynchronous task to finish is effectively lifted. Developers can now happily call the blocking `get` (*https://oreil.ly/2JFZL*) on a `Future` (*https://oreil.ly/CWUYq*) and not have to take a performance hit. But where virtual threads really shine is when it comes to aggregating the results of multiple asynchronous tasks.

Consider a scenario where you need to fetch various components of a sentence from different APIs and combine them into a cohesive phrase. For instance, you might want to retrieve an adjective and a noun to create a simple yet randomly generated phrase. With virtual threads, this task becomes remarkably straightforward:

```
public String generatePhrase() throws ExecutionException, InterruptedException {
    try (var executor = Executors.newVirtualThreadPerTaskExecutor()) {
        Future<String> adjectiveFuture = executor.submit(this::fetchAdjective);
        Future<String> nounFuture = executor.submit(this::fetchNoun);
        String adjective = adjectiveFuture.get();
        String noun = nounFuture.get();
        return adjective + " " + noun;
    }
```

```
    }
    private String fetchAdjective() {
        // Fetch adjective from an API
        return "beautiful";
    }
    private String fetchNoun() {
        // Fetch noun from an API
        return "sunset";
    }
```

In this example, we leverage the `VirtualThreadPerTaskExecutor` (*https://oreil.ly/ K6hJ6*), a convenient utility for creating virtual threads for individual tasks. We submit two tasks, one to fetch an adjective and one for a noun, using the `Executor Service`'s `submit` method.

The true elegance of virtual threads is revealed when we call `get` on the `Future` objects returned by the submitted tasks. Since virtual threads are lightweight and efficient, we can comfortably block and wait for the results without consuming excessive resources or causing performance degradation. This approach simplifies the handling of asynchronous operations, eliminating the need for complex callback structures or intricate synchronization mechanisms.

Once we have the adjective and noun, we can seamlessly concatenate them to form a phrase, such as "beautiful sunset" in this case.

The `invokeAll` method can still be utilized even when there are similar tasks with the same result type. It is particularly helpful when the goal is to compile results into a list. For instance, you might want to filter different images in a similar manner:

```
package ca.bazlur.modern.concurrency.c02;

import javax.imageio.ImageIO;
import java.awt.image.BufferedImage;
import java.io.File;
import java.io.IOException;
import java.util.List;
import java.util.concurrent.*;

public class ImageProcessingExample {

    public static void main(String[] args)
            throws InterruptedException, ExecutionException {
        try (var service = Executors.newVirtualThreadPerTaskExecutor()) {  ❶

            List<Callable<BufferedImage>> tasks = List.of(
                () -> resize("https://example.com/img1.jpg", 200, 200),
                () -> grayscale("https://example.com/img2.jpg"),
                () -> rotate("https://example.com/img3.jpg", 90)
            );  ❷

            List<Future<BufferedImage>> results = service.invokeAll(tasks);  ❸
```

```
      // Process and save transformed images
      int i = 1;
      for (Future<BufferedImage> future : results) { ❹
        BufferedImage image = future.get(); ❺
        ImageIO.write(image, "jpg",
            new File("output_image" + i + ".jpg"));
        i++;
      }
    } catch (IOException e) {
      throw new RuntimeException(e);
    }
  }

  static BufferedImage resize(String url, int width, int height) {
    //Logic to download and resize the image goes here
    return null;
  }

  static BufferedImage grayscale(String url) {
    // Logic to download and convert the image to
    // grayscale goes here
    return null;
  }

  static BufferedImage rotate(String url, double angle) {
    //Logic to download and rotate the image goes here
    return null;
  }
}
```

Let's see what we have here:

❶ Uses the virtual thread executor, but now for multiple concurrent image processing tasks.

❷ Creates a list of `Callable` tasks, each representing a different image transformation operation.

❸ Submits all tasks simultaneously with `invokeAll()`; they execute concurrently on separate virtual threads.

❹ Iterates through the results in the same order as the original task list.

❺ Retrieves each result with blocking `get()` calls that efficiently yield virtual threads during waits.

Modern applications frequently demand the ability to handle multiple tasks simultaneously while aggregating their results efficiently. Virtual threads provide an elegant solution by enabling parallel execution with seamless result collection, offering significant advantages in contemporary computing environments where I/O-bound operations dominate application performance.

The Promise of Structured Concurrency

Although all the preceding examples are valid and involve fairly straightforward ways of dealing with concurrent tasks, they are somewhat simplistic—for instance, they do not handle exceptions or timeouts very well. It's possible that the `Future::get` method throws exceptions, and without a timeout mechanism, it could potentially block indefinitely.

Java's JEP 505 introduces structured concurrency, aiming to simplify how we write robust concurrent code. The API provides a structured scope within which tasks run, and if any of them fail or timeout, all tasks within the scope are automatically canceled. Here is a brief example:

```
public static void main(String[] args) {
  try (StructuredTaskScope scope = StructuredTaskScope.open()) {
    StructuredTaskScope.Subtask<String> subtask1
        = scope.fork(() -> fetchData("https://api1.example.com"));
    StructuredTaskScope.Subtask<String> subtask2 =
        scope.fork(() -> fetchData("https://api2.example.com"));
    scope.join();
    var result = subtask2.get() + subtask1.get();
    System.out.println(result);
  } catch (InterruptedException e) {
    throw new RuntimeException(e);
  }
}
```

The preceding code requires JDK 25 with preview features enabled (`--enable-preview`).

These fail-fast scopes also let you provide timeouts and make it very easy to encapsulate exceptions. With the fail-fast scope, `subtask1` and `subtask2` are forked tasks running within the scope. If either of them fails (by raising an exception) or if the timeout elapses, all tasks running within the scope are canceled, and the exception is propagated back. This results in cleaner and more robust code, brilliantly encapsulating exception propagation and timeouts within a built-in construct.

The introduction of structured concurrency in Java represents a significant step forward in simplifying the development of concurrent applications. By providing a structured scope for running tasks, the API enables automatic cancellation and exception handling, reducing the burden on developers of managing these aspects manually.

Moreover, structured concurrency promotes a more declarative style of programming, where developers can express their intentions clearly and concisely. Instead of dealing with low-level details, such as creating and managing threads or implementing complex cancellation logic, developers can focus on the higher-level tasks and let the Structured Concurrency API handle the underlying complexities.

This is just a glimpse of structured concurrency's potential. We'll explore this fascinating subject in greater depth in subsequent chapters, examining advanced patterns, different scope types, and how structured concurrency complements virtual threads to create truly robust concurrent applications.

Managing Resource Constraints with Rate Limiting

Virtual threads are essentially an open door to unlimited concurrency, offering the potential to handle an unprecedented number of tasks simultaneously. While we've discussed this as a positive thing so far, it can be challenging in certain aspects. This is because not all parts of the software can handle the same amount of load. For example, the web application that we are building can certainly accept a million requests, thus creating a million virtual threads, but the underlying database may not be able to handle that many requests.

Before virtual threads, the thread pool helped us limit requests without the need to implement additional mechanisms. So if the thread pool has 1,000 threads, the underlying resource could, at most, have 1,000 simultaneous loads, not more. However, this presents a conundrum since virtual threads can be virtually unlimited. So now the question becomes: How do you prevent overloading services when using virtual threads?

The answer lies in implementing rate-limiting mechanisms specific to the resource you are accessing. These mechanisms can range from simple to complex, depending on the nature of the resource and the service level agreements (SLAs) you must adhere to.

Let's explore an example using a semaphore to control the number of concurrent requests to a web service. Crucially, the focus here is on the principle of rate limiting:

```
import java.net.URI;
import java.net.http.*;
import java.time.Duration;
import java.time.Instant;
import java.util.List;
import java.util.concurrent.*;
import java.util.stream.IntStream;
public class ResourceAwareRateLimitExample {
```

```java
    private static final HttpClient CLIENT = HttpClient.newBuilder()
        .connectTimeout(Duration.ofSeconds(10))  ❶
        .build();
    private static final int MAX_PARALLEL = 10;  ❷
    private static final Semaphore gate = new Semaphore(MAX_PARALLEL);  ❸
private static final String API_URL =
    "https://api.chucknorris.io/jokes/random";

    public static void main(String[] args) throws Exception {
      Instant start = Instant.now();
      List<String> jokes = fetchJokes(50);  ❹
      long ms = Duration.between(start, Instant.now()).toMillis();
      System.out.printf("Fetched %d jokes in %d ms (avg %d ms)%n",
          jokes.size(), ms, ms / jokes.size());
      jokes.stream().limit(3).forEach(j -> System.out.println("• " + j));
    }

    private static List<String> fetchJokes(int n) throws Exception {
      try (ExecutorService pool = Executors.newVirtualThreadPerTaskExecutor()) {  ❺
        List<Future<String>> futures = IntStream.range(0, n)
            .mapToObj(i -> pool.submit(ResourceAwareRateLimitExample::fetchJoke))
            .toList();
        return futures.stream()
            .map(ResourceAwareRateLimitExample::join)  ❻
            .toList();
      }
    }

    private static String fetchJoke() throws Exception {
      HttpRequest req = HttpRequest.newBuilder(URI.create(API_URL))
          .GET()
          .timeout(Duration.ofSeconds(30))  ❼
          .build();
      try {
        gate.acquire();  ❽
        HttpResponse<String> res
            = CLIENT.send(req, HttpResponse.BodyHandlers.ofString());
        if (res.statusCode() != 200)
          throw new RuntimeException("API error " + res.statusCode());
        return parseJoke(res.body());
      } finally {
        gate.release();  ❾
      }
    }

    private static String parseJoke(String json) {  ❿
      int s = json.indexOf("\"value\":\"") + 9;
      int e = json.indexOf('"', s);
      return json.substring(s, e).replace("\\\"", "\"");
    }

    private static <T> T join(Future<T> f) {
```

```
        try {
          return f.get();
        } catch (InterruptedException e) { ⓫
          Thread.currentThread().interrupt();
          throw new CompletionException(e);
        } catch (ExecutionException e) {
          throw new CompletionException(e.getCause());
        }
      }
    }
```

Let's go through what we did here:

❶ Configures a shared `HttpClient` with a 10-second connection timeout to prevent hanging on network issues.

❷ Defines the maximum number of concurrent API requests allowed at any time.

❸ Creates a counting semaphore that acts as our rate-limiting gate, initialized with the maximum parallel requests.

❹ Attempts to fetch 50 jokes, which exceeds our rate limit, demonstrating how the semaphore controls concurrency.

❺ Creates an executor that spawns a new virtual thread for each submitted task—perfect for I/O-bound operations.

❻ Blocks until all futures complete, collecting results in order of completion.

❼ Sets a per-request timeout of 30 seconds, preventing individual requests from blocking indefinitely.

❽ Acquires a permit from the semaphore, blocking if all permits are in use—this is where rate limiting happens.

❾ Releases the permit in a `finally` block, ensuring it's returned even if an exception occurs.

❿ Simple JSON parsing for demonstration—in production, use a proper JSON library like Jackson or Gson.

⓫ Improved error handling that preserves interruption status and unwraps `ExecutionException` to get the actual cause.

In this example, we've limited the concurrent tasks to 10 by setting the semaphore to count to 10. The task will be blocked whenever a new task tries to acquire the semaphore and the limit is reached. But remember, with virtual threads, blocking is cheap. This highlights the practical implications of virtual threads—even though we may introduce intentional bottlenecks for rate limiting, the efficiency of virtual threads minimizes the negative impact on the overall performance of the application.

Understanding Semaphores in Java

A *semaphore* is a synchronization mechanism that acts like a gatekeeper, controlling access to a shared resource. In Java, the `Semaphore` (*https://oreil.ly/8ACAn*) class (part of the java.util.concurrent package) offers a handy way to manage this access control.

The idea behind a semaphore is simple: it keeps track of a set number of permits. Before a thread can access a particular section of code, it needs to grab a permit. When the thread is finished, it returns the permit. If no permits are available, the thread waits until one is released.

Key methods of a semaphore are:

`acquire()` *(https://oreil.ly/SEwgu)*
: This method requests a permit. The thread will wait if none are currently available.

`release()` *(https://oreil.ly/_mtvT)*
: This method returns a permit to the semaphore, potentially allowing another waiting thread to proceed.

`availablePermits()` *(https://oreil.ly/pCyco)*
: This method lets you check how many permits are currently free.

Imagine you have a pool of only five database connections. You can use a semaphore to ensure that only five threads can use those connections at once. For instance:

```
import java.util.Optional;
import java.util.concurrent.Semaphore;

public class ResourcePool {
    private final Semaphore semaphore; ❶
    public ResourcePool(int resourceCount) {
        this.semaphore = new Semaphore(resourceCount); ❷
    }

    public Optional<String> useResource(String query) {
        try {
            semaphore.acquire(); ❸
            try {
                // Simulate obtaining and using a database connection
                return queryDatabase(query); ❹
            } finally {
                semaphore.release(); ❺
```

```
            }
        } catch (InterruptedException e) {
            Thread.currentThread().interrupt(); ❻
            return Optional.empty();
        }
    }

    private Optional<String> queryDatabase(String query) {
        // Simulate database query with some delay
        try {
            Thread.sleep(100);
        } catch (InterruptedException e) {
            Thread.currentThread().interrupt();
            return Optional.empty();
        }
        return Optional.of("Result for: " + query);
    }
}
```

Let's examine how this implementation controls access to our limited resources:

❶ The semaphore field stores our synchronization primitive. This semaphore acts as a thread-safe counter for available permits, managing concurrent access to our database connections.

❷ During construction, we set the resource limit. We initialize the semaphore with the maximum number of concurrent accesses allowed, effectively creating our connection pool size.

❸ This is where the actual rate limiting happens. The `acquire()` method blocks the current thread until a permit becomes available, implementing our resource constraint.

❹ Once a permit is acquired, we enter the critical section. This represents the section where the limited resource (database connection) is actually used.

❺ Resource cleanup is crucial in concurrent programming. We always release the permit in a `finally` block to prevent resource leaks, even if an exception occurs.

❻ Proper thread interruption handling is essential. We preserve the interrupted status for proper thread interruption handling, allowing callers to respond appropriately.

In the preceding class, the `useResource()` method is limited to access only by `resourceCount` number of threads. If more threads require access, they will have to wait until the threads with access release it.

In production systems, it's often valuable to monitor resource usage and implement timeouts to prevent indefinite blocking. Additionally, to gain an extra level of confidence in our semaphore's functionality, let's update our `ResourcePool` class.

Here's the revised code:

```
import java.util.Optional;
import java.util.Random;
import java.util.concurrent.Semaphore;
import java.util.concurrent.TimeUnit;
import java.util.concurrent.atomic.AtomicInteger;

public class MonitoredResourcePool {
  private final Semaphore semaphore;
  private final AtomicInteger activeConnections; ❶
  private final AtomicInteger peakConnections; ❷

  public MonitoredResourcePool(int resourceCount) {
    this.semaphore = new Semaphore(resourceCount, true); ❸
    this.activeConnections = new AtomicInteger(0);
    this.peakConnections = new AtomicInteger(0);
  }

  public Optional<String> useResource(String query) {
    boolean acquired = false;
    try {
      acquired = semaphore.tryAcquire(5, TimeUnit.SECONDS); ❹
      if (!acquired) {
        return Optional.empty(); ❺
      }
      int current = activeConnections.incrementAndGet();
      peakConnections.updateAndGet(peak -> Math.max(peak, current)); ❻
      return queryDatabase(query);
    } catch (InterruptedException e) {
      Thread.currentThread().interrupt();
      return Optional.empty();
    } finally {
      if (acquired) {
        activeConnections.decrementAndGet();
        semaphore.release();
      }
    }
  }

  public int getCurrentActiveConnections() {
    return activeConnections.get();
  }

  public int getPeakConnections() {
    return peakConnections.get(); ❼
  }
```

```java
    private Optional<String> queryDatabase(String query) {
        try {
            Thread.sleep(new Random().nextInt(500) + 500);
        } catch (InterruptedException e) {
            Thread.currentThread().interrupt();
            return Optional.empty();
        }
        return Optional.of("Result for: " + query);
    }
}
```

This enhanced implementation adds several production-ready features:

❶ Monitoring active connections helps with debugging and capacity planning. The `activeConnections` counter tracks current active connections for monitoring purposes only, not for enforcement of limits.

❷ Understanding peak usage patterns is crucial for capacity planning. This counter records the highest number of concurrent connections observed during the application's lifetime.

❸ Fairness prevents thread starvation in high-contention scenarios. By passing `true` as the second parameter, we create a fair semaphore that ensures threads acquire permits in FIFO order.

❹ Timeouts prevent indefinite blocking and improve system resilience. The `tryAcquire` method with timeout avoids indefinite blocking, returning control to the caller after the specified duration.

❺ Graceful degradation is better than hanging indefinitely. When unable to acquire a resource within the timeout period, we return an empty `Optional` to indicate failure.

❻ Atomic operations ensure thread-safe statistics collection. This thread-safe update of peak connections using atomic operations prevents race conditions in our monitoring code.

❼ Exposing metrics enables operational visibility. This method provides observability into resource pool usage patterns, which is essential for monitoring and alerting.

To verify that our semaphore correctly limits concurrent access, let's create a test that attempts to overwhelm the resource pool:

```java
package ca.bazlur.modern.concurrency.c02;

import java.util.ArrayList;
```

```java
import java.util.List;
import java.util.Optional;
import java.util.concurrent.*;

public class ResourcePoolTest {

  public static void main(String[] args) throws Exception {
    int maxConcurrentThreads = 5;
    int totalRequests = 50;
    var pool = new MonitoredResourcePool(maxConcurrentThreads);

    var futures = new ArrayList<Future<Optional<String>>>();

    try (var executor = Executors.newVirtualThreadPerTaskExecutor()) {
      for (int i = 0; i < totalRequests; i++) {
        final int taskId = i;
        futures.add(executor.submit(() -> pool.useResource("Query " + taskId)));
      }

      int successCount = 0;
      int timeoutCount = 0;

      for (Future<Optional<String>> future : futures) {
        Optional<String> result = future.get();
        if (result.isPresent()) {
          successCount++;
        } else {
          timeoutCount++;  ❶
        }
      }

      System.out.printf("""
              requests : %d
              successful: %d
              timed-out : %d
              peak usage: %d%n""",
          totalRequests, successCount, timeoutCount, pool.getPeakConnections());  ❷

      assert pool.getPeakConnections() <= maxConcurrentThreads
          : "Peak connections exceeded limit!";
    }
  }
}
```

Our test demonstrates the effectiveness of semaphore-based rate limiting:

❶ Tracking timeouts helps us understand system behavior under load. This counter tracks requests that couldn't acquire a permit within the timeout period, indicating resource contention.

❷ The peak connection count proves our rate limiting works correctly. This verification ensures the semaphore successfully limited concurrent access throughout the test execution.

When you run this test, you'll observe that despite submitting 50 concurrent requests, the peak connections never exceed our limit of 5. Some requests may timeout if they can't acquire a permit within five seconds, demonstrating the protective nature of our semaphore-based rate limiting.

The output appears as follows for me:

```
Total requests: 50
Successful: 32
Timed out: 18
Peak concurrent connections: 5
```

Why Use a Semaphore?

Having demonstrated how a semaphore effectively regulates concurrency, let's explore some common scenarios where this synchronization mechanism proves invaluable:

Resource management
Semaphores are ideal for limiting access to shared resources such as network sockets, database connections, or any resource with a finite capacity. Consider a scenario where your application has a license for only 10 concurrent database connections. A semaphore initialized with 10 permits ensures you never exceed this limit, preventing license violations and connection errors.

Rate limiting
Use semaphores to control the rate of requests to a web service or API, preventing overload and ensuring a smooth user experience. For example, if an external API allows only 100 requests per minute, we can use a semaphore in combination with a scheduled task that replenishes permits to maintain this rate limit.

General concurrency control
Semaphores offer a way to precisely manage the number of threads simultaneously executing a specific code section. This is crucial for maintaining stability in highly concurrent applications, especially when dealing with resources that can handle only a specific level of parallelism.

When using semaphores, keep the following important notes in mind:

Fairness
Java's `Semaphore` class allows you to configure fairness. In a fair semaphore, permits are granted in the order they were requested. However, fair semaphores can have slightly lower performance compared to nonfair ones due to the overhead of maintaining request order. Choose fairness when preventing thread starvation is more important than raw performance.

Blocking

The `acquire()` method can block a thread if no permits are available. Fortunately, the introduction of virtual threads in Java significantly reduces the overhead associated with this blocking. Unlike platform threads, blocked virtual threads don't consume OS resources, making semaphore-based synchronization much more scalable.

Error handling

Meticulously release permits within a `finally` block. This is essential to prevent resource leaks and ensure proper resource management, even in the event of exceptions.

Permit accounting

Remember that semaphores don't associate permits with specific threads. Any thread can release a permit, even one it didn't acquire. This flexibility can be useful but requires careful design to avoid accidentally increasing the effective permit count.

> ## Limitations of Semaphores
>
> Semaphores are essential for protecting limited resources, but they have a dangerous quirk: they don't track which thread acquired which permit. Any thread can release a permit, even one it never acquired.
>
> Here's how easily things can go wrong:
>
> ```
> // Start with 2 permits
> Semaphore semaphore = new Semaphore(2);
> // Thread 1: Forgets to release
> Thread.ofVirtual().start(() -> {
>     semaphore.acquire();
>     // Oops! No release
> });
> // Thread 2: Releases without acquiring
> Thread.ofVirtual().start(() -> {
>     semaphore.release(); // BUG!
>     semaphore.release(); // Double BUG!
> });
> // Result: We now have 3+ permits instead of 2!
> ```
>
> In production, this could mean exceeding database connections, overwhelming APIs, or causing memory exhaustion.
>
> Here's the bulletproof pattern:
>
> ```
> public <T> T useResource(Callable<T> task)
>   throws Exception {
>     semaphore.acquire();  // Acquire before try
>     try {
> ```

```
            return task.call();
        } finally {
            semaphore.release();   // ALWAYS releases
        }
    }
```

In conclusion, understanding semaphores gives you a powerful tool for managing shared resources in your Java applications. This is particularly valuable when working with virtual threads, as it helps ensure stability and optimal performance.

Limitations of Virtual Threads

So far, we have learned the benefits of virtual threads. They are designed to be lightweight and easily scheduled by the Java runtime, offering a more efficient way to handle concurrency. However, they come with a limitation known as *pinning*, which could potentially affect the scalability and performance of your application.

In the context of virtual threads, pinning refers to the situation where a virtual thread becomes bound to its carrier thread (the underlying platform thread on which it runs). While pinned, a virtual thread cannot unmount itself from the carrier thread even though it may hit blocking operations, effectively monopolizing that carrier thread for the duration of the pinning.

Pinning occurs in two main scenarios:

Synchronized blocks or methods
　　When a virtual thread enters a `synchronized` block or method, it becomes pinned to its carrier thread. This means that during the execution of that block or method, the carrier thread cannot be reused for other tasks.

Native methods or foreign functions
　　When a virtual thread executes a native method or a foreign function, it also becomes pinned.

The essence of virtual threads is their ability to be unmounted from carrier threads when they perform blocking operations, essentially freeing up the carrier threads for other tasks. When pinning happens, a virtual thread cannot unmount itself. This presents a challenge because we have limited carrier threads. If many virtual threads become pinned for extended periods, they can tie up these carrier threads. This blocks other virtual threads from executing, effectively limiting the concurrency benefits provided by virtual threads.

Pinning negates this advantage in the following ways:

Reduced throughput
  Because a pinned virtual thread occupies its carrier thread, other virtual threads must wait for free carrier threads, reducing the system's overall throughput.

Resource inefficiency
  Carrier threads are a finite resource tied to system capabilities. Having them blocked due to pinned virtual threads is an inefficient use of these resources.

Scalability concerns
  If a significant portion of your virtual threads becomes pinned due to frequent use of `synchronized` blocks or native methods, you might run into scalability issues.

To alleviate the effects of pinning, consider the following strategies:

- Instead of `synchronized` blocks or methods, use `ReentrantLock` (*https://oreil.ly/DkvNO*) from java.util.concurrent.locks (*https://oreil.ly/dg6lJ*), as it allows the virtual thread to be unmounted when blocked.
- Regularly review your code to identify and minimize the use of synchronized methods or blocks and native methods in the context of virtual threads.

By understanding the limitations posed by pinning in virtual threads, you can make better architectural decisions for your Java applications.

Pinning

Let's take a look at a concrete Java example that demonstrates the concept of pinning in virtual threads:

```java
import java.util.List;
import java.util.stream.IntStream;

public class ThreadPinnedExample {
  private static final Object lock = new Object();

  public static void main(String[] args) {
    List<Thread> threadList = IntStream.range(0, 10)
        .mapToObj(i -> Thread.ofVirtual().unstarted(() -> {
          if (i == 0) {
            System.out.println(Thread.currentThread()); ❶
          }
          synchronized (lock) { ❷
            try {
              Thread.sleep(25); ❸
            } catch (InterruptedException e) {
              Thread.currentThread().interrupt();
            }
          }
          if (i == 0) {
            System.out.println(Thread.currentThread()); ❹
```

```
          }
        })).toList();

    threadList.forEach(Thread::start);
    threadList.forEach(t -> {
      try {
        t.join();
      } catch (InterruptedException e) {
        Thread.currentThread().interrupt();
      }
    });
  }
}
```

Let's trace through what happens when this code executes:

❶ For the first virtual thread (when `i == 0`), we print the current thread information before entering the `synchronized` block. This captures which carrier thread the virtual thread is running on.

❷ When a virtual thread enters this `synchronized` block, it becomes pinned to its carrier thread. The pinning occurs because `synchronized` blocks currently prevent virtual threads from unmounting from their carrier threads.

❸ The sleep operation simulates a blocking I/O operation. Normally, a sleeping virtual thread would unmount from its carrier thread, allowing that carrier to run other virtual threads. However, inside a `synchronized` block, the virtual thread remains pinned, monopolizing the carrier thread for the full 25 milliseconds.

❹ After exiting the `synchronized` block, we print the thread information again. This allows us to verify whether the virtual thread remained on the same carrier thread.

When we execute this code, the output for thread 0 reveals the pinning effect:

```
VirtualThread[#21]/runnable@ForkJoinPool-1-worker-1
VirtualThread[#21]/runnable@ForkJoinPool-1-worker-1
```

Notice that the carrier thread identifier (`ForkJoinPool-1-worker-1`) remains identical before and after the synchronized block. This confirms that the virtual thread did not switch carrier threads, indicating it was pinned for the duration of the blocking operation.

Starting with JDK 24, virtual threads will no longer be pinned by `synchronized` blocks. The JVM now supports unmounting within synchronized sections, eliminating this limitation entirely. However, if you're using JDK 23 or earlier, you must still consider pinning behavior when designing concurrent applications.

Consider what happens if we scale this to 1,000 or 10,000 virtual threads, all trying to enter synchronized blocks with blocking operations. With only a handful of carrier threads available, most virtual threads will queue up waiting for a free carrier thread, defeating the purpose of using virtual threads for high concurrency.

Addressing the Pinning Problem with ReentrantLock

ReentrantLock is a synchronization mechanism in Java that offers more flexibility than the traditional synchronized block. It allows more sophisticated thread interactions and provides additional features such as fairness, try-lock, and interruptibility. One of the key advantages of using ReentrantLock is its ability to avoid the pinning problem in virtual threads.

The following example code showcases how to use ReentrantLock to avoid the pinning problem associated with virtual threads in Java. Instead of using a synchronized block, which would pin the virtual thread to its carrier, the code employs a ReentrantLock for synchronization. This allows the virtual thread to be unmounted from its carrier thread when it blocks, thus making the carrier thread available for other tasks. For example:

```
import java.util.concurrent.locks.ReentrantLock;
import java.util.stream.IntStream;

public class PreventPinningExample {
  private static final ReentrantLock lock = new ReentrantLock();  ❶

  public static void main(String[] args) {
    var threadList = IntStream.range(0, 10)
        .mapToObj(i -> Thread.ofVirtual().unstarted(() -> {
          if (i == 0) {
            System.out.println(Thread.currentThread());  ❷
          }
          lock.lock();  ❸
          try {
            Thread.sleep(25);  ❹
          } catch (InterruptedException e) {
            Thread.currentThread().interrupt();
          } finally {
            lock.unlock();  ❺
          }
          if (i == 0) {
            System.out.println(Thread.currentThread());  ❻
          }
        })).toList();

    threadList.forEach(Thread::start);
    threadList.forEach(thread -> {
      try {
        thread.join();
```

```
            } catch (InterruptedException e) {
                Thread.currentThread().interrupt();
            }
        });
    }
}
```

Let's examine the key differences from our synchronized example:

❶ We create a `ReentrantLock` instance instead of using an object monitor. This lock provides the same mutual exclusion guarantees as a `synchronized` lock, but with virtual-thread-friendly behavior.

❷ We capture the initial carrier thread information for the first virtual thread.

❸ The `lock()` method acquires the lock, similar to entering a `synchronized` block. However, unlike `synchronized`, this doesn't pin the virtual thread.

❹ During the sleep operation inside the lock, the virtual thread can unmount from its carrier thread. The carrier becomes available to run other virtual threads while this one is blocked.

❺ The unlock operation must always occur in a `finally` block. This ensures the lock is released even if an exception occurs, preventing deadlocks.

❻ After releasing the lock, we print the thread information again to observe any carrier thread changes.

When you run this example, the output reveals the crucial difference:

```
VirtualThread[#20]/runnable@ForkJoinPool-1-worker-1
VirtualThread[#20]/runnable@ForkJoinPool-1-worker-3
```

The output can be interpreted as follows:

VirtualThread[#20]/runnable@ForkJoinPool-1-worker-1
> Indicates that the virtual thread with the ID #20 is in a `runnable` state and is currently mounted on a carrier thread named `ForkJoinPool-1-worker-1`.

VirtualThread[#20]/runnable@ForkJoinPool-1-worker-3
> Shows that the same virtual thread with the ID #20 is still in a `runnable` state but has now been remounted onto a different carrier thread, named `ForkJoinPool-1-worker-3`.

This example shows that the virtual thread was initially running on one carrier thread and later moved to another. This is possible because we used `ReentrantLock` instead of a synchronized block. This essentially avoids the pinning problem and allows the Java runtime to optimally schedule the virtual thread on available carrier threads.

The key difference lies in implementation. While synchronized blocks use object monitors that currently require pinning, ReentrantLock uses park/unpark mechanisms that are virtual-thread-aware.

> ## The Park/Unpark Mechanism
>
> The park/unpark mechanism is a low-level thread coordination primitive in Java that forms the foundation for many higher-level concurrency utilities.
>
> When a thread calls LockSupport.park() (*https://oreil.ly/rvEjY*), it becomes "parked" (blocked) until:
>
> - Another thread calls unpark() with this thread as the target.
> - The thread is interrupted.
> - The call spuriously returns (rare but possible).
>
> Calling LockSupport.unpark(thread) (*https://oreil.ly/Hl-pC*) makes the target thread eligible to proceed:
>
> ```
> // Thread A
> LockSupport.park(); // Blocks until unparked
> // Thread B
> LockSupport.unpark(threadA); // Wakes up Thread A
> ```
>
> What makes park/unpark virtual-thread-friendly is that the JVM can detect when a virtual thread parks and unmount it from its carrier thread. This is different from object monitors (used by synchronized), which require the virtual thread to remain mounted.

When a virtual thread blocks on a ReentrantLock, the runtime can:

1. Save the virtual thread's state
2. Unmount it from the carrier thread
3. Use that carrier for other virtual threads
4. Later mount the virtual thread on any available carrier when the lock becomes available

Synchronized Blocks and Virtual Thread Pinning

While the `synchronized` keyword can lead to pinning, its impact varies depending on the specific code within the `synchronized` block. Let's consider a few examples:

Example 1: Minimal pinning risk

```
synchronized (this) {
  return this.a + this.b;
}
```

In this case, the operation within the `synchronized` block is extremely short. Even if the virtual thread needs to wait for the lock, it will likely be unpinned very quickly, minimizing the impact.

Example 2: Potential pinning issue

```
synchronized (this) {
  var response = httpClient.sendBlockingRequest(request);
  return response;
}
```

Here, the blocking network call (`httpClient.sendBlockingRequest`) within the `synchronized` block poses a pinning risk. The virtual thread could remain pinned for the entire duration of the network request, hindering concurrency gains.

Example 3: Similar pinning issue

```
synchronized (this) {
  this.wait();
}
```

Calls to `Object.wait()` also lead to pinning within `synchronized` blocks, as the virtual thread will remain pinned until notified.

Key takeaway

The severity of pinning caused by `synchronized` depends on the nature of operations within the block. Short, non-blocking operations are generally fine. However, blocking calls necessitate careful consideration.

Evolving landscape

Future JDK updates (*https://oreil.ly/QaB-6*) might introduce "unpinning-aware" I/O operations, potentially mitigating pinning in some scenarios. For now, when maximizing scalability with virtual threads, it's often wise to favor `ReentrantLock` for more flexible synchronization.

Special thanks to Simone Bordet (*https://oreil.ly/7vHP-*) for explaining this easily to me.

Native Method Invocation and Pinning

Similar to our previous experiments with `synchronized` blocks, let's explore how native method invocations can lead to virtual thread pinning. We'll demonstrate this by using a simple C function and Java's Foreign Function & Memory API, which is available as of JDK 22.

First, let's create a simple native function that simulates some work:

```c
#include <unistd.h>
// Function definition
int addNumbers(int number1, int number2) {
    // Pause execution for 200,000 microseconds (200 milliseconds)
    usleep(200000);

    return number1 + number2;
}
```

Let's compile this function based on our operating system:

- Linux: `gcc -shared -fPIC -o libaddNumbers.so addNumbers.c`
- macOS: `gcc -shared -fPIC -o libaddNumbers.dylib addNumbers.c`
- Windows: Use a GCC environment (like MinGW) and `gcc -shared -o addNumbers.dll addNumbers.c`

After compiling on macOS, it provided me with `libaddNumbers.dylib`. Let's invoke this native method using virtual threads:

```java
import java.lang.foreign.*;
import java.lang.invoke.MethodHandle;
import java.nio.file.Path;
import java.util.List;
import java.util.stream.IntStream;

public class ThreadPinnedNativeMethodExample {
    public static void main(String[] args) {
        List<Thread> threadList = IntStream.range(0, 10)
            .mapToObj(i -> Thread.ofVirtual().unstarted(() -> {
                if (i == 0) {
                    System.out.println(Thread.currentThread()); ❶
                }
                int sum = invokeNativeAddNumbers(56, 11); ❷
                if (i == 0) {
                    System.out.println(Thread.currentThread()); ❸
                }
            })).toList();
        threadList.forEach(Thread::start);
        threadList.forEach(t -> {
            try {
                t.join();
            } catch (InterruptedException e) {
                Thread.currentThread().interrupt();
```

```
            }
        });
    }
    public static int invokeNativeAddNumbers(int a, int b) {
        try (Arena arena = Arena.ofConfined()) { ❹
            SymbolLookup lookup = SymbolLookup.libraryLookup(
                Path.of("libaddNumbers.dylib"), arena); ❺
            MemorySegment memorySegment = lookup.find("addNumbers")
                .orElseThrow(() ->
                    new RuntimeException("addNumbers function not found"));
            Linker linker = Linker.nativeLinker();
            FunctionDescriptor addNumbersDescriptor = FunctionDescriptor.of(
                ValueLayout.JAVA_INT,     // return type
                ValueLayout.JAVA_INT,     // parameter 1
                ValueLayout.JAVA_INT);    // parameter 2
            MethodHandle addNumbersHandle = linker.downcallHandle(
                memorySegment, addNumbersDescriptor); ❻
            try {
                return (int) addNumbersHandle.invokeExact(a, b); ❼
            } catch (Throwable e) {
                throw new RuntimeException(e.getMessage());
            }
        }
    }
}
```

Let's understand what happens during execution:

❶ We capture the carrier thread information before the native call to establish a baseline.

❷ This is where the native method invocation occurs. During this call, the virtual thread becomes pinned to its carrier thread.

❸ After the native call completes, we check the carrier thread again to see if it changed.

❹ The Foreign Function & Memory (FFM) (*https://oreil.ly/TF4DO*) API is Java's modern approach to native interoperability, replacing the older Java Native Interface (JNI). Introduced as a preview feature in JDK 19 and finalized in JDK 22, it provides a safer, more performant way to call native code and manage off-heap memory. The `Arena` (*https://oreil.ly/vcHHG*) manages the lifecycle of native memory segments, ensuring proper cleanup when the `try-with-resources` block exits. To run this example with native access enabled, use: `java --enable-preview --source 21 --enable-native-access=ALL-UNNAMED ThreadPinned NativeMethodExample.java`

❺ Adjust the library path based on your OS: use `.so` for Linux, `.dylib` for macOS, or `.dll` for Windows.

❻ The downcall handle creates a bridge between Java and the native function, allowing us to invoke C code from Java.

❼ During this native invocation, the virtual thread cannot unmount from its carrier thread, causing pinning for the entire 200ms duration.

The output should look like this:

```
VirtualThread[#20]/runnable@ForkJoinPool-1-worker-1
VirtualThread[#20]/runnable@ForkJoinPool-1-worker-1
```

The identical thread identifiers before and after calling `invokeNativeAddNumbers` confirm that the virtual thread was pinned while the native method was executing.

Now we can ask the question: Why did it really happen during the native method?

Native methods cause pinning because the JVM cannot inspect or control native code execution. When a virtual thread enters native code, several constraints come into play: native code might hold thread-local state that cannot be migrated between threads, the native call stack cannot be saved and restored like Java stack frames, and native code might interact directly with OS-level thread primitives. These limitations force the virtual thread to remain mounted on its carrier thread for the entire duration of the native call.

This pinning behavior means applications with frequent native calls may not fully benefit from virtual thread scalability. To mitigate this, consider batching operations to reduce native call frequency, using asynchronous native APIs where available, or reimplementing critical native functionality in pure Java. Always measure the actual impact of native calls on your application's concurrency to determine if they're becoming a bottleneck.

JEP 491: Synchronize Virtual Threads Without Pinning

JEP 491: "Synchronize Virtual Threads Without Pinning" (*https://oreil.ly/zGYVq*), delivered in JDK 24, takes a significant step forward by reworking the synchronized keyword to be more virtual-thread-friendly. In its current state, when a virtual thread enters a synchronized block, it gets pinned to a platform thread. With this update, virtual threads will be able to acquire, hold, and release monitors independently of their carrier threads. The JVM scheduler will now allow blocked virtual threads to unmount from platform threads, freeing up resources so other tasks can continue running efficiently.

That being said, pinning isn't completely eliminated. Some edge cases such as blocking inside class initializers, waiting on class initialization by another thread, or resolving symbolic references during class loading or native code calls, will still result in pinning. While these situations are relatively rare, they could pose issues in highly concurrent applications. JEP 491 proposes monitoring these cases and refining the approach in future updates if needed.

However, there's a catch: to take advantage of these improvements, you'll need to migrate to JDK 24+. Since JDK 21 is still the long-term support (LTS) version that most applications rely on, it makes sense to remain aware of pinning issues and design applications accordingly.

For example, if we run the following code using JDK 25, we will not see the pinning issue anymore:

```
java --enable-native-access=ALL-UNNAMED ThreadPinnedNativeMethodExample.java
```

The output looks like this:

```
VirtualThread[#26]/runnable@ForkJoinPool-1-worker-1
VirtualThread[#26]/runnable@ForkJoinPool-1-worker-6
```

The Conundrum of ThreadLocal Variables in Virtual Threads

ThreadLocal (*https://oreil.ly/0TLqb*) variables in Java offer a way to confine data to a specific thread. The ThreadLocal class lets you create variables that are readable and writable only by the thread that created them. This eliminates the need for synchronization in scenarios where multiple threads might try to access the same data simultaneously.

Some classic use cases are:

Resource isolation
ThreadLocal variables are perfect for storing resources that aren't thread-safe. A classic example is SimpleDateFormat,[1] where each thread can have its own instance to avoid conflicts.

Implicit context
They're also commonly used to store contextual information specific to a thread's task, such as a database connection, user session data, or transaction IDs.

---

[1] Java now offers the DateTimeFormatter (*https://oreil.ly/2WT6n*) class, which is thread-safe and eliminates the need for ThreadLocal in this specific case.

Challenges with Virtual Threads

Virtual threads in Java are designed to be lightweight, allowing you to potentially run millions within a single application. This massive scale creates challenges when overusing ThreadLocal variables:

Memory consumption
    Each virtual thread having its own copy of a ThreadLocal variable can rapidly increase memory usage, especially if the stored data is large.

Overhead
    Initializing and cleaning up ThreadLocal variables comes with overhead. With the massive number of virtual threads, these actions can add a performance burden.

Inheritance:
    Virtual threads inherit ThreadLocal values from their parent thread like traditional threads. This inheritance can introduce subtle bugs that are difficult to trace and debug.

Let's examine a code example that demonstrates the potential drawbacks of heavily relying on ThreadLocal variables with virtual threads:

```java
import java.time.Duration;
import java.util.stream.IntStream;

public class ThreadLocalExample {

    public static void main(String[] args) {
        ThreadLocal<LargeObject> threadLocal
                = ThreadLocal.withInitial(LargeObject::new);

        var threadList = IntStream.range(0, 1000)
                .mapToObj(i -> Thread.ofVirtual().unstarted(() -> {
                    LargeObject largeObject = threadLocal.get();
                    useIt(largeObject);
                    sleep();
                })).toList();

        threadList.forEach(Thread::start);
        threadList.forEach(thread -> {
            try {
                thread.join();
            } catch (InterruptedException e) {
                Thread.currentThread().interrupt();
            }
        });
    }

    private static void useIt(LargeObject largeObject) {
```

```
            System.out.println(largeObject.data.length);
    }

    private static void sleep() {
        try {
            Thread.sleep(Duration.ofMinutes(5));
        } catch (InterruptedException e) {
            throw new RuntimeException(e);
        }
    }

    static class LargeObject {
        private byte[] data = new byte[1024 * 500]; // 500 KB
    }
}
```

This example demonstrates the creation of a 500 KB `LargeObject`. Each of the 1,000 virtual threads stores its own copy of a `LargeObject` within a `ThreadLocal`. By opening JConsole[2] after executing the program, we can observe the memory usage (Figure 2-3).

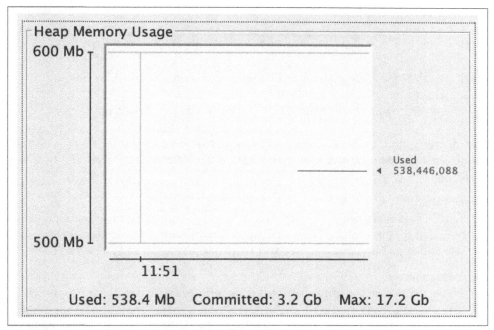

Figure 2-3. Heap memory usage on JConsole when using `ThreadLocal`

---

2 JConsole is a graphical monitoring tool bundled with the Java Development Kit (JDK).

It is evident from this observation that memory usage has accumulated. However, if we execute the same program without using `ThreadLocal`, the memory usage drops immediately, despite the involvement of 1,000 virtual threads (Figure 2-4).

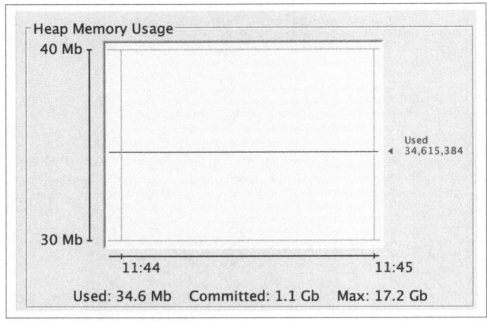

Figure 2-4. Heap memory usage on JConsole when not using `ThreadLocal`

The memory and overhead challenges associated with `ThreadLocal` in a virtual thread environment motivate the exploration of alternatives. Here are two key strategies:

Scoped values
    Scoped values are designed with virtual threads in mind. Their immutability and bounded lifetimes make them well-suited for passing data between threads in a safe and efficient manner. We'll cover scoped values in depth in Chapter 5.

Rethinking sharing
    The advent of virtual threads prompts us to re-evaluate our overall approach to data sharing. Explore if it's possible to restructure your application to minimize the need for `ThreadLocal` altogether, potentially leading to more scalable designs.

Monitoring

Now that we understand the limitations of virtual threads, it's clear they arise mainly from two sources: pinning and the use of `ThreadLocal`. Crafting new applications with these limitations in mind is one thing, but we don't always have that luxury. Often, we're working with legacy applications, some boasting millions of lines of code. Migrating to virtual threads in such cases requires a keen eye for compatibility issues. Fortunately, we're not left to our own devices here; there are tools specifically designed to flag potential problems.

Monitoring ThreadLocals

To track the usage of `ThreadLocal`, you can start the JVM with the `-Djdk.traceVirtualThreadLocals` flag. This will print stack traces whenever a `ThreadLocal` variable is accessed within a virtual thread, highlighting potential mismanagement or overuse.

We can use the following command to monitor `ThreadLocal` activity in our `ThreadLocalExample`:

```
java -Djdk.traceVirtualThreadLocals ThreadLocalExample.java
```

Executing this will yield an output like the following:

```
VirtualThread[#23]/runnable@ForkJoinPool-1-worker-4
...
VirtualThread[#25]/runnable@ForkJoinPool-1-worker-6
    java.base/java.lang.ThreadLocal.setInitialValue(ThreadLocal.java:236)
    java.base/java.lang.ThreadLocal.get(ThreadLocal.java:194)
    java.base/java.lang.ThreadLocal.get(ThreadLocal.java:172)
    com.example.myapp.ThreadLocalExample.
                lambda$main$0(ThreadLocalExample.java:13)
    java.base/java.lang.VirtualThread.run(VirtualThread.java:329)
```

Each entry provides valuable insight into where and how `ThreadLocal` is used, allowing us to refine our approach to ensure compatibility with virtual threads.

Upon examination of the output, several patterns emerge. Initially, we see the `ThreadLocal.setInitialValue()` being invoked, an anticipated action since each virtual thread must initialize its thread-local variable. The stack traces with `java.base/java.lang.ThreadLocal.setInitialValue(ThreadLocal.java:236)` confirm this.

Furthermore, when a thread needs to retrieve its thread-local variable, it calls `ThreadLocal.get()`. The output, marked by instances of `java.base/java.lang.ThreadLocal.get(ThreadLocal.java:194)`, underscores these moments of access.

Most importantly, the stack trace sheds light on the specific locations within your code where `ThreadLocal` is accessed. The lines with `com.example.myapp.ThreadLocal Example.lambda$main$0(ThreadLocalExample.java:13)` point directly to these critical points in your application, giving you the exact references needed for further investigation or refactoring.

As it becomes apparent that every virtual thread initializes its own `ThreadLocal` instance, it reconfirms our concern: the potential for escalated memory use, particularly when virtual threads are many in number. This aspect requires careful consideration when migrating to virtual threads.

Simultaneously, the stack trace gives us invaluable information for debugging. It provides a window into precisely where `ThreadLocal` is being used. With this, we can enhance the performance of our application, ensuring that `ThreadLocal` is not only used judiciously but also replaced or restructured if it becomes a bottleneck.

Monitoring Pinning

Similar to our approach with `ThreadLocal`, we can monitor existing source code for pinning issues. We have multiple tools available at our disposal. These tools range from JVM flags to the Java Flight Recorder (JFR) and `jcmd` (*https://oreil.ly/nnqx2*) for thread dumps. Let's begin by examining the utility of the JVM flag.

Using the JVM flag

The system property `jdk.tracePinnedThreads` is designed to trigger a stack trace whenever a thread encounters a blocking operation while pinned. When the JVM is run with `-Djdk.tracePinnedThreads=full`, it prints a complete stack trace that includes not just the Java frames but also the native frames and those frames holding monitors, which are highlighted. For a more succinct output that focuses on the core issue, `-Djdk.tracePinnedThreads=short` will limit the trace to just the problematic frames.

To illustrate this, let's execute the `ThreadPinnedExample.java` with the JVM flag:

```
java -Djdk.tracePinnedThreads=full ThreadPinnedExample.java
```

Here's a snippet of what the output might look like:

```
VirtualThread[#20]/runnable@ForkJoinPool-1-worker-1
VirtualThread[#21]/runnable@ForkJoinPool-1-worker-2 reason:MONITOR
    java.base/java.lang.VirtualThread$VThreadContinuation.onPinned(VirtualThread
    .java:199)
    java.base/jdk.internal.vm.Continuation.onPinned0(Continuation.java:393)
    java.base/java.lang.VirtualThread.parkNanos(VirtualThread.java:635)
    java.base/java.lang.VirtualThread.sleepNanos(VirtualThread.java:812)
    java.base/java.lang.Thread.sleepNanos(Thread.java:489)
    java.base/java.lang.Thread.sleep(Thread.java:522)
    ca.example.myapp.
.ThreadPinnedExample.lambda$main$0(ThreadPinnedExample.java:20) <== monitors:1
    java.base/java.lang.VirtualThread.run(VirtualThread.java:329)
VirtualThread[#20]/runnable@ForkJoinPool-1-worker-1
```

This output documents each instance where a thread becomes pinned. In particular, the `reason:MONITOR` tag indicates a thread is waiting to acquire a monitor, which can be an invaluable clue in detecting potential bottlenecks. The stack trace not only provides the *where* but also the *why*—in this case, highlighted by the line ending with <== monitors:1, denoting a thread holding a monitor.

By dissecting this output, we can make informed decisions about optimizing thread usage and minimizing pinning by identifying the affected area of code and potentially replacing it.

Using the Java Flight Recorder

Java Flight Recorder (JFR) is an invaluable tool that extends beyond traditional monitoring, offering specialized capabilities for observing and debugging the nuances of virtual threads. This powerful feature set facilitates a thorough and effective debugging process, which is vital as we navigate the complexities of concurrent programming.

JFR provides powerful tools to monitor virtual thread behavior. Here's a look at the most important events:

- jdk.VirtualThreadStart and jdk.VirtualThreadEnd mark the birth and termination of a virtual thread. While not enabled by default, turning them on gives you detailed tracking of thread lifecycles, which can be helpful for debugging or fine-grained analysis.

- jdk.VirtualThreadPinned is a crucial event, enabled by default, that signals when a virtual thread becomes pinned to a carrier thread for an extended period (the threshold is configurable, 20ms being the default). Pinning events indicate potential performance bottlenecks where the efficiency gains of virtual threads are lost.

- jdk.VirtualThreadSubmitFailed is another default-enabled event, and it signals failures to start or unpark virtual threads. It can point to resource exhaustion or unexpected bottlenecks within the JVM's thread management.

To monitor specific events like jdk.VirtualThreadStart and jdk.VirtualThread End, we have two main approaches: utilizing JDK Mission Control (*https://oreil.ly/4p_Ek*) for a GUI-driven experience or creating a custom JFR configuration file for more direct control.

Creating a custom JFR configuration file (*.jfc*) is a straightforward way to track the events we're most interested in. This tailored file enables selective monitoring, focusing your resources and analyzing relevant data points.

Here's a basic template for a *.jfc* file designed to record pivotal virtual thread events:

```
<?xml version="1.0" encoding="UTF-8"?>
<configuration version="2.0" label="Virtual Thread Events"
    description="JFR configuration to record virtual thread events">
  <event name="jdk.VirtualThreadStart">
```

```xml
      <setting name="enabled">true</setting>
    </event>
    <event name="jdk.VirtualThreadEnd">
      <setting name="enabled">true</setting>
    </event>
    <event name="jdk.VirtualThreadPinned">
      <setting name="enabled">true</setting>
    </event>
    <event name="jdk.VirtualThreadSubmitFailed">
      <setting name="enabled">true</setting>
    </event>
</configuration>
```

To put this into action, let's put the XML content into a file named *VThreadEvents.jfc*.

To understand how to monitor virtual threads effectively, let's dive into a code example designed to showcase JFR in action. Here's the Java program, and we'll break it down afterward:

```
import java.time.Duration;
import java.util.concurrent.locks.Lock;
import java.util.concurrent.locks.ReentrantLock;

public class JFRVirtualThreadDemo {
  private static final Object syncLock = new Object();
  private static final Lock reentrantLock = new ReentrantLock();
  public static void main(String[] args) {
    // Triggering lifecycle events for virtual threads
    Thread vThreadStartEnd = Thread.ofVirtual().unstarted(() -> {
      System.out.println("Virtual thread started and will end soon.");
    }); ❶
    vThreadStartEnd.start();
    joinThread(vThreadStartEnd);
    // Pinning with a synchronized block
    Thread vThreadPinnedSync = Thread.ofVirtual().unstarted(() -> {
      synchronized (syncLock) { ❷
        sleepUninterruptibly(Duration.ofMillis(500));
      }
    });
    vThreadPinnedSync.start();
    joinThread(vThreadPinnedSync);
    // No pinning with ReentrantLock
    Thread vThreadWithLock = Thread.ofVirtual().unstarted(() -> {
      reentrantLock.lock();
      try {
        sleepUninterruptibly(Duration.ofMillis(500)); ❸
      } finally {
        reentrantLock.unlock();
      }
    });
    vThreadWithLock.start();
    joinThread(vThreadWithLock);
  }
```

```java
    private static void joinThread(Thread thread) {
      try {
        thread.join();
      } catch (InterruptedException e) {
        Thread.currentThread().interrupt();
      }
    }

    private static void sleepUninterruptibly(Duration duration) { ❹
      boolean interrupted = false;
      try {
        long remainingNanos = duration.toNanos();
        long end = System.nanoTime() + remainingNanos;
        while (true) {
          try {
            Thread.sleep(remainingNanos / 1_000_000,
                (int) (remainingNanos % 1_000_000));
            return;
          } catch (InterruptedException e) {
            interrupted = true;
            remainingNanos = end - System.nanoTime();
          }
        }
      } finally {
        if (interrupted) {
          Thread.currentThread().interrupt();
        }
      }
    }
}
```

Let's examine what each section demonstrates:

❶ This simple virtual thread showcases basic lifecycle events. JFR will record both `VirtualThreadStart` and `VirtualThreadEnd` events, showing how quickly virtual threads complete short tasks.

❷ The `synchronized` block causes thread pinning. When the virtual thread sleeps inside this block, it remains pinned to its carrier thread for the entire 500ms duration, which JFR will capture as a `VirtualThreadPinned` event.

❸ Despite using a lock, `ReentrantLock` doesn't cause pinning. The virtual thread can unmount from its carrier during sleep, demonstrating why `ReentrantLock` is preferred for virtual threads.

❹ This helper method ensures the thread sleeps for the full duration, even if interrupted, making our timing measurements more predictable for demonstration purposes.

Now that we've prepared everything, it's time to start a recording and execute our example code. Here's the command to initiate the JFR recording:

```
java -XX:StartFlightRecording=filename=recording.jfr,settings=VThreadEvents.jfc \
JFRVirtualThreadDemo.java
```

This will record only the events we've specified in our custom *.jfc* file.

After running our application, we can analyze the *recording.jfr* file using tools like JDK Mission Control, or we can print the events to the console using:

```
jfr print --events jdk.VirtualThreadStart,jdk.VirtualThreadEnd,\
jdk.VirtualThreadPinned,jdk.VirtualThreadSubmitFailed recording.jfr
```

This way, we'll get insights specifically into the virtual thread behavior of our Java application:

```
jdk.VirtualThreadStart {
  startTime = 10:23:14.936 (2024-03-23)
  javaThreadId = 23
  eventThread = "" (javaThreadId = 23, virtual)
}
jdk.VirtualThreadEnd {
  startTime = 10:23:14.939 (2024-03-23)
  javaThreadId = 23
  eventThread = "" (javaThreadId = 23, virtual)
}
jdk.VirtualThreadStart {
  startTime = 10:23:14.940 (2024-03-23)
  javaThreadId = 35
  eventThread = "" (javaThreadId = 35, virtual)
}
jdk.VirtualThreadPinned {
  startTime = 10:23:14.941 (2024-03-23)
  duration = 504 ms
  eventThread = "" (javaThreadId = 35, virtual)
}
jdk.VirtualThreadEnd {
  startTime = 10:23:15.445 (2024-03-23)
  javaThreadId = 35
  eventThread = "" (javaThreadId = 35, virtual)
}
jdk.VirtualThreadStart {
  startTime = 10:23:15.446 (2024-03-23)
  javaThreadId = 37
  eventThread = "" (javaThreadId = 37, virtual)
}
jdk.VirtualThreadEnd {
  startTime = 10:23:15.948 (2024-03-23)
  javaThreadId = 37
  eventThread = "" (javaThreadId = 37, virtual)
}
```

These logs show how quickly virtual threads are created and finished, highlighting how they're meant for short tasks. Additionally, the logs reveal when virtual threads are pinned. Pinning times tell us how long a virtual thread remains attached to a carrier thread, which can help identify potential slowdowns.

Additionally, we can load the *recording.jfr* file to JDK Mission Control or Azul Mission Control (*https://oreil.ly/qKQZ9*) and analyze it (Figure 2-5).

Figure 2-5. Java Flight Recorder analysis using Azul Mission Control

Viewing Virtual Threads in jcmd Thread Dumps

While tools like JDK Mission Control offer sophisticated analysis, sometimes a quick thread dump is a useful diagnostic tool. The `jcmd` (*https://oreil.ly/nnqx2*) utility provides this functionality, and importantly, it lets us capture information about virtual threads.

To generate thread dumps, first obtain the process ID (PID) of your running Java application using tools like `ps` or `jps`.[3] Then, choose your desired format for the thread dump.

---

3 We can identify a process's PID by using the `ps` command for general processes or `jps` specifically for Java applications. Use `ps -ef | grep <process_name>` to list all processes and filter by name (replace *<process_name>* with the actual name). The first column shows the PID. For Java processes, use `jps` or `jps -l` for a detailed listing.

Monitoring | 81

Plain text

```
jcmd <PID> Thread.dump_to_file -format=text <file>
```

JSON

```
jcmd <PID> Thread.dump_to_file -format=json <file>
```

Replace `<PID>` with the actual process ID and `<file>` with the desired output filename.

For example, you can execute the following command to generate a JSON thread dump:

```
jcmd 12345 Thread.dump_to_file -format=json threaddump.json
```

The JSON format is particularly useful for automated debugging and analysis tools that can consume JSON data. It's a machine-readable format that allows you to programmatically analyze thread states, which can be beneficial in complex systems with many threads.

The `jcmd` thread dump will list virtual threads that are blocked in network I/O operations and virtual threads that are created by the `ExecutorService` interface. However, it has limitations as it will not include:

- Object addresses
- Locks
- Java Native Interface (JNI) statistics
- Heap statistics
- Other information commonly found in traditional thread dumps

This focus on essential information makes it easier to pinpoint issues specifically related to thread execution and blocking, without the noise of additional, often irrelevant, details.

By using `jcmd` along with JFR, we can get a comprehensive view of how virtual threads are performing in our application, enabling us to debug and optimize more effectively.

Programmatic thread dumps in Java

In addition to using the command-line utility, you can also generate thread dumps programmatically within your Java application. The following Java code snippet demonstrates this technique:

```java
import java.io.IOException;
import java.lang.ProcessHandle;
import java.time.Duration;
import java.util.List;
```

```
import java.util.concurrent.Executors;
import java.util.concurrent.TimeUnit;
import java.util.stream.IntStream;

public class ThreadDumpDemo {
  private static final int THREAD_COUNT = 1_000;
  private static final Duration WORK_DURATION = Duration.ofSeconds(5);
  private static final Duration DELAY_BEFORE_DUMP = Duration.ofSeconds(2);

  public static void main(String[] args) {
    long pid = ProcessHandle.current().pid();  ❶
    String outputFile = "dump.json";
    try (var executor = Executors.newVirtualThreadPerTaskExecutor()) {
      IntStream.range(0, THREAD_COUNT).forEach(i ->
          executor.submit(() -> sleep(WORK_DURATION)));  ❷
      executor.submit(() -> {
        sleep(DELAY_BEFORE_DUMP);  ❸
        runJcmdDump(pid, outputFile);
      });
    }
  }

  private static void sleep(Duration d) {
    try {
      TimeUnit.NANOSECONDS.sleep(d.toNanos());
    } catch (InterruptedException e) {
      Thread.currentThread().interrupt();
    }
  }

  private static void runJcmdDump(long pid, String file) {
   ProcessBuilder pb = new ProcessBuilder(List.of(
    "/bin/sh", "-c",
    String.format("jcmd %d Thread.dump_to_file -format=json %s",
        pid, file)));  ❹
    try {
      Process p = pb.start();
      int exit = p.waitFor();
      if (exit != 0) {
        System.err.printf("jcmd exited %d%n", exit);
        p.getInputStream().transferTo(System.err);
        p.getErrorStream().transferTo(System.err);
      }
    } catch (IOException | InterruptedException e) {
      Thread.currentThread().interrupt();
      System.err.println("Failed to run jcmd: " + e.getMessage());
    }
  }
}
```

Let's understand how this program captures thread state:

❶ We obtain the current PID using the `ProcessHandle` (*https://oreil.ly/DmzRe*) API. This PID is essential for the `jcmd` tool to identify which JVM process to dump.

❷ We create 1,000 virtual threads, each sleeping for 5 seconds. This simulates a heavily concurrent workload, ensuring that many active threads are present when the dump is obtained.

❸ The thread dump is triggered after a two-second delay. This timing ensures that most virtual threads are still active (or sleeping) when we capture the system state.

❹ We use `ProcessBuilder` (*https://oreil.ly/gHhAl*) to execute the `jcmd` command with JSON output format. The JSON format provides structured data that's easier to parse programmatically than traditional text dumps.

This program demonstrates how to programmatically trigger and capture thread dumps using Java's `ProcessBuilder`. It schedules a large number of virtual threads and then generates a thread dump when the last thread is about to be scheduled. The dump is saved to a file, and the PID is printed to the console for reference.

The generated *dump.json* file provides rich information about the system state:

```json
{
  "threadDump": {
    "processId": "76586",
    "time": "2024-03-23T15:01:41.901030Z",
    "runtimeVersion": "21+35-2513",
    "threadContainers": [
      {
        "container": "<root>",
        "parent": null,
        "owner": null,
        "threads": [
          {
            "tid": "1",
            "name": "main",
            "stack": [
              "java.base\/java.io.FileInputStream.readBytes(Native Method)",
              "java.base\/java.io.FileInputStream.read(FileInputStream.java:287)",
              "java.base\/java.io.BufferedInputStream.read1(BufferedInputStream.java:345)",
              "java.base\/java.io.BufferedInputStream.implRead(BufferedInputStream.java:420)",
              ... (additional stack trace elements)"
            ]
          },
          ....
          "... (additional threads)"
        ],
        "threadCount": "7"
      },
      {
        "container": "java.util.concurrent.ThreadPerTaskExecutor@768b771c",
        "parent": "<root>",
        "owner": null,
```

```
      "threads": [
        {
          "tid": "20",
          "name": "",
          "stack": [
            "java.base\/java.lang.VirtualThread.parkNanos(VirtualThread.java:631)",
            "java.base\/java.lang.VirtualThread.sleepNanos(VirtualThread.java:803)",
            "java.base\/java.lang.Thread.sleep(Thread.java:507)",
            "ThreadDumpDemo.sleepOfSeconds(ThreadDumpDemo.java:38)",
            "ThreadDumpDemo.lambda$main$0(ThreadDumpDemo.java:29)",
            "java.base\/java.util.concurrent.ThreadPerTaskExecutor$TaskRunner
                .run(ThreadPerTaskExecutor.java:314)",
            "java.base\/java.lang.VirtualThread.run(VirtualThread.java:311)"
          ]
        }
        "... (additional threads)"
      "... (additional thread containers)"
    ]
  }
}
```

Now let's see what it reveals:

Main thread

The thread with `tid: "1"` named `main` indicates the main thread. This is where our application starts. It's currently doing a file input operation.

System threads

Threads like `Reference Handler`, `Finalizer`, `Signal Dispatcher`, and `Notification Thread` are JVM-managed threads that handle garbage collection, reference objects, and other JVM-level tasks.

Common-cleaner thread

This thread is responsible for cleaning the reference objects after they are processed by the garbage collector.

Many virtual threads

We see lots of threads that are likely virtual threads. These are the numerous unnamed threads with `tid`s such as 20, 22, 23, etc. They are virtual threads, given their stack traces include `java.lang.VirtualThread.parkNanos` and `java.lang.VirtualThread.sleepNanos`, likely due to our `sleepOfSeconds` calls.

In a real troubleshooting scenario, you'd look for these clues in a thread dump:

Blocked threads

Threads stuck in the `BLOCKED` or `WAITING` state often indicate problems like deadlocks or resource contention.

Resource usage

Combine the thread dump with CPU and memory usage data to see if the system is overloaded, which can also create bottlenecks.

Generating Thread Dumps with HotSpotDiagnosticsMXBean

Java Management Extensions (JMX) offer powerful tools for monitoring applications. The `HotSpotDiagnosticMXBean` (*https://oreil.ly/H4dl2*) within the com.sun.management package (*https://oreil.ly/bVf_E*) has been enhanced with a new method that lets you specify the desired format of your thread dumps. This includes JSON for structured analysis, or the traditional plain-text format.

Here's how to generate a JSON thread dump programmatically:

```
public static void takeThreadDump(String outputFile) {
  var hotSpotDiagnosticMXBean
      = ManagementFactory.getPlatformMXBean(HotSpotDiagnosticMXBean.class);
  try {
    // Ensure that the output file path is absolute
    if (!new File(outputFile).isAbsolute()) {
      throw new IllegalArgumentException("Output path must be absolute.");
    }
    hotSpotDiagnosticMXBean.dumpThreads(outputFile,
        HotSpotDiagnosticMXBean.ThreadDumpFormat.JSON);
  } catch (IOException e) {
    throw new RuntimeException("An error occurred while taking thread dump", e);
  }
}
```

The `dumpThreads` (*https://oreil.ly/uekb2*) is a new method that has been added which takes an argument from the `ThreadDumpFormat` (*https://oreil.ly/Npslp*) enum, allowing you to choose between `TEXT_PLAIN` (*https://oreil.ly/_dQ4n*) or `JSON` (*https://oreil.ly/s5RUt*). Also, you need to make sure to always provide an absolute path for the `outputFile` to avoid errors. This method can be used with JMX tools for both local and remote diagnostics.

Practical Tips for Migrating to Virtual Threads

Now that we have discussed the benefits and limitations of virtual threads and how to debug them, here are some tips when migrating:

Library updates are key
> The best way to avoid pinning issues is to use libraries specifically updated for virtual threads. These libraries will use modern synchronization tools that avoid tying up carrier threads.

When updates aren't available
> If we can't update libraries, we can move legacy I/O and other blocking operations to traditional thread pools (`Executors.newFixedThreadPool()`). This keeps blocking code contained.

The semaphore's dilemma
> Semaphores can limit how many virtual threads enter a pinning-prone code section. However, use them very carefully. Setting the limit too low will choke off your application's concurrency and negate the benefits of virtual threads.

While the advent of virtual threads brings significant benefits, it's important to consider several factors to leverage their potential and fully avoid common pitfalls:

Ecosystem evolution
> Many libraries are still adapting to virtual threads. We need to be patient and check for updates regularly.

Resource trade-offs
> Virtual threads let us run more tasks concurrently, but this could lead to other resource bottlenecks. We may still need ways to limit usage.

Know your framework
> We need to research how our preferred frameworks and languages work with virtual threads. There might be specific patterns to avoid.

As we adopt virtual threads, we need to up our game on monitoring. Focus on these key metrics:

CPU
> We want to see those scalability gains! Track CPU usage patterns to ensure you're efficiently using virtual threads and minimizing unexpected pinning events.

Memory and garbage collection
> Virtual threads shift memory usage patterns. We may need to adjust our heap sizes or fine-tune garbage collection if there are changes in behavior.

Latency and throughput
> This is the ultimate test. Are our users experiencing faster response times? Is our system handling a higher volume of requests under load? These metrics will quantify the real-world impact of our migration.

Reaffirming the Benefits of Virtual Threads

We've explored the mechanics of virtual threads, monitoring techniques, and potential areas for caution; let's revisit the core advantages that make them a compelling addition to Java's concurrency toolkit:

Simplified concurrency
> Virtual threads fundamentally streamline the way we write concurrent code. Their lightweight nature allows us to express tasks and workflows more naturally, reducing cognitive overhead and the potential for errors compared to traditional thread management.

Enhanced scalability
> Applications using virtual threads can often handle far greater levels of concurrency without hitting resource limits imposed by operating system threads. This scalability is especially valuable for modern applications handling numerous simultaneous connections or requests.

Resource efficiency
> Virtual threads consume minimal memory and are scheduled intelligently by the JVM. This translates directly into better hardware utilization, potentially reducing operational costs or enabling you to do more with the same hardware resources.

Compatibility
> A significant advantage of virtual threads is their integration with existing Java paradigms. You can often introduce them into your applications to reap performance benefits without major code refactoring.

Reduced CPU overhead
> Because virtual threads don't directly consume CPU time when idle (e.g., waiting for I/O), they allow your application to dedicate more processing power to active tasks, improving overall responsiveness.

Streamlined server-side programming
> Virtual threads promise to revitalize the classic "request-per-thread" model for server-side applications, making it far more scalable than when using traditional threads.

It's About Scalability

The notion of scalability in Java is all about the way an application handles an increase in workload. Traditionally, the way threads interact with I/O operations has been the great bottleneck to scalability. We can think of platform threads as being like bank tellers where people are waiting in line, but they don't do anything while they're waiting for information to process or for a network reply.

This is where virtual threads totally change the game. They're so lightweight that you can have thousands or even millions of them running in parallel without stressing your system. What's more, during I/O waits, virtual threads can gracefully "unmount" from their underlying carrier threads, freeing up valuable memory in the process. This means your system can juggle far more tasks at the same time.

With virtual threads, we can finally unleash the full power of modern CPUs. Their ability to support a massive number of virtual threads helps us squeeze every bit of performance out of our hardware. More threads translate into higher throughput and a more responsive application, even when it's being hammered with requests.

The benefits for your scalable bank (application) are:

Serving more customers (concurrent requests)
    Now your bank—or rather, your application—can handle a much larger volume of customer requests without getting bogged down.

Reduced wait times (improved throughput)
    This efficient use of resources means faster overall service, with more customers being helped in the same amount of time.

Optimized resource utilization (lower memory footprint)
    Virtual threads are lean so that you can serve more customers with the same number of tellers (underlying resources).

Virtual threads represent a huge leap for scalable Java applications. By breaking free from the constraints of traditional threads, they pave the way for systems that are more efficient, responsive, and capable of handling ever-growing demands.

In Closing

The introduction of virtual threads in Java represents a significant shift in the history of the Java concurrency model, significantly increasing scalability and performance for applications run on services. As you begin utilizing virtual threads in your applications, exploit their ability to handle a vast number of concurrent tasks with minimal resource overhead. This can lead to more performant, responsive, and scalable applications.

Start by introducing virtual threads in parts of your application use cases likely to benefit the most, such as I/O-bound operations. Gradually ramp up their usage while closely monitoring the impact on performance and resource usage.

Keep a vigilant eye on thread activity, identify potential bottlenecks, and ensure you are fully leveraging the advantages of virtual threads. Remember the limitations of pinning and `ThreadLocal`. Consider employing modern synchronization tools like `ReentrantLock` to avoid unnecessary pinning. Stay informed about the latest library and framework support to take advantage of optimizations and new features.

Reevaluate your concurrency patterns and fully embrace virtual threads' simpler and more natural concurrency models. By embracing virtual threads, you can simplify and make your concurrency more coherent, significantly improving your applications' performance and scalability, resulting in cleaner and easier-to-maintain code.

As Java continues to evolve, staying informed and adaptable will ensure that you can fully leverage these powerful new capabilities, unlocking the full potential of your applications.

CHAPTER 3

The Mechanics of Modern Concurrency in Java

The knowledge of anything, since all things have causes, is not acquired or complete unless it is known by its causes.
  —Ibn Sina (Avicenna), circa 1025 A.D.

Knowing how to use something is important, but understanding how it works is essential. By understanding its inner workings, we not only gain greater appreciation for it, but we can also quickly fix any problems that arise. That's why knowing how virtual threads were implemented and their internals is crucial for a well-grounded Java developer. In this chapter, we will explore how virtual threads work internally and are implemented.

We must know two concepts to understand how virtual threads are implemented. One is the `ForkJoinPool`, and the second is *continuation*. `ForkJoinPool` is a scheduler that schedules virtual threads. Continuation is an aspect of how virtual threads can pause their execution and then resume where they were paused. We will begin by introducing the thread pool, and then gradually get into the depth of the `ForkJoin Pool` and how it's implemented slightly differently to accommodate virtual threads.

Thread Pool

In the first chapter, we discussed the Java Executor framework, which is essentially the implementation of a thread pool. But we didn't quite explain how a thread pool works and most importantly, why we needed one.

As the name suggests, a thread pool is a group of threads that are created at the application's startup and continue running throughout the application. The strategy of creating a thread pool may differ for different kinds of pools, but the essential idea is that it will have a number of threads ready and keep them running. The thread pool will have a queue to hold the tasks. It will pick tasks from the queue and execute them as soon as threads are available. Once it finishes the execution, it will pick the next one and keep on executing tasks while the tasks are available in the queue. If no tasks are available, it will wait until a new task is available. If all the threads are busy executing different tasks, any additional tasks are placed in the queue and wait there until the threads become available.

Why Do We Need a Thread Pool?

While creating a thread is easy (as we saw in Chapter 1), creating many threads ad hoc can be problematic. If we continue to create threads on an ad hoc basis as our demands grow, we may eventually hit the maximum number of threads allowed by the operating system, causing the application to crash—an undesirable outcome. We want to control the number of threads we can create in a running application, and a thread pool gives us this control. It also gives us a natural way of rate limiting a resource that otherwise could be overwhelmed by too many concurrent tasks. By defining how many threads are optimal for our application and setting this limit at the start, we can prevent resource exhaustion, especially when a large number of concurrent tasks might be submitted. For example, consider a web application—if a new thread is created for each incoming request, a sudden burst of requests could cause the application to crash.

In addition to providing control, a thread pool allows tasks to execute immediately without waiting for a new thread to be created, leading to faster response times. A thread pool manages threads' lifecycles. This minimizes the complexity of manually handling threads and reduces the risk of errors like thread leaks. Moreover, it gives us the sense of tasks as units of work and shifts our focus to our business logic, which we want to execute concurrently rather than dealing with the nuts and bolts of threads.

Now that we know what a thread pool is and why it's essential, let's implement a simple one from scratch to understand how it works internally.

Building a Simple Thread Pool in Java

Our `SimpleThreadPool` class will demonstrate the core concepts of a thread pool. Let's break down its implementation:

```java
class Worker extends Thread {
    public Worker(ThreadGroup threadGroup, String name) {
        super(threadGroup, name);
    }
    @Override
    public void run() {
        while (running) {
            try {
```

```
            Runnable task = queue.take();
            task.run();
        } catch (InterruptedException e) {
            Thread.currentThread().interrupt();
        }
    }
  }
}
```

This `Worker` class is an inner class of the `SimpleThreadPool` class, so it has direct access to the `Queue` that we will use to hold the tasks as a form of `Runnable`. Each `Worker` class is an independent thread that continuously pulls tasks from the shared queue and executes them. The `running` flag controls the worker's lifecycles. The flag is a field of our pool, so we can gracefully shut down the pool when we want to. The idea is that as long as we have a task in the queue and the pool is running, this thread will keep trying to pull tasks from the queue. We will use a blocking queue so if no task is there, the thread will wait until it gets one.

All `Worker` threads are grouped under a `ThreadGroup` (*https://oreil.ly/jHIrv*), which gives us easier management. If we want to shut down all the threads by signaling interrupt, we can just interrupt the group; we don't need to interrupt individually, although, under the hood, that actually happens.

Now, let's look at the implementation of our `SimpleThreadPool`:

```
import java.util.concurrent.BlockingQueue;
import java.util.concurrent.LinkedBlockingDeque;

public class SimpleThreadPool implements AutoCloseable {

    private final BlockingQueue<Runnable> queue;
    private final ThreadGroup threadGroup;
    private volatile boolean running = true; ❶

    public SimpleThreadPool(int poolSize, int queueSize) {
        Worker[] threads = new Worker[poolSize];
        this.queue = new LinkedBlockingDeque<>(queueSize); ❷
        this.threadGroup = new ThreadGroup("SimpleThreadPool");

        for (int i = 0; i < poolSize; i++) {
            threads[i] = new Worker(threadGroup, "Worker-" + i);
            threads[i].start(); ❸
        }
    }

    public void submit(Runnable task) {
        try {
            queue.put(task); ❹
        } catch (InterruptedException e) {
            Thread.currentThread().interrupt();
        }
```

```
    }

    public void shutdown() {
        this.running = false;
        threadGroup.interrupt(); ❺
    }

    @Override
    public void close() {
        while (!queue.isEmpty()) { ❻
            try {
                Thread.sleep(100);
            } catch (InterruptedException e) {
                Thread.currentThread().interrupt();
                return; // exit gracefully
            }
        }
        shutdown();
    }

    class Worker extends Thread {
        public Worker(ThreadGroup threadGroup, String name) {
            super(threadGroup, name);
        }

        @Override
        public void run() {
            while (running) {
                try {
                    Runnable task = queue.take();
                    task.run();
                } catch (InterruptedException e) {
                    // pool doesn't use interrupts for shutdown;
                    // if ever interrupted, just exit
                    Thread.currentThread().interrupt();
                }
            }
        }
    }
}
```

The implementation reveals several important design decisions:

❶ The `volatile` keyword ensures all threads see changes to the `running` flag immediately, preventing workers from missing the shutdown signal.

❷ `LinkedBlockingDeque` provides thread-safe operations for task submission and retrieval. Its bounded capacity prevents memory exhaustion from unbounded task accumulation.

❸ Workers start immediately upon creation, ready to process tasks as soon as they're submitted.

❹ The `put()` method blocks if the queue is full, providing natural backpressure when the pool is overwhelmed.

❺ Interrupting the thread group signals all workers simultaneously, triggering coordinated shutdown.

❻ The graceful shutdown waits for pending tasks to complete, ensuring no work is lost during pool closure.

The class has two primary methods: `submit()` and `shutdown()`. It also implements the `AutoCloseable` interface so that we can use a `try`-with-resources pattern, which is why we also have a close method. Its constructor initializes the thread pool with a specified number of worker threads (`poolSize`) and a queue of a given size (`queueSize`). It creates and starts the worker threads. We have used the `LinkedBlockingDeque` (*https://oreil.ly/Xcv3-*) to store the tasks. It provides thread-safe operations for adding and retrieving tasks, ensuring that workers can access the queue concurrently without issues.

Using the `submit()` method, a task is added to the queue for execution by a thread from the pool. The `shutdown()` method sets the running flag to false and interrupts all threads in the pool, signaling them to stop. In the `close()` method, we gracefully shut down the thread pool. It waits a little while for the query to empty before initiating a shutdown. That way, we can ensure all the pending tasks are proceeding.

Now that we've built our `SimpleThreadPool`, let's see it in action. Here's an example of how you might use it:

```java
package ca.bazlur.modern.concurrency.c03;

public class SimpleThreadPoolDemo {
  public static void main(String[] args) throws InterruptedException {
    try (var threadPool = new SimpleThreadPool(4, 100)) {
      for (int i = 0; i < 100; i++) {
        int finalI = i;
        threadPool.submit(() -> runTask(finalI));
      }
    }

    Thread.sleep(10_000);
    System.out.println("Main thread finished");
  }

  private static void runTask(int id) {
```

Thread Pool | 95

```
      System.out.printf("Task %d on %s%n", id,
          Thread.currentThread().getName());
      try {
        Thread.sleep(100);// simulate work being done
      } catch (InterruptedException e) {
        Thread.currentThread().interrupt();
      }
    }
  }
}
```

In this example, we create a `SimpleThreadPool` with four worker threads and a queue capacity of one hundred. We submit a hundred tasks to the pool, and each task simply prints its ID and the name of the thread executing it. The try-with-resources block ensures that the `close()` method of the `SimpleThreadPool` is called when execution exits the block, allowing for graceful shutdown.

When you run this code, you'll see output like:

```
Task 1 is being executed by Worker-2
Task 0 is being executed by Worker-0
Task 2 is being executed by Worker-3
Task 3 is being executed by Worker-1
```

This demonstrates how `SimpleThreadPool` efficiently manages the execution of multiple tasks using a limited number of threads. We can experiment with different pool sizes and queue capacities to observe their impact on performance and resource utilization.

However, this example is very simplified so that we understand the basic concept. We would typically use the `ExecutorService` in a real-world application, as it provides a more robust and feature-rich thread pool implementation. For example, some thread pools have a minimum and maximum number of threads, which means that at any point in time, only a minimum number of threads will be around, but if need be, the thread pool can increase to a maximum number.

The Executor Framework

The Executor framework is designed to maximize performance while being easy to use. It provides multiple implementations that conform to a common interface, `ExecutorService` (*https://oreil.ly/JQWme*). To get instances of different thread pool implementations, we use a factory class called `Executors` (*https://oreil.ly/lDFVL*), which offers various factory methods tailored for different types of thread pools.

For example, if we want a fixed-size thread pool with 10 threads, we can use the following code:

```
ExecutorService service = Executors.newFixedThreadPool(10);
```

Under the hood, the `newFixedThreadPool` (*https://oreil.ly/dttrO*) method creates an instance of `ThreadPoolExecutor` (*https://oreil.ly/tRWwo*), utilizing the thread count we provide along with some additional arguments. In fact, most of the other methods in the `Executors` class also use `ThreadPoolExecutor`, configuring it differently based on the arguments to achieve various behaviors.

To delve a bit deeper, let's examine the constructor of `ThreadPoolExecutor`:

```
public ThreadPoolExecutor(int corePoolSize,
                          int maximumPoolSize,
                          long keepAliveTime,
                          TimeUnit unit,
                          BlockingQueue<Runnable> workQueue,
                          ThreadFactory threadFactory,
                          RejectedExecutionHandler handler) {}
```

Then let's look at the parameters it takes:

`corePoolSize`
: The number of threads to keep in the pool, even if they are idle, unless `allowCoreThreadTimeOut` (*https://oreil.ly/cnxif*) is set.

`maximumPoolSize`
: The maximum number of threads allowed in the pool.

`keepAliveTime`
: When the number of threads is greater than the core, this is the maximum time that excess idle threads will wait for new tasks before terminating.

`unit`
: The time unit for the `keepAliveTime` argument, e.g., nanosconds, milliseconds, seconds, etc.

`workQueue`
: The queue to use for holding tasks before they are executed. This queue will hold only the `Runnable` tasks submitted using the `execute` method.

`threadFactory`
: The factory to use when the executor creates a new thread.

`handler`
: The handler to use when execution is blocked because the thread bounds and queue capacities are reached.

Understanding these parameters helps us see how different configurations of thread pools are achieved through the factory methods in the `Executors` class. For instance, `newFixedThreadPool()` sets both `corePoolSize` and `maximumPoolSize` to the same value, creating a pool with a fixed number of threads that remain alive unless explicitly shut down.

Frameworks often use this class to manage task execution efficiently. For instance, the Spring Framework wraps `ThreadPool` in a `ThreadPoolTaskExecutor` (*https://oreil.ly/Btpa_*) to handle asynchronous operations seamlessly. Setting the appropriate pool size is crucial to achieving optimum performance.

When configuring a thread pool, two key sizes must be considered: the core pool size and the maximum pool size. The *core pool size* is the minimum number of threads always kept alive in the pool, even if idle. Maintaining a core set of threads is essential; as we know, creating new threads is expensive. By keeping these threads readily available, the system can quickly assign tasks without incurring the overhead of thread creation. These threads remain waiting when there are no tasks to execute, and they are ready to handle new tasks as they arrive.

However, having too many idle threads can waste unnecessary resources such as CPU cycles and memory. This is why setting an appropriate minimum number of threads is crucial. The *maximum pool size* defines the upper limit on the number of threads that can be active in the pool at any given time. This allows the thread pool to adjust to increased demand by scaling up when more tasks are submitted.

Determining the optimal core and maximum pool sizes is vital for performance tuning. These values can vary significantly depending on the workload and the hardware on which the application is running. Unfortunately, there is no one-size-fits-all answer. Developers often have to experiment and monitor performance metrics to find the right balance, adjusting the thread pool sizes based on empirical results. The general idea is that if the workload is CPU-bound (for example, number crunching), the number of threads should match the available CPU cores. Adding more threads can degrade performance because it increases context switching and synchronization overhead. However, if the workload is I/O-bound (e.g., database calls), having more threads than CPUs can be beneficial, as idle threads waiting on I/O can allow other tasks to be executed.

The virtual threads we discussed in the previous chapter offer a way to eliminate the complexities associated with thread pool management for the I/O-bound workload. However, while virtual threads provide a significant advantage, the use cases for existing thread pools will not disappear entirely. Legacy systems, compatibility considerations, and specific performance requirements may still require traditional thread pools. For example, a recent study (*https://oreil.ly/NNN5x*) done with OpenLiberty[1] found that their own `ThreadPool` implementation performed better than virtual

---

1 OpenLiberty is a lightweight, cloud-native Java runtime optimized for building microservices and cloud-based applications, supporting Jakarta EE, MicroProfile, and other open standards.

threads. That's why it's paramount to understand how to configure and utilize existing thread pools effectively.

Let's briefly discuss available types of thread pools in the JDK under the Executor framework.

FixedThreadPool

The `FixedThreadPool` (*https://oreil.ly/4NKEP*) creates a pool with a fixed number of threads. If all threads are busy, new tasks will wait in the queue until a thread becomes available. This approach helps maintain a consistent number of active threads, which is useful when you have a predictable workload.

Let's see an example:

```
try (ExecutorService fixedPool = Executors.newFixedThreadPool(4)) {
  for (int i = 0; i < 10; i++) {
    fixedPool.submit(() -> {
      System.out.println(Thread.currentThread().getName()
          + " is executing a task");
    });
  }
}
```

When to use: This is best suited for applications requiring a constant number of threads working concurrently, such as server applications where you need to maintain a predictable concurrency level. For instance, if you have a limited number of resources or database connections, a fixed pool can help ensure that you don't overwhelm your system.

CachedThreadPool

The `CachedThreadPool` (*https://oreil.ly/MUcqT*) dynamically creates new threads when needed and reuses previously created threads if they are idle. This is highly beneficial when the workload fluctuates in size, as it allows the thread pool to adjust to the demand dynamically:

```
try (ExecutorService cachedPool = Executors.newCachedThreadPool()) {
  for (int i = 0; i < 10; i++) {
      cachedPool.submit(() -> {
          System.out.println(Thread.currentThread().getName()
              + " is executing a task");
      });
  }
}
```

When to use: This is ideal when you have a large number of short-lived tasks, or when tasks arrive in unpredictable bursts. It's not suitable for situations where tasks are long-running, as it could lead to too many active threads being created.

SingleThreadExecutor

The `SingleThreadExecutor` (*https://oreil.ly/xdp-9*) ensures that tasks are executed sequentially using a single thread. It's like having a single worker handling tasks in the order they are received:

```java
try (var singleThreadPool = Executors.newSingleThreadExecutor()) {
  for (int i = 0; i < 5; i++) {
    singleThreadPool.submit(() -> {
      System.out.println(Thread.currentThread().getName()
          + " is executing a task");
    });
  }
}
```

When to use: Use this executor when you need tasks to run in strict sequence or when they must not run concurrently. It's often used when you're working with a shared resource that needs to be accessed by only one task at a time, ensuring no race conditions occur.

ScheduledThreadPoolExecutor

The `ScheduledThreadPoolExecutor` (*https://oreil.ly/Utb7K*) schedules tasks to run after a delay or at fixed intervals:

```java
try (ScheduledExecutorService scheduledPool
            = Executors.newScheduledThreadPool(2)) {
        scheduledPool.scheduleAtFixedRate(() -> {
            System.out.println(Thread.currentThread().getName()
                + " is running a scheduled task");
        }, 0, 5, TimeUnit.SECONDS);
    }
```

When to use: It is ideal for periodic tasks such as sending notifications, performing system health checks, or running maintenance tasks at regular intervals. It ensures that tasks are executed at the desired frequency without manual intervention.

WorkStealingPool

The `WorkStealingPool` creates a pool of threads that dynamically balances the workload between threads using a work-stealing algorithm. This type of pool optimizes the usage of available processors:

```java
try (ExecutorService workStealingPool = Executors.newWorkStealingPool()) {
  for (int i = 0; i < 10; i++) {
      workStealingPool.submit(() -> {
          System.out.println(Thread.currentThread().getName()
              + " is executing a task");
      });
  }
}
```

When to use: When you have a high number of small, independent tasks and want to maximize the utilization of CPU cores.

There is a special type of thread pool in Java called the `ForkJoinPool` (*https://oreil.ly/rsb95*). It is designed for divide-and-conquer tasks, where large problems can be split into smaller, independent tasks that can be processed in parallel. In fact, this `ForkJoinPool` uses a work-stealing algorithm under the hood. We'll explore the details of the `ForkJoinPool` later in this chapter.

Callable and Future: Handling Task Results

So far, we've been submitting tasks using `Runnable` (*https://oreil.ly/XI_fh*), but no results have been returned. But sometimes, we need to get a result after a task is completed. This is where `Callable` (*https://oreil.ly/TvnqA*) and `Future` (*https://oreil.ly/y6fnZ*) come in.

Callable

The interface looks like this:

```
public interface Callable {
    V call() throws Exception;
}
```

It is also a functional interface like `Runnable`; the only difference is that it can return a result and throw exceptions.

Let's see an example:

```
import java.util.Map;
import java.util.concurrent.*;

public class CallableExample {
  static final Map<Integer, Long> cache = new ConcurrentHashMap<>(
      Map.of(0, 0L, 1, 1L) ❶
  );
  public static void main(String[] args) throws Exception {
    try (ExecutorService threadPool = Executors.newCachedThreadPool()) {
      Future<Long> fibonacciNumber = threadPool.submit(new Callable<Long>() { ❷
        @Override
        public Long call() throws Exception {
          return fibonacci(50); ❸
        }
      });
    }
  }

  private static Long fibonacci(int n) {
    if (cache.containsKey(n)) {
      return cache.get(n);
```

```
    } else {
      long result = fibonacci(n - 1) + fibonacci(n - 2);
      cache.put(n, result); ❹
      return result;
    }
  }
}
```

Let's examine the key components:

❶ We use a `ConcurrentHashMap` to cache Fibonacci results, making our recursive implementation efficient and thread-safe for concurrent access.

❷ The `submit` method accepts a `Callable<Long>` and returns a `Future<Long>`. This `Future` represents the eventual result of the asynchronous computation.

❸ Unlike `Runnable.run()`, the `call()` method returns a value, in this case, the 50th Fibonacci number.

❹ The `cache` ensures we don't recalculate values, crucial for recursive algorithms where the same values are computed multiple times.

In the preceding code, we submitted a job to calculate the 50th Fibonacci number. We used the `Callable` interface to submit the job. Since the interface is functional, we can also use a lambda expression:

```
Future fibonacciNumber = threadPool.submit(() -> fibonacci(50));
```

But look, it returns the result wrapped with another interface, `Future`. Let's find out why.

Future

`Future` has several methods:

```
public interface Future<V> {
    boolean cancel(boolean mayInterruptIfRunning);
    boolean isCancelled();
    boolean isDone();
    V get() throws InterruptedException, ExecutionException;
    V get(long timeout, TimeUnit unit)
        throws InterruptedException, ExecutionException, TimeoutException;
}
```

However, we usually use the `get()` and `isDone()` methods for most use cases.

When you submit a task using `Callable`, a `Future` is returned immediately, even if the task hasn't finished. The `isDone()` method checks if the task is complete, and the `get()` method retrieves the result.

The `get()` method is a blocking operation. It will block the calling thread until the result is available.

Let's consider an example where we want to calculate multiple Fibonacci numbers:

```
public static void main(String[] args) {
    List<Future<Long>> futures = new ArrayList<>();
    List<Integer> fibonacciIndices = List.of(10, 20, 30, 40, 50);

    try (ExecutorService threadPool = Executors.newCachedThreadPool()) {
        for (int index : fibonacciIndices) {
            futures.add(threadPool.submit(() -> fibonacci(index)));
        }
        for (Future<Long> future : futures) {
            System.out.println("Fibonacci number: " + future.get());
        }
    } catch (ExecutionException | InterruptedException e) {
        throw new RuntimeException(e);
    }
}
```

In this example, multiple `Callable` tasks are submitted and executed in parallel. However, when we call `future.get()` within the loop, the main thread blocks until that specific task completes. The advantage here is that other threads continue their work while the main thread is blocked.

The ForkJoinPool

Since Java 7, we have had a special thread pool, the `ForkJoinPool`, in addition to the generic `ThreadPoolExecutor`. Although it looks like any other pool, it has a special purpose. While `ForkJoinPool` implements the `ExecutorService` interface, it differs significantly from the traditional `ThreadPoolExecutor` in its core design and operational principles. It employs a work-stealing mechanism where each thread has its own task queue. Idle threads can steal tasks from the tails of other threads' deques. We will discuss the work-stealing algorithm in a moment. While the traditional pool deals with a shared queue where tasks are assigned to idle threads, this can lead to contention and overhead as the threads compete for tasks.

The traditional thread pool usually maintains a fixed or bounded number of threads, and thread creation and termination are less dynamic. On the other hand, `ForkJoin Pool` can adaptively adjust the number of active threads based on workload and processor availability. It can also dynamically add, suspend, or resume threads to maintain efficiency.

The traditional thread pool often relies on explicit synchronization mechanisms like locks and condition variables to manage task access and thread synchronization. On the other hand, the `ForkJoinPool` minimizes the need for explicit synchronization due to the work-stealing algorithm. This allows threads to operate more autonomously, which reduces contention and overhead, thus giving us excellent performance.

Traditional thread pools don't recognize that some tasks could be dependent on other tasks. So if a subtask starts executing on a thread and then has to wait for another task, the running thread will not be able to make progress until the child task is completed by another thread. This is a problem. On the other hand, the `ForkJoinPool` is designed in such a way that tasks can be recursively decomposed into smaller subtasks, creating a tree-like structure. If a task is dependent on its child tasks, it can suspend its own execution and execute other pending tasks while waiting. Let's see an example.

Imagine we need to write a program to calculate the 20th Fibonacci number. For the sake of the demonstration, we'll need to make it multithreaded, so the assumption is we'll get it faster. We will begin with a fixed number of threads, let's say 100:

```java
import java.util.Map;
import java.util.concurrent.*;

public class FibonacciNumberWithTraditionalThreadPool {
  private static final Map<Integer, Long> cache = new ConcurrentHashMap<>(
      Map.of(0, 0L, 1, 1L)
  );
  private static long getFibonacci(int i, ExecutorService pool) {
    if (cache.containsKey(i)) {
      return cache.get(i);
    }
    Future<Long> future1 = pool.submit(() -> getFibonacci(i - 1, pool));  ❶
    Future<Long> future2 = pool.submit(() -> getFibonacci(i - 2, pool));  ❷
    try {
      long l1 = future1.get();  ❸
      long l2 = future2.get();
      long result = l1 + l2;
      cache.put(i, result);
      return result;
    } catch (InterruptedException | ExecutionException e) {
      throw new RuntimeException(e);
    }
  }

  public static void main(String[] args) {
    try (var pool = Executors.newFixedThreadPool(100)) {  ❹
      Future<Long> future = pool.submit(() -> getFibonacci(20, pool));
      Long l = future.get();
      System.out.println("Fibonacci number is: " + l);
```

```
      } catch (ExecutionException | InterruptedException e) {
        throw new RuntimeException(e);
      }
    }
  }
}
```

Let's examine what we have done here:

❶ Each task submits two subtasks to calculate Fibonacci ($n - 1$).

❷ And Fibonacci ($n - 2$), creating a binary tree of tasks.

❸ The parent task blocks waiting for its children to complete, holding a thread hostage.

❹ Despite having 100 threads, the pool quickly exhausts as each thread waits for its subtasks.

The preceding Java code calculates the 20th Fibonacci number using a thread pool and caching for efficiency. It employs a recursive `getFibonacci()` function that breaks down the problem into smaller subproblems, submitting each to a thread pool. `ConcurrentHashMap` (*https://oreil.ly/v5zUs*) acts as a cache to store previously computed results, preventing redundant calculations.

However, if we run this code, we will soon find out that it doesn't produce any result; rather, it creates a deadlock. We are limited to 100 threads here. When we call the `getFibonacci()` method, it creates two child tasks and submits them to the pool; essentially, the thread running the parent task keeps waiting until the children finish their work. Each child's task continues doing similar things, creating more tasks. While doing so, the pool runs out of threads, and they keep on waiting. Since the child tasks are in the queue and not getting executed, the other threads get stuck, essentially creating a deadlock. We can solve the deadlock by providing more threads, but we know that threads are limited.

If we generate a thread dump using the following command:

```
jcmd 36427 Thread.dump_to_file -format=json threaddump.json
```

We will see something like Figure 3-1.

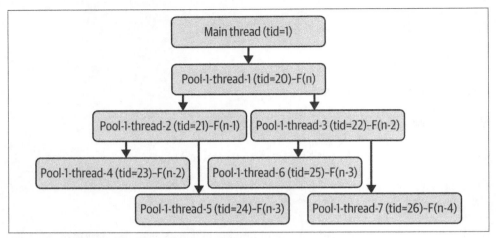

Figure 3-1. Fibonacci calculation in `ForkJoinPool`

On the other hand, if we do the same thing with a `ForkJoinPool`, it won't face a similar issue. Since `ForkJoinPool` is designed especially for the decomposition of work into multiple subproblems while waiting on the dependent tasks, it can suspend its tasks and keep working on pending tasks, and it continues working without an issue.

For instance:

```java
import java.util.Map;
import java.util.concurrent.*;
import java.util.Map;
import java.util.concurrent.*;

public class FibonacciNumberWithForkJoinPool {
  private static final Map<Integer, Long> cache = new ConcurrentHashMap<>(
      Map.of(0, 0L, 1, 1L)
  );

  static class FibonacciTask extends RecursiveTask<Long> { ❶
    private final int n;
    public FibonacciTask(int n) {
      this.n = n;
    }
    @Override
    protected Long compute() {
      if (cache.containsKey(n)) {
        return cache.get(n);
      }
      FibonacciTask f1 = new FibonacciTask(n - 1);
      f1.fork(); ❷
      FibonacciTask f2 = new FibonacciTask(n - 2);
      long result = f2.compute() + f1.join(); ❸
      cache.put(n, result);
```

```
      return result;
    }
  }

  public static void main(String[] args) {
    try (var pool = new ForkJoinPool()) { ❹
      Long result = pool.invoke(new FibonacciTask(20));
      System.out.println("Fibonacci number is: " + result);
    }
  }
}
```

Let's examine how `ForkJoinPool` avoids the deadlock:

❶ `RecursiveTask` (*https://oreil.ly/4kYNM*) is designed specifically for Fork/Join decomposition, providing the framework for splitting work.

❷ The `fork()` (*https://oreil.ly/Pcvmt*) method asynchronously submits the subtask to the pool, placing it in the current thread's deque.

❸ Here's the key difference: `compute()` (*https://oreil.ly/8TBFk*) executes `f2` directly on the current thread (avoiding thread consumption), while `join()` (*https://oreil.ly/JkAAe*) waits for `f1`. If `f1` isn't complete, the thread can steal other work instead of blocking.

❹ `ForkJoinPool` uses a default configuration optimized for the number of available processors.

This Java code calculates the 20th Fibonacci number using a `ForkJoinPool`, which is designed for efficient parallel execution of recursive tasks. We also used a `Concurrent HashMap` to store previously computed Fibonacci numbers to prevent redundant calculations. It uses a `FibonacciTask` class that extends `RecursiveTask`, which allows tasks to be split and executed in parallel.

If we run the code, we will immediately get results.

Now that we have covered why `ForkJoinPool` is special, let's discuss why it is used to implement virtual threads.

In Java, contention arises when threads need exclusive access to shared resources such as objects, variables, or I/O streams. Usually, those resources are guarded using synchronization, locks, etc. These synchronization mechanisms ensure the program's correctness, but the application's performance can degrade if there are too many contentions. For example, if threads spend more time waiting to acquire locks, it leads to longer execution times. So, if we can design our program with fewer contentions, the performance is likely to increase. In fact, the ForkJoinPool is designed to have lower contention, which is why it yields excellent performance.

Why ForkJoinPool for Virtual Threads?

Like the regular thread pool, the `ForkJoinPool` also comprises a predefined number of worker threads. If we don't specify the amount of parallelism (essentially the number of threads) in the constructor argument, it starts with the number of available processors in the system it runs.

The `ForkJoinPool` can be used for both CPU-bound and I/O-bound workloads; however, it is essential to understand that having more threads than available processors does not benefit CPU-intensive work. In CPU-intensive work, each thread competes for CPU time, and since we have a fixed number of cores available, having more threads than available cores means more context switch overhead. Only a number of threads equal to the available CPU cores can run simultaneously, so excess threads just wait and add no benefit. On the other hand, I/O-intensive work benefits from more threads, as some of them would be blocked while others can continue working. In the previous chapter, we discussed how virtual threads benefit I/O-intensive workloads. We will get into how `ForkJoinPool` relates to virtual threads, but first, let's explore what's happening under the hood in this pool.

Each worker thread maintains its own deque (double-ended queue), namely Work Queue, of tasks. Tasks are typically pushed and popped from one end (following LIFO [last-in, first-out] order) by the worker thread. Another thread can steal a task from the other end (using FIFO [first-in, first-out] order. When a worker thread breaks down tasks as part of the divide-and-conquer algorithm, it places the newly created subtasks directly into its own work queue (Figure 3-2).

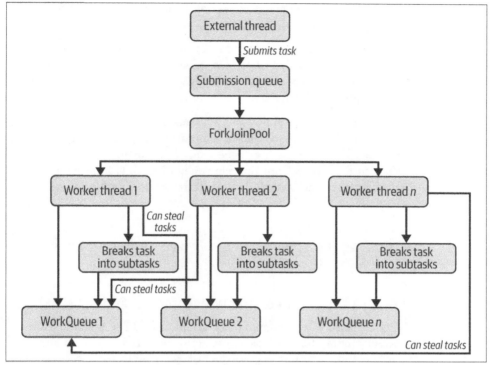

Figure 3-2. `ForkJoinPool` task flow—external threads submit tasks, which are distributed to worker threads that manage their own queues and can steal tasks from one another

External threads submit tasks (which are not part of the worker threads), and they enter the system through submission queues. These queues are similar to `WorkQueues` but are managed by the `ForkJoinPool` itself. Synchronization mechanisms like locks are not explicitly used; instead, atomic operations like compare-and-swap (CAS) are used to efficiently manage concurrent access.

We can use a "busy bees" metaphor to describe the worker threads. They are constantly scanning for work to keep themselves occupied. Since we have only a limited number of these worker threads, we want to ensure they're always doing something worthwhile. When a worker runs out of tasks in its own queue, it becomes a "stealer" and attempts to steal a task from another worker's queue. That's where the "work-stealing" magic happens!

At first glance, one might assume that this task stealing would lead to contention when both a worker and a stealer try to access the same queue. Well, that is why, to minimize contention, two threads pick tasks from two different ends of the queue.

Typically, the queue owner uses the pop method, taking from the top (LIFO), and the stealers take from the bottom (FIFO).

The "push" method adds new tasks to the head of the queue. When a worker "pops" a task, it takes the most recently added one. This makes the queue work like a stack (LIFO). This might be another place to ask questions, as you might wonder if this is unfair to older tasks waiting in the queue.

The answer to that question is as follows—CPUs have caches that store recently accessed data. By prioritizing the newest tasks, we increase the chances that the data needed for those tasks is already in the cache. This leads to fewer "cache misses" (when the CPU has to fetch data from the main memory), thus improving performance. But what about the older tasks? Well, that's where the stealer thread comes into the picture. It polls them from the tail of the queue.

In addition to these strategies, the `ForkJoinPool` uses clever CAS operations to manage the queue. These operations are designed to be superefficient, even when many threads are involved.

Implementing a Lock-Free Counter with Compare-And-Set (CAS)

The CAS technique is used when designing concurrent algorithms. It allows for the safe and concurrent modification of a shared value without resorting to the traditional locking mechanism. Instead of acquiring a lock, a thread using CAS compares the current value of a variable with an expected value and swaps it with a new value only if the current value matches the expected one.

Consider the following example of a CAS-based atomic counter using Java's VarHandle (https://oreil.ly/3lC84). The counter is updated atomically using a CAS operation, ensuring thread safety without needing explicit locks:

```
import java.lang.invoke.MethodHandles;
import java.lang.invoke.VarHandle;

public class AtomicCounter {
  private volatile int counter = 0;
  private static final VarHandle COUNTER_HANDLE;
  static {
    try {
      COUNTER_HANDLE = MethodHandles.lookup().findVarHandle(
          AtomicCounter.class, "counter", int.class); ❶
    } catch (ReflectiveOperationException e) {
      throw new Error(e);
    }
  }

  public void increment() {
    int current;
```

```
      int next;
      do {
        current = counter;  ❷
        next = current + 1;
      } while (!COUNTER_HANDLE.compareAndSet(this, current, next));  ❸
    }

    public int get() {
      return counter;
    }

    public static void main(String[] args) throws InterruptedException {
      AtomicCounter atomicCounter = new AtomicCounter();
      Thread.ofPlatform().start(() -> {
        for (int i = 0; i < 100; i++) {
          atomicCounter.increment();
        }
      });
      Thread.ofPlatform().start(() -> {
        for (int i = 0; i < 100; i++) {
          atomicCounter.increment();
        }
      });
      Thread.sleep(100);
      System.out.println("Final Counter Value: " + atomicCounter.get());  ❹
    }
  }
```

Let's examine how CAS ensures thread safety:

❶ `VarHandle` provides low-level access to variables with atomic operations. It's more performant than reflection-based approaches and offers stronger guarantees than `volatile` alone.

❷ We read the current value and calculate the next value. This is our "expected" state.

❸ The CAS operation atomically checks if the counter still equals the current value. If yes, it updates to the next and returns true. If another thread modified it, the operation returns false, and we retry.

❹ The final value should be exactly 200, demonstrating that no increments were lost despite concurrent access.

In this code, we have created two platform threads that increment the counter 100 times each. With the CAS operation, the value would update safely without any issues. With CAS, threads do not block each other. Instead, each thread attempts to update a shared variable atomically. If the operation fails (because another thread updated the value first), the thread retries the operation until it succeeds. This

> approach is non-blocking and generally more efficient, particularly under light contention, because it reduces the overhead of acquiring and releasing locks. This is precisely why `ForkJoinPool` uses CAS operations for its work-stealing queues; they keep threads productive rather than waiting.

The `ForkJoinPool` was initially designed to help speed up parallel processing by utilizing all available processor cores. This was done by employing the divide-and-conquer algorithm. The basic idea is that we can divide a big task into smaller tasks until they are simple enough to compute independently. However, one thing we have to keep in mind is that `ForkJoinPool` is the manager of the pool of threads, but it doesn't break the tasks into smaller ones itself; rather, *it is the developer's responsibility to determine how to break the tasks down*. That's where `RecursiveTask` (*https://oreil.ly/4kYNM*), `RecursiveAction` (*https://oreil.ly/JNpA4*), etc. come into the picture. The developer usually extends these classes to create their task class and add the logic into it. When a task is split into multiple child tasks, the parent task waits until its subtasks are executed; once the subtasks have finished executing, the task joins (merges) all the results into one result. While the parent task waits for the completion of its child tasks, the worker thread can either continue working on other tasks in its queue or steal tasks from other workers if it runs out of tasks. This is uniquely different from other thread pools.

However, the use of this `ForkJoinPool` gradually expanded to many other use cases, especially with event-style tasks, which are typically designed to execute independently and do not require joining (i.e., waiting for a task's result). In such a case, a `ForkJoinPool` can be created using the appropriate constructor argument in async mode. In async mode, `ForkJoinPool` switches to FIFO , which is more suitable for tasks that do not rely on a recursive, divide-and-conquer model. It ensures that tasks are processed in the order they are submitted, which is vital for tasks representing events or external triggers.

Consider the following example:

```java
import java.util.concurrent.ForkJoinPool;

public class AsyncModeExample {

  public static void main(String[] args) {
    try (ForkJoinPool forkJoinPool = new ForkJoinPool(4,
        ForkJoinPool.defaultForkJoinWorkerThreadFactory, null, true)) {
      for (int i = 0; i < 10; i++) {
        forkJoinPool.submit(new EventTask("Event " + i));
      }
    }
  }

  record EventTask(String eventName) implements Runnable {
```

```
    public void run() {
      System.out.println("Processing " + eventName
          + " in thread: " + Thread.currentThread().getName());
      try {
        Thread.sleep(1000);
      } catch (InterruptedException e) {
        Thread.currentThread().interrupt();
      }
      System.out.println("Completed " + eventName
          + " in thread: " + Thread.currentThread().getName());
    }
  }
}
```

In this example code, we have first created the instance of `ForkJoinPool` by passing async mode `true` to the constructor. The same can be achieved by using `Executors.newWorkStealingPool()`.

The bottom line is that `ForkJoinPool` is much more efficient and performant, which is why it has been chosen to schedule virtual threads. When using virtual threads, the async mode is used. The threads in the `ForkJoinPool` execute all the virtual threads and act as a scheduler.

Continuation

A *continuation* is an abstract concept that carries different meanings across fields like mathematics, computer science, and everyday language. In programming, a continuation refers to the ability of a program to save its current execution state and resume later from where it stopped.

It's similar to how a thread executes and, during a context switch, takes a snapshot of its state so it can resume later. However, in the case of continuations, this concept applies at a more granular level, even at the method level.

For instance, imagine a method with a few lines of code. Normally, when the method is called, it executes all the lines sequentially. If the method exits early and is called again, it starts from the beginning. But with a continuation, the method can "pause" at a specific point and, when called again, resume exactly from where it stopped, preserving the execution state.

Continuations have many practical uses in programming, including exception handling, non-blocking I/O operations, concurrency control, generators, etc.[2]

---

2 A *generator* is a function that can yield multiple values over time, pausing its execution between yields. When the generator is called again, it resumes execution from the point where it left off, similar to how continuations work.

Let's explore how continuations work.

As of Java 21, continuations are available through an internal package. While using these internal APIs directly in production code is not recommended, understanding how they work can still be valuable. We can explore a sample implementation to experiment and learn more about continuations. Consider the following code:

```
import jdk.internal.vm.Continuation;
import jdk.internal.vm.ContinuationScope;
// --add-exports java.base/jdk.internal.vm=ALL-UNNAMED

public class ContinuationExample {
    public static void main(String[] args) {
        ContinuationScope scope = new ContinuationScope("main");
        Continuation continuation = new Continuation(scope, () -> {
            System.out.println("Hello from continuation");
            Continuation.yield(scope);
            System.out.println("Hello again from continuation");
            Continuation.yield(scope);
            System.out.println("Done from continuation");
        });
        System.out.println("Before starting continuation");
        continuation.run();
        System.out.println("After starting continuation");
        continuation.run();
        System.out.println("After starting continuation again");
        continuation.run();
    }
}
```

In this example, we use the `Continuation` (*https://oreil.ly/vfTNY*) and `ContinuationScope` (*https://oreil.ly/CRbK7*) classes from the jdk.internal.vm package. These classes are not part of the public Java API and require adding special JVM arguments (`--add-exports java.base/jdk.internal.vm=ALL-UNNAMED`) to make them accessible.

Continuation is part of the internal API; don't use it in your production code; the preceding code is only for illustration purposes. Internal APIs can change or be removed without notice, which can lead to undesirable situations.

The `ContinuationScope` is used to create a unique scope for continuation, and the `Continuation` is essentially a piece of code that can be paused and resumed.

If we run the preceding code, we will have the following output:

```
Before starting continuation
Hello from continuation
After starting continuation
```

```
Hello again from continuation
After starting continuation again
Done from continuation
```

The first line in the main prints Before starting continuation. When continuation.run() is called, the continuation starts executing. It prints Hello from continuation and then yields as we have called Continuation.yield(scope). At this point, the continuation pauses, and control returns to main, which then prints After starting continuation. When continuation.run() is called again, it resumes from where it left off. It prints Hello again from continuation and yields once more. Control returns to main, which prints After starting continuation again. Finally, continuation.run() resumes the continuation, and it prints Done from continuation. Since there are no more yields, the continuation is completed.

Essentially, this is how continuations work inside virtual threads. When we start executing something, if the method is being executed on the virtual thread and it starts an I/O operation, the continuation calls the Continuation.yield(scope) method to pause the virtual thread and remove it from being executed by a carrier thread. Later, when the I/O operation is complete, the virtual thread gets scheduled again to complete its execution.

Now, a fair question would be, how does Continuation do it?

We know that anything we execute gets executed by a thread, specifically a platform thread. Each thread has a stack and stack frames. When we execute code, the stack grows and moves downwards with each method invocation. Consider Figure 3-3.

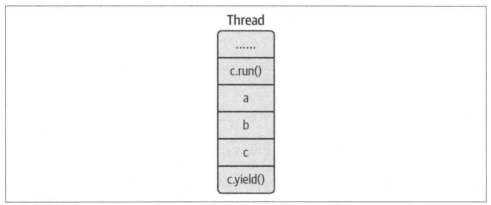

Figure 3-3. A stack and stack frame of a Continuation.run()

We have a platform thread that has been running, and at a certain point, it starts running the Continuation c by invoking c.run(). The run() method has a method a that calls b, and b calls c, and at c, we get c.yield(). That means, at this point, the Continuation will pause its execution and return. This Continuation c will be executed by another platform thread later, but for the current thread, it needs to return. The thread will finish its current work when the c.run() returns. But c.run() hasn't really finished its work; it paused. So what it really does is take all the frames from a to c.yield() and put them aside somewhere in the Continuation object (Figure 3-4).

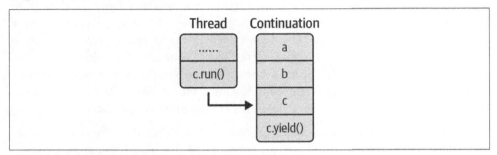

Figure 3-4. Stack moving out from the running thread after c.yield

The next time this Continuation c is mounted again, the opposite happens. All the thread frames get copied over to the thread stack, c.yield() returns, and execution continues where it left off. The stack then looks like Figure 3-5.

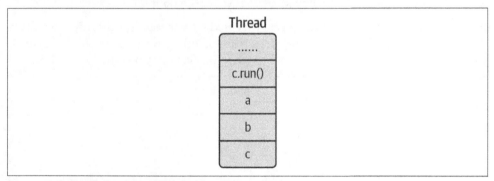

Figure 3-5. Stack frames are copied back when continuation resumes

From a high level, that's what happens; the stack frame gets copied over when a virtual thread aka continuation is unmounted and then copied back to the mounted thread again. However, this can be a costly operation, especially for deep call stacks. Each time a continuation gets suspended, the entire stack will be copied over. That's where an intelligent lazy copy mechanism is implemented in JVM.

Lazy copying is an optimization technique that avoids unnecessary copying of stack frames. What it does is, when first-time continuation is suspended, it copies over the entire stack frame to the Continuation object. Now, when this Continuation object is resumed, it doesn't copy the entire stack frame back to the thread, rather, it copies one or two frames (Figure 3-6).

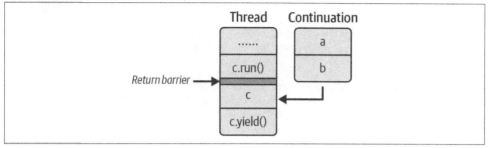

Figure 3-6. Stack copied back via lazy-copy mechanism, which doesn't copy all frames

Here, `c.yield()` returns to c, and c should return to b; however, b isn't in the stack. Instead, it employs a mechanism called *return barriers*. These are small pieces of code injected at function return points. When a function returns, the return barrier checks if the current frame needs to be copied to any continuation stacks. So, c doesn't return to b but to some VM code that will store all frames. Now it copies over b and may continue calling another method, say d. And then, if now `c.yield()` happens, only b, d, will be copied over to the `Continuation` object.

> I believe this provides a sufficient explanation of how Java continuation works in our day-to-day programming. However, if you want to know a bit more, I would suggest reading the source code of Project Loom (*https://oreil.ly/556J8*). There is also an excellent talk (*https://oreil.ly/Dly1t*) by Ron Pressler about continuations that covers pretty much everything.

Building Our Own Virtual Threads from Scratch

To illustrate the core concept of how virtual threads use continuation, we will create a simplified version of our own custom thread-like abstraction, which we'll call `Nano Thread`. Using Java's `Continuation` API, we can simulate the behavior of virtual threads. In this section, we'll break down the code step by step, starting with the `Nano ThreadScheduler`, followed by the `NanoThread` class, and finally, a simulation of file transfer operations.

The NanoThread class

The `NanoThread` class represents our custom virtual thread, which is built around the `Continuation` API. A `NanoThread` is created by passing in a `Runnable`, which is then encapsulated within a `Continuation`. Let's look at the following code:

```java
import jdk.internal.vm.Continuation;
import jdk.internal.vm.ContinuationScope;
import java.util.concurrent.atomic.AtomicInteger;

public class NanoThread {
    public static final NanoThreadScheduler NANO_THREAD_SCHEDULER
                    = new NanoThreadScheduler();
    private static final AtomicInteger COUNTER
                    = new AtomicInteger(1);
    public static final ContinuationScope SCOPE
                    = new ContinuationScope("nanoThreadScope");
    private final Continuation continuation;
    private final int nid;

    private NanoThread(Runnable runnable) {
        this.nid = COUNTER.getAndIncrement();
        this.continuation = new Continuation(SCOPE, runnable);
    }

    public static void start(Runnable runnable) {
        var nanoThread = new NanoThread(runnable);
        NANO_THREAD_SCHEDULER.schedule(nanoThread);
    }

    public void run() {
        continuation.run();
    }

    public static NanoThread currentVThread() {
        return NanoThreadScheduler.CURRENT_NANO_THREAD.get();
    }

    @Override
    public String toString() {
        return "NanoThread-" + nid + "-" + Thread.currentThread().getName();
    }
}
```

In this class, we introduce a `NanoThread` that is assigned a unique ID using `COUNTER` and manages a `Continuation`. Each `NanoThread` is initialized with a `Runnable` that encapsulates the logic to be executed.

The `run()` method is where the magic happens—it simply invokes `Continuation.run()`, allowing the thread to execute the code within the `Runnable`. If, at any point, the `NanoThread` yields its execution (using `Continuation.yield()`), it will pause and later resume from where it left off, simulating the behavior of a virtual thread.

The `start()` method initiates the `NanoThread` and hands it over to the scheduler for execution.

The NanoThread scheduler

The `NanoThreadScheduler` class plays a critical role in managing and executing `Nano Thread` instances. It uses a Fork/Join Pool to handle task scheduling and a `Scheduled ExecutorService` (*https://oreil.ly/ERUCr*) to simulate I/O-bound operations, which is a common reason threads pause and yield their execution.

Let's take a look at the scheduler:

```java
import java.util.concurrent.ExecutorService;
import java.util.concurrent.Executors;
import java.util.concurrent.ScheduledExecutorService;
public class NanoThreadScheduler {
    public static final ThreadLocal<NanoThread> CURRENT_NANO_THREAD
                                                = new ThreadLocal<>();

    public static final ScheduledExecutorService IO_EVENT_SCHEDULER =
        Executors.newSingleThreadScheduledExecutor();
    private final ExecutorService workStealingPool =
        Executors.newWorkStealingPool(2);

    public void schedule(NanoThread nanoThread) {
        workStealingPool.submit(() -> {
            CURRENT_NANO_THREAD.set(nanoThread);
            nanoThread.run();
            CURRENT_NANO_THREAD.remove();
        });
    }
}
```

The `NanoThreadScheduler` maintains a thread-local variable `CURRENT_NANO_THREAD` to track which `NanoThread` is currently executing on a worker thread. We also define an `IO_EVENT_SCHEDULER` to simulate I/O operations that introduce delays, a critical feature for understanding the behavior of virtual threads.

The `schedule()` method submits `NanoThread` instances to the Fork/Join Pool, where the actual execution takes place. This pool operates with two worker threads, continuously checking for tasks in the queue. We can certainly add more threads to it, but for our illustration, two threads are sufficient.

Simulating I/O operations with file transfer

In our example, we simulate an I/O-bound task—a file transfer. This is where the `IO_EVENT_SCHEDULER` becomes important, as it schedules tasks with random delays to mimic real-world I/O behavior:

```java
import jdk.internal.vm.Continuation;
import java.util.Random;
import java.util.concurrent.TimeUnit;
import static ca.bazlur.mcj.chap3.custom.NanoThread.NANO_THREAD_SCHEDULER;
import static ca.bazlur.mcj.chap3.custom.NanoThread.SCOPE;
```

```java
import static ca.bazlur.mcj.chap3.custom.NanoThreadScheduler.CURRENT_NANO_THREAD;
import static ca.bazlur.mcj.chap3.custom.NanoThreadScheduler.IO_EVENT_SCHEDULER;

public class FileOperation {
    private final Random random = new Random();

    public void transfer(String filePath) {
        System.out.println("Start transferring file: " + filePath);
        NanoThread nanoThread = NanoThread.currentVThread();
        IO_EVENT_SCHEDULER.schedule(() ->
                NANO_THREAD_SCHEDULER.schedule(nanoThread),
                random.nextInt(1000), TimeUnit.MILLISECONDS);
        CURRENT_NANO_THREAD.remove();
        Continuation.yield(SCOPE);
        System.out.println("Transfer completed for file: " + filePath);
    }
}
```

The `FileOperation` class defines a `transfer()` method that simulates a file transfer. It schedules the `NanoThread` to resume execution after a random delay (simulating an I/O wait time) using the `IO_EVENT_SCHEDULER`.

In this process, the current `NanoThread` yields, giving up its execution and allowing other threads to run. When the `Continuation.yield(SCOPE)` is executed in the transfer method, the worker thread in the Fork/Join Pool assumes the work is done if the run method returns, so it goes on to execute other `NanoThreads`. Once the delay has passed, the `IO_EVENT_SCHEDULER` reschedules the `NanoThread`, allowing it to continue from where it left off.

Putting it all together

Finally, we create a demo to simulate the concurrent transfer of multiple files using our `NanoThread` system:

```java
import java.time.Duration;

public class NanoThreadDemo {

  public static void main(String[] args) throws Exception {
    FileOperation fileOperation = new FileOperation();
    for (int i = 0; i < 4; i++) {
      int finalI = i;
      NanoThread.start(() -> {
        System.out.println("Transfer: "
            + "File_" + finalI + " Running in VThread: "
            + NanoThread.currentVThread());

        fileOperation.transfer("File_" + finalI);

        System.out.println("Transfer: " + "File_" + finalI
            + " Completed in VThread: " + NanoThread.currentVThread());
```

```
        });
    }

    // Let's wait for a minute to allow the
    // schedulers to run all our nano threads
    Thread.sleep(Duration.ofMinutes(1));
  }
}
```

In this `Demo` class, we create four `NanoThreads`, each simulating a file transfer. We initiate the transfers concurrently, allowing them to yield and resume based on random delays.

Let's run this code using the following command:

```
java --add-exports java.base/jdk.internal.vm=ALL-UNNAMED NanoThreadDemo.java
```

We will get an output like this:

```
Transfer: File_1 Running in VThread: NanoThread-2-ForkJoinPool-1-worker-2
Transfer: File_0 Running in VThread: NanoThread-1-ForkJoinPool-1-worker-1
Start transferring file: File_1
Start transferring file: File_0
Transfer: File_2 Running in VThread: NanoThread-3-ForkJoinPool-1-worker-2
Start transferring file: File_2
Transfer: File_3 Running in VThread: NanoThread-4-ForkJoinPool-1-worker-2
Start transferring file: File_3
Transfer completed for file: File_3
Transfer: File_3 Completed in VThread: NanoThread-4-ForkJoinPool-1-worker-1
Transfer completed for file: File_0
Transfer: File_0 Completed in VThread: NanoThread-1-ForkJoinPool-1-worker-1
Transfer completed for file: File_1
Transfer: File_1 Completed in VThread: NanoThread-2-ForkJoinPool-1-worker-1
Transfer completed for file: File_2
Transfer: File_2 Completed in VThread: NanoThread-3-ForkJoinPool-1-worker-1
```

If you look closely at the preceding output, you will quickly discover that `File_1` started execution by `NanoThread-2-ForkJoinPool-1-worker-2`, but when it completes, it was executed by `NanoThread-2-ForkJoinPool-1-worker-1`. The `Nano Thread` remains the same; however, the underlying worker thread switches. This is precisely what happens in virtual threads as well. Even if a virtual thread starts on a worker thread, if it yields because of I/O, it may end up on a completely different worker when it schedules again (Figure 3-7).

Note that this implementation is only for illustration purposes.

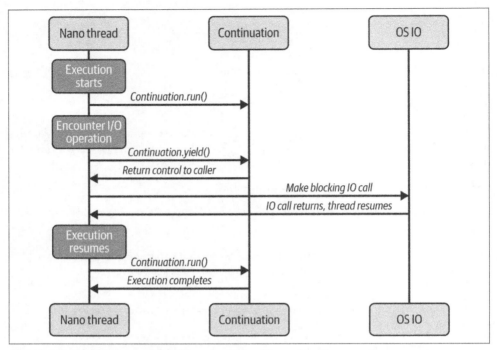

Figure 3-7. High-level design of the novel `NanoThread` *to illustrate the concept*

Virtual Threads and I/O Polling

In reality, when virtual threads start an I/O operation, the `Continuation` gets paused. What really happens is that the thread calls the `LockSupport.park()` method (*https://oreil.ly/rvEjY*). It looks like this:

```
public static void park() {
    if (Thread.currentThread().isVirtual()) {
        VirtualThreads.park();
    } else {
        U.park(false, 0L);
    }
}
```

In `VirtualThreads.park()`, after a few steps, it invokes the `yieldContinuation()` method. This effectively removes the virtual thread from the carrier threads (the real platform threads executing virtual threads).

Now, the key question is: what unparks the virtual thread when data arrives on the socket?

The JVM uses a JVM-wide read poller. At its core, this poller is a basic event loop that monitors synchronous networking operations like `read()`, `connect()`, and `accept()`

when they are invoked in a virtual thread and are not immediately ready. When an I/O operation becomes ready (e.g., when data arrives on the socket), the poller gets notified and unparks the corresponding parked virtual thread. This mechanism is mirrored for write operations, with a similar write poller.

On macOS, the poller uses `kqueue` (*https://oreil.ly/cB2Fe*); on Linux, it uses `epoll` (*https://oreil.ly/ksG8z*); and on Windows, it uses `wepoll` (*https://oreil.ly/JYXmb*), which provides an epoll-like API on top of the Ancillary Function Driver for Winsock.

The poller maintains a map of file descriptors to virtual threads. When a file descriptor is registered with the poller (e.g., a socket), an entry is added to this map that associates the file descriptor with the virtual thread waiting for the I/O operation to complete. The poller's event loop, upon waking up with an event (such as data being available on a socket), uses the event's file descriptor to look up the corresponding virtual thread in the map and then unparks it, allowing it to resume execution.

If you're interested in learning more, I recommend reading the poller's source code (*https://oreil.ly/MEBWI*) in the OpenJDK repository. You'll see how the JVM efficiently handles I/O for virtual threads by leveraging platform-specific mechanisms like `epoll` and `kqueue` to ensure that virtual threads don't waste resources while waiting for I/O.

In Closing

Nearly all the blocking points in the JDK libraries have been rewritten to accommodate virtual threads. Most of the blocking operations now work in such a way that, when a virtual thread encounters a blocking call, it unmounts, freeing its carrier thread, the underlying OS thread, to take on new work. This approach ensures that the system can handle a large number of virtual threads without exhausting system resources.

By grasping these concepts, we will gain more confidence in working with virtual threads and become more well-rounded developers.

CHAPTER 4
Structured Concurrency

Simplicity is prerequisite for reliability.
—Edsger W. Dijkstra

In our previous chapters, we have seen how virtual threads open up a world of possibilities by letting us handle blocking tasks in Java concurrency. With thousands of lightweight virtual threads capable of spawning without significant overhead, blocking calls are no longer a concern. However, one critical issue still needs to be addressed: managing the relationships and dependencies between tasks when they are broken down and distributed across multiple threads.

Imagine a scenario where a parent task has several dependent subtasks, each running on a different thread. If the parent task terminates unexpectedly, its subtasks continue to execute independently. The results of these subtasks become irrelevant, yet they still consume resources.

Moreover, if the parent must be completed only when all its subtasks are complete, any failure among the subtasks should ideally lead to the cancellation of the entire operation. This lack of coordination can lead to numerous orphaned threads. These orphaned threads will exhaust valuable memory and processor time by doing unnecessary work. Often, such inefficiencies involve considerable costs.

In traditional concurrency models, such as Java's `ExecutorService` and `Future`, task hierarchies are not inherently supported, which makes it difficult to propagate cancellations or handle errors in a structured manner. This results in a fragmented and often error-prone approach to concurrent programming.

Structured concurrency is a paradigm that addresses these challenges by treating groups of related tasks as a single unit of work. It ensures that the lifecycles of subtasks are bound to the parent task, providing a transparent and manageable structure for concurrent execution. This not only simplifies error handling and cancellation but also enhances the reliability and observability of concurrent code.

In this chapter, we will explore structured concurrency in Java, examining its benefits and how it addresses the limitations of traditional concurrency models. We will introduce the `StructuredTaskScope` (*https://oreil.ly/eOySX*) API, discuss how it helps manage task hierarchies, and provide practical examples to illustrate its use. By the end of this chapter, you will have a solid understanding of how to implement structured concurrency in your Java applications and how to write more robust and maintainable concurrent code.

The Challenge of Unstructured Concurrency

In Java, concurrency has traditionally been managed using abstractions like `ExecutorService` and `Future`. While these classes provide a means of executing tasks concurrently, they also present some challenges, especially when tasks must be coordinated.

Consider a common scenario: a web application needs to fetch product details and associated reviews for display. An approach using `ExecutorService` could be implemented to perform these operations in parallel, thereby improving response time.

To illustrate this, let's construct the Java code for our scenario piece by piece. We'll begin by defining the data structures that will hold our product information and reviews. Java records are well-suited for these simple data carriers due to their conciseness and simplicity. We'll also define a custom `ProductServiceException` to more effectively handle errors specific to our product service logic:

```
record Product(Long id, String name, String description) {}
record Review(Long id, String comment, int rating, Long productId) {}
record ProductInfo(Product product, List<Review> reviews) {}

class ProductServiceException extends RuntimeException {
  public ProductServiceException(String message, Throwable cause) {
    super(message, cause);
  }
  public ProductServiceException(String message) {
    super(message);
  }
}
```

With our data models and custom exception in place, we need to simulate the actual work of fetching data. Real-world data retrieval typically involves network latency, which can be mimicked using helper methods. The `ProductService` class, which we'll define shortly, will include these private helper methods: `sleepForAWhile()` to introduce a delay, `log()` to log messages with a concise thread identifier for better readability, and `fetchProduct()` and `fetchReviews()` to simulate the data fetching operations. These methods will print messages indicating their progress, including the name of the executing thread, to help visualize concurrency.

Now, we can implement the central `ProductService` class. The key method here is `fetchProductInfo()`. This method utilizes an `ExecutorService` (specifically, `Executors.newVirtualThreadPerTaskExecutor()`, which is suitable for I/O-bound operations as it creates lightweight virtual threads for each task) to concurrently run the product- and review-fetching tasks. It then uses `Future.get()` to await their completion and retrieve their results. The helper methods for simulating work are included as private instance methods within this class for proper encapsulation:

```
public class ProductService {
    public ProductInfo fetchProductInfo(Long productId) {
        log("Fetching product & reviews for id: " + productId);

        try (var ExecutorService
                = Executors.newVirtualThreadPerTaskExecutor()) {  ❶

            Future<Product> productTask =
                ExecutorService.submit(() -> fetchProduct(productId));  ❷
            Future<List<Review>> reviewsTask =
                ExecutorService.submit(() -> fetchReviews(productId));  ❸
            Product product = productTask.get();  ❹
            log("Product retrieved for id: " + productId);
            List<Review> reviews = reviewsTask.get();  ❺
            log("Reviews retrieved for id: " + productId);
            log("All info fetched for id: " + productId);
            return new ProductInfo(product, reviews);  ❻

        } catch (ExecutionException | InterruptedException e) {  ❼
            Throwable cause = e.getCause() != null ? e.getCause() : e;
            log("Error processing product info for id: " +
                productId + ": " + cause.getMessage());

            if (e instanceof InterruptedException) {
                Thread.currentThread().interrupt();
            }

            throw new ProductServiceException(
                "Fetch failed for id: " + productId, cause);
        }
    }
}
```

Now let's go through what we have done here:

❶ We created a virtual thread executor that spawns a new virtual thread for each submitted task.

❷ Submits the product-fetching operation to run concurrently.

❸ Submits the review-fetching operation to run concurrently.

❹ Blocks until the product task completes and retrieves the result.

❺ Blocks until the review task completes and retrieves the result.

❻ Combines both results into the final `ProductInfo` object.

❼ Catches both execution and interruption exceptions with appropriate handling.

To complete our concurrent product service example, we need several supporting methods that simulate real-world operations:

```java
private Product fetchProduct(Long productId) {
    log("Fetching product id: " + productId);
    sleepForAWhile(Duration.ofSeconds(1)); // Simulate network call
    return new Product(productId, "Sample Product",
        "A great product description.");
}
private List<Review> fetchReviews(Long productId) {
    log("Fetching reviews for id: " + productId);
    sleepForAWhile(Duration.ofSeconds(2)); // Simulate network call
    return List.of(
        new Review(1L, "Excellent!", 5, productId),
        new Review(2L, "Good value.", 4, productId)
    );
}

private void sleepForAWhile(Duration duration) {
    try {
        Thread.sleep(duration);
    } catch (InterruptedException e) {
        Thread.currentThread().interrupt();
        throw new RuntimeException("Thread interrupted during sleep", e);
    }
}

private static void log(String message) {
    Thread currentThread = Thread.currentThread();
    String threadName = currentThread.isVirtual()
        ? "VThread[#" + currentThread.threadId() + "]"
        : currentThread.getName();  ❶
    String currentTime = LocalTime.now()
        .format(DateTimeFormatter.ofPattern("HH:mm:ss.SSS"));
    System.out.printf("%s %-15s: %s%n", currentTime, threadName, message);
}

void main() { ❷
    ProductService productService = new ProductService();
    long testProductId = 1L;
```

```
        log("Attempting to fetch product info for ID: " + testProductId);
        try {
            ProductInfo productInfo = productService.fetchProductInfo(testProductId);
            log("Successfully retrieved: " + productInfo);
        } catch (ProductServiceException e) {
            log("Service Error: " + e.getMessage() +
                (e.getCause() != null ? " | Caused by: " +
                e.getCause().getMessage() : ""));
        }
    }
}
```

Let's examine the key implementation details in this code:

❶ This custom logging format helps us track which threads are executing our concurrent operations. Virtual threads generally don't have a name, but their `toString()` method gives us verbose names like `VirtualThread[#34]/runnable@ForkJoinPool-1-worker-1`, and we shorten this to `VThread[#34]` for clarity while still distinguishing virtual threads from platform threads.

❷ Runs the complete example, showing both the concurrent execution flow and error handling, producing the output we analyze next.

With all components in place, let's execute the complete example to observe the concurrent behavior. Run the following command in your terminal to see how virtual threads handle our parallel operations:

```
java ProductService.java
```

And the output would look as follows:

```
00:50:27.625 main         : Attempting to fetch product info for ID: 1
00:50:27.627 main         : Fetching product & reviews for id: 1
00:50:27.631 VThread[#34]: Fetching product id: 1
00:50:27.631 VThread[#36]: Fetching reviews for id: 1
00:50:28.638 main         : Product retrieved for id: 1
00:50:29.652 VThread[#36]: Fetched reviews for id: 1
00:50:29.653 main         : Reviews retrieved for id: 1
00:50:29.653 main         : All info fetched for id: 1
00:50:29.660 main         : Successfully retrieved Product Info:
ProductInfo[product=Product[id=1, name=Sample Product, description=A great
product description.], reviews=[Review[id=1, comment=Excellent!, rating=5,
productId=1], Review[id=2, comment=Good value., rating=4, productId=1]]]
```

At first glance, this approach seems perfectly reasonable. We've split the work into two concurrent tasks: fetching the product details and fetching its reviews. However, if we carefully consider this, we have a few problems here. As both methods execute concurrently, each method can succeed or fail independently.

Imagine a scenario where the product database is temporarily unavailable. The `fetchProduct()` task might throw an exception, which will end up stopping the main request thread. However, oblivious to this failure, the `fetchReviews()` task continues to execute in its own thread. This is a thread leak that can potentially hog resources and add unnecessary load to the server (Figure 4-1).

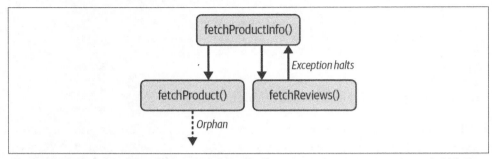

Figure 4-1. Parent task spawns two child tasks; however, an exception in one child halts the parent, leaving the other child task orphaned

If the user decides to abandon the request, the server might want to halt the request thread by interrupting. However, this won't cancel the subtasks; the `fetchProduct()` and `fetchReviews()` tasks will continue running even after the `fetchProductInfo()` method fails. This results in two threads leaking and a waste of precious CPU cycles on a request that's no longer relevant.

The `fetchProductInfo()` method returns results based on the results of both subsequent methods. So, the `fetchProductInfo()` method either succeeds with both results or fails. However, what if `fetchProduct()` takes a significantly longer time than `fetchReviews()`, and while it's fetching the product, `fetchReviews()` fails? In this case, the `fetchProductInfo()` method unnecessarily waits for `fetchProduct()`, which will ultimately be abandoned.

To illustrate these problems in action, let's modify our methods to simulate a realistic failure scenario. We'll create a situation where one task takes significantly longer while the other fails quickly:

```
private Product fetchProduct(Long productId) {
  log("Fetching product id: " + productId);
  if (productId == 1L) {
    log("Product id: " + productId
        + " - simulating long network call (5 seconds).");
    sleepForAWhile(Duration.ofSeconds(5));
    log("Product id: " + productId + " fetch complete.");
    return new Product(productId,
        "Long-Fetched Product", "This product takes time to fetch.");
  }
  log("Product id: " + productId +
      " - simulating standard network call (1 second).");
  sleepForAWhile(Duration.ofSeconds(1));
```

```
      log("Product id: " + productId + " fetch complete.");
      return new Product(productId, "Sample Product",
          "A great product description.");
    }

    private List<Review> fetchReviews(Long productId) {
      log("Fetching reviews for id: " + productId);
      if (productId == 1L) {
        log("Reviews for id: " + productId
            + " - simulating quick failure after 1 second.");
        sleepForAWhile(Duration.ofSeconds(1));
        throw new ProductServiceException("Simulated failure " +
            "fetching reviews for product " + productId);
      }
      log("Reviews for id: " + productId
          + " - simulating network call (2 seconds).");
      sleepForAWhile(Duration.ofSeconds(2));
      List<Review> reviews = List.of(
          new Review(1L, "Excellent!", 5, productId),
          new Review(2L, "Good value.", 4, productId)
      );
      log("Fetched reviews for id: " + productId);
      return reviews;
    }
```

In the preceding method, we've introduced a conditional behavior based on `product Id == 1L` to create a controlled scenario: the product fetch will take five seconds (simulating a slow database), while the reviews fetch will fail after just one second. This timing mismatch perfectly demonstrates our resource leak problem.

Now, if we rerun the code, the output would be as follows:

```
00:58:02.885 main           : Attempting to fetch product info for ID: 1
00:58:02.887 main           : Fetching product & reviews for id: 1
00:58:02.890 VThread[#36]   : Fetching reviews for id: 1
00:58:02.890 VThread[#34]   : Fetching product id: 1
00:58:02.890 VThread[#36]   : Reviews for id: 1 - simulating quick failure after
1 second.
00:58:02.891 VThread[#34]   : Product id: 1 - simulating long network call
(5 seconds).
00:58:07.899 VThread[#34]   : Product id: 1 fetch complete.
00:58:07.900 main           : Product retrieved for id: 1
00:58:07.905 main           : Error processing product info for id:
1: Simulated failure fetching reviews for product 1
00:58:07.906 main           : Service Error: Fetch failed for id:
1 | Caused by: Simulated failure fetching reviews for product 1
```

The log output reveals the exact problem we described. Even though `fetchReviews()` throws an exception, the `productFetch()` method continues its execution, taking a full five seconds to retrieve the product. This delay is unnecessary because the result can no longer be used.

This example exposes the core issue with unstructured concurrency. It treats tasks as independent entities, ignoring their relationships and dependencies. The result is a breeding ground for error, resource leaks, and performance bottlenecks. Even further down the road, it makes it difficult to diagnose issues. Observability tools such as thread dumps will show each method call as stacks of unrelated threads with no hint of the task–subtask relationship.

It's like the goto (*https://oreil.ly/i40L7*) statement back in the old days. As a result of using goto, the execution jumps to arbitrary points in the code, making it challenging to trace the program's logic. Similarly, tasks or threads can be executed in an arbitrary order in unstructured concurrency, making it hard to predict the program's state at any given time.

Structured concurrency represents a paradigm shift that can solve these problems, making programming in the presence of concurrency clean and straightforward.

The Promise of Structured Concurrency

Structured concurrency arrives as a fresh approach to Java concurrency. Rather than treating concurrent tasks as independent entities, it organizes them in a way that mirrors the logical structure of our programs.

The core principle is straightforward: when a task spawns multiple concurrent subtasks, they must all return to the same point in the parent task's code. Think of it like a manager delegating work to team members; everyone reports back before the project can be considered complete.

In this model, the parent task acts as a supervisor, monitoring its subtasks and waiting for their completion or intervening when problems arise. This constraint may seem simple, but it has profound implications for the reliability and maintainability of concurrent code. Every subtask, regardless of whether it succeeds or fails, must report back to its parent before the operation can conclude.

Now let's discuss some of the benefits that it brings.

First, structured concurrency provides a unified mechanism for error and cancellation handling across a group of related (sibling) tasks. For example, if one subtask encounters an error or is canceled, its sibling tasks are automatically terminated, and the error propagates gracefully up the task hierarchy.

Second, it prevents thread leaks by enforcing a strict parent-child lifecycle for tasks. Tasks cannot outlive their intended scope because the parent ensures all subtasks are properly cleaned up upon completion, leading to more predictable system behavior.

Furthermore, structured concurrency enhances observability by providing a clear and intuitive representation of task dependencies. Tools such as thread dumps and specialized profilers can then easily trace these task relationships. This improved traceability facilitates faster troubleshooting and root cause analysis when issues arise.

The paradigm also encourages a more declarative programming style, allowing developers to focus on the business logic of their tasks rather than the intricate details of thread management. This shift results in cleaner, more maintainable code that is easier to understand and modify, which ultimately reduces development time and costs.

Finally, because structured concurrency often works on top of virtual threads, this combination enables the creation of a vast number of concurrent tasks with minimal overhead. Structured concurrency provides the essential framework for orchestrating these virtual threads, ensuring their safe and efficient execution, even at a large scale.

Structured concurrency is positioned to become a fundamental component of Java concurrent programming. By addressing the core problems of unstructured concurrency, it offers a path toward more reliable and maintainable systems.

Let's examine the Structured Concurrency API and see how it addresses the challenges we've discussed.

Understanding the API

At the heart of the Structured Concurrency API lies the `StructuredTaskScope` (*https://oreil.ly/k9kPw*) in the java.util.concurrent (*https://oreil.ly/2tqNo*) package. In this section, we'll explore its main features, how it works, and how it can be used to simplify and improve concurrent programming in Java.

StructuredTaskScope

The `StructuredTaskScope` (*https://oreil.ly/k9kPw*) interface is central to the structured concurrency model in Java. It allows developers to manage groups of related tasks, ensuring that their lifecycles are bound together. This makes error handling, cancellation, and result aggregation more straightforward and reliable.

The `StructuredTaskScope` is a sealed interface, parameterized by the types T and R, which represent the result type of the tasks executed within the scope:

```
public sealed interface StructuredTaskScope<T,R>
                                                extends AutoCloseable
```

Let's explore its key methods:

`<U extends T> StructuredTaskScope.Subtask<U> fork(Callable<? extends U> task)`
> Creates and starts a new subtask within the scope. The task is executed concurrently in a separate thread (typically a virtual thread). The method returns a Subtask (*https://oreil.ly/eB1YZ*) object representing the running subtask.

`<U extends T> StructuredTaskScope.Subtask<U> fork(Runnable task)`
   Creates and starts a new subtask within the scope to run the provided action. The action executes concurrently in a separate thread (typically a virtual thread). Because the task is a `Runnable`, it produces no result; therefore, `Subtask.get()` returns `null` on successful completion. The method returns a `Subtask` object representing the running subtask.

`join()`
   Returns the result after waiting for all subtasks to complete or the scope to be canceled. This method blocks the calling thread (which must be the scope owner) until all subtasks finish. If a timeout is configured and expires, the scope is canceled and `TimeoutException` is thrown. After waiting completes, the joiner's `result()` method is invoked to get the result or throw an exception. If the `result()` method throws an exception, `FailedException` is thrown with that exception as the cause. This method can only be called once by the scope owner.

`close()`
   This method closes the scope, ensuring that all subtasks have been completed or canceled. It is typically called implicitly when using the try-with-resources (*https://oreil.ly/RkRYx*) statement.

The `StructuredTaskScope` is an interface; it cannot be instantiated directly. However, a key feature of this API is the static factory method `open()`. This method has the following signature:

```
static <T> StructuredTaskScope<T,Void> open()
```

This method creates a new `StructuredTaskScope` that can be used to fork subtasks returning results of any type. The scope's `join()` method waits for all subtasks to complete successfully or for any subtask to fail. While `open()` has other overloaded methods, we will discuss those in a subsequent section. Because `StructuredTask Scope` extends `AutoCloseable`, we will use it within a try-with-resources block, ensuring automatic closure. It's important to note that the `close()` method should not be invoked manually in such cases.

StructuredTaskScope is intended to be used in a strictly structured manner. If its `close()` method is invoked before all nested task scopes (if we have them) have been closed, the scope will: 1. Attempt to close the underlying construct of each nested scope (in the reverse order of their creation). 2. Close itself. 3. Throw a `Structure ViolationException` to indicate the improper closure sequence. We should instead rely on the try-with-resource statement.

Now that we have some understanding of structured concurrency and its API, let's implement the fetchProductInfo method using StructuredTaskScope. This method will gather product information concurrently by fetching product details and reviews:

```
public ProductInfo fetchProductInfo(Long productId) {
    log("Fetching product & reviews for id: " + productId);
    try (var scope = StructuredTaskScope.open()) {  ❶
        StructuredTaskScope.Subtask<Product> productTask =
            scope.fork(() -> fetchProduct(productId));  ❷
        StructuredTaskScope.Subtask<List<Review>> reviewsTask =
            scope.fork(() -> fetchReviews(productId));  ❸
        scope.join();  ❹
        return new ProductInfo(productTask.get(), reviewsTask.get());  ❺
    } catch (InterruptedException e) {
        Thread.currentThread().interrupt();
        throw new ProductServiceException(
            "Fetch failed for id: " + productId);  ❻
    }
}
```

Let's trace through what happens when this structured approach executes:

❶ The fetchProductInfo() method initiates a StructuredTaskScope within a try-with-resources block for automatic cleanup.

❷ Creates the first subtask to fetch the Product and starts it running concurrently.

❸ Creates the second subtask to retrieve the List<Review> and starts it running concurrently alongside the product task.

❹ Calls scope.join(), which blocks until both subtasks complete, one fails, or the scope is canceled.

❺ If both subtasks succeed, join() returns normally, and the method constructs a ProductInfo instance using results from productTask.get() and reviewsTask.get().

❻ If either subtask fails, join() interrupts the other running subtask, waits for it to terminate, and throws a StructuredTaskScope.FailedException with the original exception as its cause.

The structured concurrency feature explored in this chapter is currently available as a preview in JDK 25.

We can enable it using the `--enable-preview` flag during compilation and runtime. To compile and run your code, use the following commands:

- *With* javac: `javac --release 25 --enable-preview Main.java`
- *With* java: `java --enable-preview Main`
- *With the source code launcher:* `java --enable-preview Main.java`
- *With JShell:* `jshell --enable-preview`

We anticipate this feature will soon be integrated into future JDK releases without requiring any modifications to the code.

To see how structured concurrency handles failures, let's modify the `fetchProduct()` method to simulate a scenario where the product is not found:

```
private Product fetchProduct(Long productId) {
  log("Fetching product id: " + productId);
  if (productId == 1L) {
    throw new ProductServiceException("Product not found"); ❶
  }
  sleepForAWhile(Duration.ofSeconds(1)); // Simulate network call
  return new Product(productId, "Sample Product",
      "A great product description.");
}
```

❶ Immediately throws an exception for product ID 1 to simulate a "not found" scenario

When we run the program with this modification, the output demonstrates the structured concurrency behavior:

```
04:46:34.321 main : Attempting to fetch product info for ID: 1
04:46:34.321 main : Fetching product & reviews for id: 1
04:46:34.325 VThread[#34]: Fetching product id: 1
04:46:34.325 VThread[#36]: Fetching reviews for id: 1
Exception in thread "main"
    java.util.concurrent.StructuredTaskScope$FailedException:
    ca.bazlur.mcj.chap4.ProductServiceException:
    at java.base/java.util.concurrent.StructuredTaskScopeImpl
      .join(StructuredTaskScopeImpl.java:257)
    at ca.bazlur.mcj.chap4.FailingProductServiceWithStructuredConcurrency
      .fetchProductInfo(FailingProductServiceWithStructuredConcurrency)
    at ca.bazlur.mcj.chap4.FailingProductServiceWithStructuredConcurrency
      .main(FailingProductServiceWithStructuredConcurrency)
```

```
Caused by: ca.bazlur.mcj.chap4.ProductServiceException:
    Product not found
    at ca.bazlur.mcj.chap4.FailingProductServiceWithStructuredConcurrency
        .fetchProduct(FailingProductServiceWithStructuredConcurrency)
    at ca.bazlur.mcj.chap4.FailingProductServiceWithStructuredConcurrency
        .lambda$fetchProductInfo$0(FailingProductServiceWithStructuredConcurrency)
    at java.base/java.util.concurrent.StructuredTaskScopeImpl$SubtaskImpl
        .run(StructuredTaskScopeImpl.java)
    at java.base/java.lang.VirtualThread.run(VirtualThread.java:456)
```

The stack trace reveals exactly what we hoped to see. Because the `fetchProduct()` subtask threw an exception, `StructuredTaskScope` immediately canceled the concurrently running `fetchReviews()` subtask. The `scope.join()` method then threw a `StructuredTaskScope.FailedException`, wrapping the original `ProductService Exception` that occurred in `fetchProduct()` as its cause so that the parent thread can handle the error gracefully (Figure 4-2).

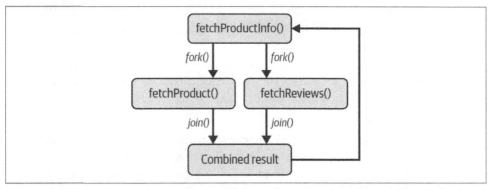

Figure 4-2. A `StructuredTaskScope` workflow where `fetchProductInfo()` forks fetch Product() and `fetchReviews()`, joins their results, and ensures cancellation on failure

This structured version not only addresses the limitations of our previous unstructured approach but also brings significant benefits. If either task fails, the other is canceled automatically, preventing the resource waste we saw earlier. If the parent task is canceled, the scope closes and automatically terminates both subtasks. The `join()` method ensures that both tasks complete before results are retrieved, preventing the incomplete data issues that plagued our original implementation.

Beyond the technical improvements, the structured code is more concise, easier to understand, and less prone to errors. It clearly reflects the intent of the operation: fetching both the product and reviews in parallel, but only proceeding if both succeed. There is no ambiguity about what should happen when things go wrong.

By embracing structured concurrency, we can create concurrent code that is more efficient, reliable, and maintainable. This reliability instills a sense of security, knowing that our code will perform as expected.

Scopes and Subtasks: Relationship and Lifecycle

Now that we understand structured concurrency and its APIs, let's explore the relationship between scopes and their subtasks.

Structured concurrency uses `StructuredTaskScope` as a parent container to manage its child subtasks, handling their lifecycle and execution. Each subtask represents a unit of concurrent work running on virtual threads within the scope. This parent-child relationship ensures a coordinated and predictable execution flow.

The `StructuredTaskScope` defines a bounded context for concurrent operations, managing the entire lifecycle of its subtasks to ensure they execute and terminate in a disciplined manner.

Forking subtasks

To initiate concurrent work, the scope's owner uses the `fork()` method. The API provides two distinct overloads for this purpose:

fork(Callable<? extends U> task)
: This method is used for subtasks that are designed to return a value. It takes a `Callable` and, upon execution in a new virtual thread, its `call()` method will be invoked.

fork(Runnable task)
: This method is used for subtasks that perform an action but do not return a result. It works identically to the `Callable` version, but if the subtask completes successfully, its corresponding `Subtask.get()` method will simply return `null`.

The fork process

Regardless of which `fork()` method is called, the process is the same:

- A `Subtask` object is created to represent the asynchronous task. This `Subtask` acts as a handle.
- An internal `Joiner` policy object is consulted via its `onFork()` method. If the policy determines the subtask should not run (e.g., if the scope is already canceled), `fork()` returns the handle and no new thread is started.
- Otherwise, a new virtual thread is started to execute the task.

The `fork()` method immediately returns the `Subtask` handle. The scope's owner can only use this handle to get the result with `Subtask.get()` or the exception with `Subtask.exception()` after the scope has been joined via the `join()` method.

Subtask completion

When a subtask finishes its work, the thread executing it notifies the joiner by invoking its onComplete() method, passing the Subtask handle, which now contains the final state (e.g., SUCCESS, UNAVAILABLE, or FAILED). We will discuss Joiner in a later section.

The scope owner uses join() to wait for the subtask policy to be satisfied. For the default scope created by StructuredTaskScope.open(), this means waiting until either all subtasks complete successfully or one subtask fails. If a subtask fails, the scope automatically cancels any other running subtasks. The join() method then throws a FailedException that wraps the original exception from the subtask that failed.

Finally, when the scope is closed (either explicitly or via a try-with-resources block), it guarantees a clean shutdown by waiting for all subtask threads to terminate before allowing the parent thread to proceed. This prevents resource leaks and ensures the structured nature of the concurrent operations.

Joining Policies with Joiner

A core feature of StructuredTaskScope is its ability to define flexible joining policies through a Joiner object. A Joiner is a powerful mechanism that manages the lifecycle of subtasks by dictating the conditions under which the join() method completes and what kind of result, or outcome, it produces.

Instead of a few fixed policies, Java provides the Joiner interface. A simplified view of its structure shows both the outcome methods and the lifecycle hooks:

```
public interface Joiner<T, R> {
    R result();  ❶
    Throwable exception();  ❷
    default boolean onFork(Subtask<? extends T> subtask) { ... }  ❸
    default boolean onComplete(Subtask<? extends T> subtask) { ... }  ❹
}
```

Let's look at what this method entails:

❶   Outcome method that defines the successful result to return from scope.join()

❷   Outcome method that defines the exception to throw from scope.join()

❸   Lifecycle hook called every time fork() is invoked to track new subtasks

❹   Lifecycle hook called when any subtask finishes, containing the core policy logic

The first two methods, `result()` and `exception()`, are outcome methods that define the contract for the final outcome of `scope.join()`. An implementation must provide logic for one of these to return either a successful value or an exception to be thrown.

The `onFork()` method is a lifecycle hook that allows the `Joiner` to be aware of and track new subtasks as they are created. The `onComplete()` method is where the core policy logic typically resides, checking if the completion of a specific subtask satisfies the overall joining condition (such as "is this the first success?" or "have all tasks now failed?").

Common Joining Policies

The `Joiner` provides several static factory methods for creating common policies:

`Joiner.awaitAllSuccessfulOrThrow()`
    This is the default policy. It is used when we call `StructuredTaskScope.open()`. Its internal `onComplete()` logic tracks the completion count. If a subtask fails, it cancels the scope. It only allows `join()` to complete successfully when all forked subtasks have succeeded.

`Joiner.anySuccessfulResultOrThrow()`
    This implements a "race to win" policy. Its `onComplete()` logic checks if the completing subtask was successful. If so, it immediately cancels the scope, and its `result()` method returns the successful result.

`Joiner.allSuccessfulOrThrow()`
    This policy's `onComplete()` hook collects the result of every subtask that completes successfully. It waits for all subtasks to finish and then makes the collected results available in a `Stream`.

`Joiner.awaitAll()`
    This policy waits for all subtasks to complete, whether they succeed or fail. It is useful when you need to know the outcome of every task and handle each one individually. The `scope.join()` method returns a `Stream<Subtask>` that you can process to inspect the state, result, or exception of each subtask.

`Joiner.allUntil(Predicate<Subtask> isDone)`
    This is the most flexible factory method, allowing for custom cancellation logic. It takes a `Predicate` that is tested against every subtask upon its completion. If the predicate returns true, the scope is canceled. This allows for complex policies, such as "cancel after two subtasks fail." If the predicate never returns true, it behaves like `awaitAll()`, waiting for all subtasks to finish. In either case, `scope.join()` returns a `Stream<Subtask>` of all subtasks that were forked.

This `Joiner`-based approach allows for fine-grained control over the scope's completion criteria and its return value, from waiting for all subtasks to succeed, to racing them to find the first available result, to collecting multiple results in a stream.

Let's explore each of these policies with practical examples.

Wait for all to succeed or first to fail

When you create a `StructuredTaskScope` using the `open()` method, it defaults to a policy where all subtasks must succeed. This "all-or-nothing" approach is internally managed by `Joiner.awaitAllSuccessfulOrThrow()`. This means that if even one subtask fails, the entire scope is shut down. Any remaining, in-progress subtasks are immediately canceled, and the error from the failing subtask is propagated back to the parent task. This design ensures that you only get a result if every part of your operation completes successfully, preventing the use of incomplete or partial results.

Let's illustrate this with a practical example. We will first create data records similar to those we made earlier in the chapter:

```
record Product(long productId, String name) {}
record Review(String user, int rating) {}
record ProductInfo(Product product, List<Review> reviews) {}
```

Next, we need the methods that will run as our concurrent subtasks. To make the concurrency visible, we'll add `log()` statements and use `Thread.sleep()` to simulate network latency. We will also create a specific method, `fetchProductThatFails()`, to demonstrate the error-handling path:

```
// A subtask that succeeds after a 1-second delay
private Product fetchProduct(long productId)
    throws InterruptedException {
  log(" -> Fetching product details... (will take 1s)");
  Thread.sleep(Duration.ofSeconds(1));  ❶
  log(" <- Product details fetched.");
  return new Product(productId, "Sample Product");
}
// A subtask that will always fail
private Product fetchProductThatFails(long productId) {
  log(" -> Fetching product details... (will fail)");
  throw new ProductServiceException("Product ID " + productId + " not found");  ❷
}
// A subtask that succeeds after a 2-second delay
private List<Review> fetchReviews(long productId)
    throws InterruptedException {
  log(" -> Fetching product reviews... (will take 2s)");
  Thread.sleep(Duration.ofSeconds(2));  ❸
  log(" <- Product reviews fetched.");
  return List.of(new Review("Inaya", 5), new Review("Rushda", 4));
}
```

Each method serves a specific purpose in our demonstration:

❶ Simulates a one-second network call for product data

❷ Immediately throws an exception to simulate a "product not found" scenario

❸ Simulates a two-second network call for review data.

We defined the log() method in the previous section. Let's convert it into a utility method so that we can reuse it in other contexts:

```java
import java.time.LocalTime;
import java.time.format.DateTimeFormatter;
public class Utils {
  public static void log(String message) {
    Thread currentThread = Thread.currentThread();
    String threadName = currentThread.isVirtual()
        ? "VThread[#" + currentThread.threadId() + "]"
        : currentThread.getName();
    String currentTime = LocalTime.now()
        .format(DateTimeFormatter.ofPattern("HH:mm:ss.SSS"));
    System.out.printf("%s %-12s: %s%n", currentTime, threadName, message);
  }
}
```

Now let's define our main logic using the default policy:

```java
public ProductInfo fetchProductInfo(long productId, boolean shouldFail)
    throws InterruptedException {
  Instant start = Instant.now();
  // Using open() provides the default "fail-fast" policy
  try (var scope = StructuredTaskScope.open()) { ❶
    StructuredTaskScope.Subtask<Product> productTask = shouldFail
        ? scope.fork(() -> fetchProductThatFails(productId)) ❷
        : scope.fork(() -> fetchProduct(productId)); ❸
    StructuredTaskScope.Subtask<List<Review>> reviewsTask
        = scope.fork(() -> fetchReviews(productId)); ❹
    // Waits for both to succeed, or throws FailedException on first failure
    log("... Scope joining. Waiting for subtasks...");
    scope.join(); ❺
    log("... Scope joined successfully.");
    // Only reachable if join() succeeds
    return new ProductInfo(productTask.get(), reviewsTask.get()); ❻
  } catch (StructuredTaskScope.FailedException ex) {
    // This block executes only in the failure scenario
    log("... Scope join failed. A subtask threw an exception.");
    throw new RuntimeException("Failed to fetch product info", ex.getCause()); ❼
  } finally {
    Instant end = Instant.now();
    log("Total time taken: " + Duration.between(start, end).toMillis() + "ms");
  }
}
```

Let's trace through the execution flow:

❶ Creates a scope with the default `awaitAllSuccessfulOrThrow()` policy

❷ Conditionally forks a task that will fail (for demonstration)

❸ Forks a task that will succeed after one second

❹ Forks a task that will succeed after two seconds

❺ Waits for all subtasks to complete successfully or fails fast on first error

❻ Retrieves results only if all subtasks succeeded

❼ Handles the failure case by wrapping the original exception

This is the core of our example. The `fetchProductInfo()` method uses `Structured TaskScope` to orchestrate the subtasks. A boolean flag, `shouldFail`, will allow us to easily switch between the success and failure paths.

Here's our complete demonstration class:

```
public class DefaultPolicyDemo {
  // ... (method implementations from above)
  void main() {
    var demo = new DefaultPolicyDemo();
    log("--- Running Success Scenario ---");
    log("... Expecting to take ~2 seconds (the time of the slowest task)...\n");
    try {
      ProductInfo result = demo.fetchProductInfo(123L, false); ❶
      log("\nSuccess! Result: " + result);
    } catch (Exception e) {
      log("\nCaught unexpected exception in success scenario: " +
        "" + e.getMessage());
    }
  }
}
```

The main method demonstrates the success path:

❶ Runs the success scenario by passing `false` for the `shouldFail` parameter

Let's run the code:

```
java --enable-preview DefaultPolicyDemo.java
```

Understanding the API | 143

Please note that we are using JDK 25, and structured concurrency is a preview feature.

The output would be as follows:

```
20:35:18.357 main         : --- Running Success Scenario ---
20:35:18.358 main         : ... Expecting to take ~2 seconds (the time of the slowest task)...
20:35:18.362 main         : ... Scope joining. Waiting for subtasks...
20:35:18.363 VThread[#36] : -> Fetching product reviews... (will take 2s)
20:35:18.363 VThread[#34] : -> Fetching product details... (will take 1s)
20:35:19.367 VThread[#34] : <- Product details fetched.
20:35:20.369 VThread[#36] : <- Product reviews fetched.
20:35:20.370 main         : ... Scope joined successfully.
20:35:20.371 main         : Total time taken: 2012ms
20:35:20.378 main         :
Success! Result: ProductInfo[product=Product[productId=123, name=Sample Product], reviews=[Review[user=Inaya, rating=5], Review[user=Rushda, rating=4]]]
```

The main thread creates the scope and immediately forks two subtasks, `fetchProduct()` and `fetchReviews()`, which are picked up by virtual threads (`VThread[#34]` and `VThread[#36]`) and start executing at nearly the same instant. While they run in parallel, the main thread blocks at the `scope.join()`, waiting for the outcome. After one second, the `fetchProduct()` task completes, but the main thread continues to wait as the slower `fetchReviews()` task is still running. Once `fetchReviews()` completes after two seconds, and now that all subtasks have succeeded, the `join()` method finally returns. The total time taken is ~2,000ms, indicating that the tasks ran in parallel, as the operation's duration is bounded by its longest-running subtask.

Now, let's turn our attention to the failure scenario. To do this, we'll modify the main method to call `fetchProductInfo()` with the `shouldFail` flag set to `true`. This will cause it to use the `fetchProductThatFails()` method, which we've designed to immediately throw an exception.

Next, we'll modify our main method to execute this path:

```
void main() {
  var demo = new DefaultPolicyDemo();
  log("--- Running Failure Scenario ---");
  log("... Expecting to fail almost instantly...\n");
  try {
    demo.fetchProductInfo(456L, true); ❶
  } catch (Exception e) {
    // We expect the RuntimeException thrown from our catch block
    log("\nCaught expected exception in failure scenario: " + e.getMessage());
    log("Cause: " + e.getCause()); ❷
```

```
    }
}
```

The failure scenario demonstrates immediate error handling:

❶ Runs the failure scenario by passing `true` for the `shouldFail` parameter

❷ Shows the original cause of the failure wrapped in our `RuntimeException`

The output would be as follows:

```
22:20:11.405 main            : --- Running Failure Scenario ---
22:20:11.406 main            : ... Expecting to fail almost instantly...
22:20:11.411 main            : ... Scope joining. Waiting for subtasks...
22:20:11.412 VThread[#34]    : -> Fetching product details... (will fail)
22:20:11.412 VThread[#36]    : -> Fetching product reviews... (will take 2s)
22:20:11.413 main            : ... Scope join failed. A subtask threw an exception.
22:20:11.414 main            : Total time taken: 7ms
22:20:11.414 main            :
Caught expected exception in failure scenario: Failed to fetch product info
22:20:11.414 main            : Cause: ca.bazlur.mcj.chap4.
ProductServiceException: Product ID 456 not found
```

This output clearly demonstrates the power of the fail-fast policy. Although both the failing `fetchProductThatFails()` task and the two-second `fetchReviews()` task are forked onto virtual threads, the entire operation is over in just seven milliseconds. The moment the first subtask fails, the `Joiner` policy cancels the other running subtask and causes `scope.join()` to immediately throw a `FailedException`. The system does not waste time waiting for the `fetchReviews()` task to complete, as its result would be irrelevant. This rapid error propagation and prevention of wasted work is a core advantage of using structured concurrency for "all-or-nothing" operations.

To fully appreciate the benefits of the default fail-fast policy, let's compare it with a traditional `ExecutorService` approach for the same task:

```
ProductInfo fetchProductInfoWithExecutor(Long productId)
    throws ExecutionException, InterruptedException {
  Instant start = Instant.now();
  try (ExecutorService service
                        = Executors.newVirtualThreadPerTaskExecutor()) { ❶
    Future<Product> productFuture
        = service.submit(() -> fetchProductThatFails(productId)); ❷
    Future<List<Review>> reviewFuture
        = service.submit(() -> fetchReviews(productId)); ❸
    Product product = productFuture.get(); ❹
    List<Review> reviews = reviewFuture.get(); ❺
    return new ProductInfo(product, reviews);
  } finally {
    Instant end = Instant.now();
    System.out.printf("Time taken: %dms%n",
        end.toEpochMilli() - start.toEpochMilli());
```

```
            }
    }
```

The traditional approach shows its limitations:

① Creates an `ExecutorService` with virtual threads

② Submits the failing product task and gets a `Future`

③ Submits the reviews task and gets another task

④ Blocking `get` method invocation waiting for the product result (which will fail)

⑤ Would block waiting for the review results, but is never reached due to an exception

If we call this method from the main method, the output reveals the inefficiency:

```
22:46:10.211 main             : --- Running Failure Scenario with Executor ---
22:46:10.212 main             : ... Expecting to fail almost instantly...
22:46:10.215 VThread[#36]     : -> Fetching product reviews... (will take 2s)
22:46:10.215 VThread[#34]     : -> Fetching product details... (will fail)
22:46:12.221 VThread[#36]     : <- Product reviews fetched.
Time taken: 2010ms
22:46:12.227 main             :
Caught expected exception in failure scenario: ca.bazlur.mcj.chap4.ProductService
Exception: Product ID 456 not found
22:46:12.227 main             : Cause: ca.bazlur.mcj.chap4.ProductServiceException:
Product ID 456 not found
```

When we dissect the console log, the critical inefficiency of this unstructured approach becomes clear. We see that even though our `fetchProductThatFails()` task on `VThread[#34]` fails almost instantly, the `fetchReviews()` task on `VThread[#36]` continues running, completely unaware. The log confirms this by printing the `Product reviews fetched` message after the full two-second delay. This happens because the `ExecutorService` provides no concept of a shared scope; from its perspective, the two `Futures` are independent, and a failure in one has no bearing on the other. As a result, our program is blocked while the reviews task runs to completion, wasting system resources on a result we will ultimately discard.

Race for the first successful result

With the `Joiner.anySuccessfulResultOrThrow()` policy, we can orchestrate a race among our concurrent subtasks, declaring a winner as soon as one completes successfully. We can think of this as a "first-past-the-post" approach. The moment we have a winner, the `Joiner` cancels all other running subtasks.

To illustrate this policy, we'll set up a scenario where we fetch product details from three different sources, each with a different response time. We want to proceed with whichever result we get first.

First, we need to define our three `fetch` methods. We'll give each a different `Thread.sleep()` duration and add `log()` statements. This will allow us to observe the race and the ensuing cancellation in action when we run the code:

```java
private Product fetchProductFromCache(long productId) throws
    InterruptedException {
  log(" -> Checking cache... (will take 500ms)");
  Thread.sleep(Duration.ofMillis(500)); ❶
  log(" <- Cache has the result!");
  return new Product(productId, "Product from Cache");
}
// A slower source (2000ms)
private Product fetchProductFromDatabase(long productId)
    throws InterruptedException {
  try {
    log(" -> Querying database... (will take 2s)");
    Thread.sleep(Duration.ofSeconds(2)); ❷
    log(" <- Database has the result!");
    return new Product(productId, "Product from DB");
  } catch (InterruptedException e) {
    // This block will execute when the scope cancels this task
    log(" <- Database query was canceled."); ❸
    Thread.currentThread().interrupt();
    throw e;
  }
}
// The slowest source (3000ms)
private Product fetchProductFromAPI(long productId)
    throws InterruptedException {
  try {
    log(" -> Calling external API... (will take 3s)");
    Thread.sleep(Duration.ofSeconds(3)); ❹
    log(" <- API has the result!");
    return new Product(productId, "Product from API");
  } catch (InterruptedException e) {
    // This block will also execute upon cancellation
    log(" <- API call was canceled."); ❺
    Thread.currentThread().interrupt();
    throw e;
  }
}
```

Each method simulates a different data source with varying response times:

❶ The cache responds fastest at 500ms, making it the likely winner.

❷ The database takes two seconds and includes cancellation handling.

❸ Logs when the database query gets interrupted due to scope cancellation.

❹ The API is slowest at three seconds and also handles cancellation.

❺ Logs when the API call gets interrupted due to scope cancellation.

Now, we'll write our orchestrator method. This time, when we open the scope, we'll pass in the `Joiner.anySuccessfulResultOrThrow()` joiner to set up the race:

```
public Product fetchProduct(long productId) {
  Instant start = Instant.now();
  // The Joiner specifies the "race-to-win" policy
  try (var scope
          = StructuredTaskScope.open(
              StructuredTaskScope
                .Joiner.<Product>anySuccessfulResultOrThrow())) { ❶
    scope.fork(() -> fetchProductFromDatabase(productId)); ❷
    scope.fork(() -> fetchProductFromCache(productId)); ❸
    scope.fork(() -> fetchProductFromAPI(productId)); ❹
    // join() now returns the result of the first successful subtask
    return scope.join(); ❺
  } catch (InterruptedException | StructuredTaskScope.FailedException e) {
    // FailedException is thrown if ALL subtasks fail
    throw new RuntimeException(e); ❻
  } finally {
    Instant end = Instant.now();
    log("Total time taken: %dms%n"
        .formatted(Duration.between(start, end).toMillis()));
  }
}
```

The orchestrator method sets up the race conditions:

❶ Creates a scope with the race-to-win policy that returns the first successful result

❷ Forks the database task (two-second delay)

❸ Forks the cache task (500ms delay)—likely winner

❹ Forks the API task (three-second delay)

❺ Waits for the first successful completion and returns that result

❻ Handles the case where all subtasks fail (throws `FailedException`)

When we execute this code, we expect to see the cancellation happen live. Let's call this method from the main method:

```
public class RacePolicyDemo {
  // ... (method implementations from above)
  void main() {
    var demo = new RacePolicyDemo();
    log("--- Running Race Scenario ---");
    log("... Three tasks will race. " +
        "Expecting to finish in ~500ms (the fastest task)...\n");
    try {
      Product winningProduct = demo.fetchProduct(123L);  ❶
      log("Race finished! Winning result: " + winningProduct);
    } catch (Exception e) {
      log("Caught unexpected exception: " + e.getMessage());
      e.printStackTrace();
    }
  }
}
```

The main method demonstrates the race scenario:

❶ Starts the race between three different data sources and expects the fastest to win

For this code to work we need the following record as well:

```
public record Product(long productId, String source) {
}
```

Let's execute the code:

```
java --enable-preview RacePolicyDemo.java
```

The output will be as follows:

```
23:03:23.917 main         : --- Running Race Scenario ---
23:03:23.917 main         : ... Three tasks will race. Expecting to finish in
~500ms (the fastest task)...
23:03:23.923 VThread[#36]: -> Checking cache... (will take 500ms)
23:03:23.923 VThread[#38]: -> Calling external API... (will take 3s)
23:03:23.923 VThread[#34]: -> Querying database... (will take 2s)
23:03:24.429 VThread[#36]: <- Cache has the result!
23:03:24.431 VThread[#34]: <- Database query was canceled.
23:03:24.431 VThread[#38]: <- API call was canceled.
23:03:24.439 main         : Total time taken: 513ms
23:03:24.442 main         : Race finished! Winning result: Product[productId=123,
source=Product from Cache]
```

When we look at our console output, we can see a perfect demonstration of the race-to-win policy. We see that all three of our fetch methods are forked and start running in parallel. However, after about 500ms, our fastest task, fetchProductFromCache(), succeeds. At that exact moment, our Joiner policy considers its condition met, and we see it immediately cancel the other two running subtasks; we have proof of this in the was canceled messages that get printed to the error stream. Our join method then returns the winning result from the cache, and our entire operation concludes in just over 500ms, without us having to waste time waiting for the slower tasks.

Gather all results or fail fast

We've seen the default policy, which fails if any subtask fails. This next policy, `allSuccessfulOrThrow`, behaves identically in the case of a failure, but offers a more convenient way to handle results upon success.

Like the default policy, `allSuccessfulOrThrow()` maintains a strict "all-or-nothing" strategy. If any subtask fails, it promptly cancels all other running subtasks, and the `scope.join()` method throws a `FailedException`.

The key difference is what happens on success. Instead of `join()` returning void, it returns a `java.util.Stream<Subtask<T>>`. This stream contains the handles to all the successfully completed subtasks, in the order they were forked, making it easy to process all the results at once. We should use this `Joiner` when all of our subtasks return the same result type (e.g., `String`, `Product`, etc.) and we need all of them to succeed.

The default `awaitAllSuccessfulOrThrow()` policy is better suited for when our subtasks return results of different types, since we would handle each subtask's result individually anyway.

Let's imagine we need to validate a list of user IDs by checking them against an external service. We want to do this concurrently, but the entire batch is only valid if every user ID is successfully validated.

First, we'll define a simple method that simulates validating a user. We'll also create a version that fails for a specific ID:

```
public record ValidatedUser(long userId, String status) {
}

private ValidatedUser validateUser(long userId)
    throws InterruptedException {
  log(" -> Validating user %d...".formatted(userId));
  Thread.sleep(Duration.ofMillis(100 + new Random().nextInt(500))); ❶
  log(" <- User %d is valid.".formatted(userId));
  return new ValidatedUser(userId, "VALID");
}

private ValidatedUser validateUserWithFailure(long userId)
    throws InterruptedException {
  if (userId == 3L) {
    log(" -> Validating user %d... (will fail)".formatted(userId));
    throw new IllegalArgumentException("Invalid user ID: " + userId); ❷
  }
```

```
    return validateUser(userId);
}
```

The validation methods simulate real-world behavior:

❶ Adds random delay between 100–600ms to simulate network variability

❷ Specifically fails for user ID 3 to demonstrate error handling

Now, we'll write a method that takes a list of user IDs, forks a validation task for each, and uses `allSuccessfulOrThrow()` to collect the results:

```
public List<ValidatedUser> validateAllUsers(List<Long> userIds)
    throws InterruptedException {
  log("Validating a batch of " + userIds.size() + " users...");
  try (var scope
          = open(Joiner.<ValidatedUser>allSuccessfulOrThrow())) {  ❶
    var subtasks = userIds.stream()
        .map(id -> scope.fork(() -> validateUserWithFailure(id)))  ❷
        .toList();
    // join() returns a Stream<Subtask<ValidatedUser>> on success
    // or throws FailedException on the first failure
    var resultStream = scope.join();  ❸
    log("...All users validated successfully. Processing stream...");
    return resultStream
        .map(Subtask::get)  ❹
        .toList();
  } catch (FailedException ex) {
    log("All users validated successfully. Processing stream");
    throw new RuntimeException("Batch validation failed",
        ex.getCause());  ❺
  }
}
```

The batch validation method demonstrates collecting multiple results:

❶ Creates a scope with the `allSuccessfulOrThrow()` policy for collecting all results

❷ Forks a validation subtask for each user ID and collects the subtask handles

❸ Waits for all validations to complete and returns a `Stream` of successful subtasks

❹ Extracts the actual `ValidatedUser` results from each subtask

❺ Handles batch failure by wrapping the original validation exception

A Note on var and Type Inference

To keep our code concise, we've used the `var` keyword. While this improves readability by reducing boilerplate, it's helpful for us to know the explicit types being used.

In the `validateAllUsers` method:

- `var scope` is inferred as `StructuredTaskScope<Validated User>`
- `var subtasks` is inferred as `List<Subtask<ValidatedUser>>`
- `var resultStream` is inferred as `Stream<Subtask<Validated User>>`

Now, let's put everything together into our complete `BatchValidationDemo.java` class. To maintain the conciseness of the code we present, we will use static imports for the nested classes of `StructuredTaskScope`, such as `Joiner` and `Subtask`, as well as for the `open()` method itself:

```
import static java.util.concurrent.StructuredTaskScope.*;
public class BatchValidationDemo {
  // ... (method implementations from above)
  void main() {
    var demo = new BatchValidationDemo();
    List<Long> successfulBatch = List.of(1L, 2L, 4L, 5L);
    // Contains the failing ID '3'
    List<Long> failingBatch = List.of(1L, 2L, 3L, 4L, 5L); ❶
    log("--- Running Success Scenario ---");
    try {
      List<ValidatedUser> results = demo.validateAllUsers(successfulBatch); ❷
      log("\nBatch validation complete. Results:");
      results.forEach(validatedUser -> log(validatedUser.toString()));
    } catch (Exception e) {
      log("Caught unexpected exception: " + e.getMessage());
    }
    log("\n==============================================\n");
    log("--- Running Failure Scenario ---");
    try {
      demo.validateAllUsers(failingBatch); ❸
    } catch (Exception e) {
      log("Caught expected exception: " + e.getMessage());
    }
  }
}
```

The `main` method tests both scenarios:

❶ Creates a batch containing user ID 3, which will trigger our failure condition

❷ Tests the success scenario with user IDs that will all validate successfully

❸ Tests the failure scenario where one validation fails and cancels the others

Now, let's run the code:

```
java --enable-preview BatchValidationDemo.java
```

The output would be as follows:

```
00:29:49.275 main          : --- Running Success Scenario ---
00:29:49.276 main          : Validating a batch of 4 users...
00:29:49.286 VThread[#39]:   -> Validating user 4...
00:29:49.286 VThread[#36]:   -> Validating user 2...
00:29:49.286 VThread[#34]:   -> Validating user 1...
00:29:49.286 VThread[#42]:   -> Validating user 5...
00:29:49.452 VThread[#39]:   <- User 4 is valid.
00:29:49.480 VThread[#42]:   <- User 5 is valid.
00:29:49.614 VThread[#34]:   <- User 1 is valid.
00:29:49.696 VThread[#36]:   <- User 2 is valid.
00:29:49.697 main          : All users validated successfully. Processing stream
00:29:49.698 main          :
Batch validation complete. Results:
00:29:49.701 main          : ValidatedUser[userId=1, status=VALID]
00:29:49.702 main          : ValidatedUser[userId=2, status=VALID]
00:29:49.702 main          : ValidatedUser[userId=4, status=VALID]
00:29:49.702 main          : ValidatedUser[userId=5, status=VALID]
00:29:49.702 main          :
===============================================
00:29:49.702 main          : --- Running Failure Scenario ---
00:29:49.702 main          : Validating a batch of 5 users...
00:29:49.703 VThread[#48]:   -> Validating user 4...
00:29:49.703 VThread[#47]:   -> Validating user 3... (will fail)
00:29:49.703 VThread[#45]:   -> Validating user 1...
00:29:49.703 VThread[#46]:   -> Validating user 2...
00:29:49.703 VThread[#49]:   -> Validating user 5...
00:29:49.704 main          : ...Validation failed for one of the users.
00:29:49.704 main          : Caught expected exception: Batch validation failed
```

When we assess the output, we can clearly observe the two distinct outcomes of our "all-or-nothing" policy.

In the success scenario, all four validation tasks are forked onto virtual threads and run concurrently. The `main` thread waits at `join()` until the last task completes, after which `join()` returns the `Stream` of results, which we then print.

In the failure scenario, all five tasks are forked, but the task for `userId=3` immediately fails. The `Joiner` detects this failure and cancels the entire scope. The `join()` call never returns a `Stream`; instead, it immediately throws a `FailedException`. Our `catch` block catches this exception and prints the final error message. The key observation is that none of the other tasks print a `<- User X is valid` message, because they were all canceled before they could complete. This confirms the fail-fast behavior and demonstrates how the policy protects the integrity of our batch operation.

Wait for all

We've seen policies that either fail fast or require all tasks to succeed. The `awaitAll()` policy takes a different approach: it waits for all subtasks to complete, regardless of whether they succeed or fail. This makes it ideal for scenarios where we care about side effects or need to process all results, even partial ones.

Unlike `allSuccessfulOrThrow()`, the `awaitAll()` policy never cancels running subtasks when one fails. All forked tasks are allowed to run to completion. The `scope.join()` method always returns `null`, since this joiner focuses on task completion rather than result collection.

The key advantage is resilience. When some operations can fail but we still want the benefit of processing successful ones, `awaitAll()` ensures no work is wasted. We should use this joiner when our subtasks perform side effects (like logging, metrics collection, or file processing) or when we need to gather as much data as possible, even if some sources are unavailable.

The `awaitAll()` policy is particularly useful for monitoring systems, batch processing jobs, and fan-in server architectures where partial success is acceptable and valuable.

Let's imagine we need to send notifications about a critical system event to multiple channels (email, SMS, push notifications). We want maximum reach, so even if one channel fails, the others should still deliver the notification.

First, we'll define a simple record to track notification results, along with methods that simulate sending notifications with varying reliability:

```
public record NotificationResult(String channel, boolean success,
                                String message) {
    public static NotificationResult success(String channel, String message) {
        return new NotificationResult(channel, true, message);
    }

    public static NotificationResult failure(String channel, String error) {
        return new NotificationResult(channel, false, error);
    }
}
// Shared state to collect results (side effects)
private final List<NotificationResult> notificationResults =
    new CopyOnWriteArrayList<>();  ❶
private final AtomicInteger successCount = new AtomicInteger(0);  ❷
private final AtomicInteger failureCount = new AtomicInteger(0);  ❸
```

The shared state tracks notification outcomes:

① Thread-safe list to collect results from concurrent notification attempts

② Atomic counter for successful deliveries across all channels

③ Atomic counter for failed deliveries to track overall reliability

Now let's implement the notification methods with varying reliability:

```
    private void sendEmailNotification(String message)
        throws InterruptedException {
      log(" -> Sending email notification...");
      Thread.sleep(Duration.ofMillis(200 + new Random().nextInt(300)));
      // Email is generally reliable (90% success rate)
      if (new Random().nextDouble() < 0.9) { ①
        log(" <- Email sent successfully");
        notificationResults.add(
            NotificationResult.success("EMAIL", "Delivered to inbox"));
        successCount.incrementAndGet();
      } else {
        log(" <- Email failed: SMTP server unavailable");
        notificationResults.add(
            NotificationResult.failure("EMAIL", "SMTP server unavailable"));
        failureCount.incrementAndGet();
        throw new RuntimeException("Email delivery failed"); ②
      }
    }

    private void sendSmsNotification(String message)
        throws InterruptedException {
      log(" -> Sending SMS notification...");
      Thread.sleep(Duration.ofMillis(150 + new Random().nextInt(400)));
      // SMS is less reliable (70% success rate)
      if (new Random().nextDouble() < 0.7) { ③
        log(" <- SMS sent successfully");
        notificationResults.add(
            NotificationResult.success("SMS", "Delivered to mobile"));
        successCount.incrementAndGet();
      } else {
        log(" <- SMS failed: Carrier gateway timeout");
        notificationResults.add(
            NotificationResult.failure("SMS", "Carrier gateway timeout"));
        failureCount.incrementAndGet();
        throw new RuntimeException("SMS delivery failed");
      }
    }

    private void sendPushNotification(String message)
        throws InterruptedException {
      log(" -> Sending push notification...");
      Thread.sleep(Duration.ofMillis(100 + new Random().nextInt(200)));
      // Push notifications are most reliable (95% success rate)
```

```
    if (new Random().nextDouble() < 0.95) { ❹
      log(" <- Push notification sent successfully");
      notificationResults.add(
          NotificationResult.success("PUSH", "Delivered to device"));
      successCount.incrementAndGet();
    } else {
      log(" <- Push notification failed: Device token expired");
      notificationResults.add(
          NotificationResult.failure("PUSH", "Device token expired"));
      failureCount.incrementAndGet();
      throw new RuntimeException("Push notification delivery failed");
    }
  }
```

Each notification method simulates real-world reliability patterns:

❶ Email has a 90% success rate, simulating typical SMTP reliability.

❷ Even on failure, we record the result before throwing an exception.

❸ SMS has a 70% success rate, reflecting carrier gateway challenges.

❹ Push notifications have a 95% success rate and are the most reliable channel.

Now, we'll write a method that sends notifications to all channels concurrently using `awaitAll()` to ensure all channels are attempted, regardless of individual failures:

```
public void sendCriticalAlert(String alertMessage) throws InterruptedException {
  log("Sending critical alert: " + alertMessage);

  try (var scope = open(Joiner.<Void>awaitAll())) { ❶
    // Fork notification tasks - each performs side effects
    scope.fork(() -> {
      sendEmailNotification(alertMessage);
      return null; // awaitAll() ignores return values ❷
    });
    scope.fork(() -> {
      sendSmsNotification(alertMessage);
      return null;
    });
    scope.fork(() -> {
      sendPushNotification(alertMessage);
      return null;
    });
    log("Waiting for all notification attempts to complete");
    // join() always returns null for awaitAll()
    // All tasks complete regardless of individual failures
    Void result = scope.join(); ❸
    log("...All notification attempts completed.");
    // Process the side effects (collected results)
    logNotificationSummary(); ❹
```

```
    } catch (InterruptedException e) {
      log("...Notification sending was interrupted");
      Thread.currentThread().interrupt();
      throw e;
    }
  }
```

The alert method demonstrates the awaitAll() pattern:

❶ Creates a scope with an awaitAll() policy that waits for all tasks regardless of failures.

❷ Returns null since awaitAll() focuses on completion, not result collection.

❸ join() always returns null but ensures all tasks have completed.

❹ Processes the side effects collected during task execution.

Let's add the summary method that processes our collected results:

```
private void logNotificationSummary() {
  log("\n--- Notification Summary ---");
  log("Total channels attempted: " + (successCount.get() + failureCount.get()));
  log("Successful deliveries: " + successCount.get());
  log("Failed deliveries: " + failureCount.get());
  log("\nDetailed results:");
  notificationResults.forEach(result -> {
    String status = result.success() ? "✓" : "✗";
    log(status + " " + result.channel() + ": " + result.message());
  });
  if (successCount.get() > 0) {
    log("\n◉ Alert successfully delivered through " +
        successCount.get() + " channel(s)");
  } else {
    log("\n⚠ Alert failed to deliver through any channel!");
  }
}
```

A Note on var and Type Inference, Part 2

In the sendCriticalAlert method:

- var scope is inferred as StructuredTaskScope<Void>

- open() is statically imported: import static java.util.con current.StructuredTaskScope.open;

Now, let's put everything together into our complete `AwaitedAllDemo.java` class. To keep the code we present concise, we will use static imports for `StructuredTask Scope`'s nested classes, like `Joiner`, and the `open()` method itself:

```
import module java.base;
import static ca.bazlur.mcj.chap4.Utils.log;
import static java.util.concurrent.StructuredTaskScope.*;
import static java.util.concurrent.StructuredTaskScope.open;

public class AwaitAllDemo {
    public record NotificationResult(String channel,
                                     boolean success,
                                     String message) {
        // factory methods and implementation shown above
    }

    private final List<NotificationResult> notificationResults =
        new CopyOnWriteArrayList<>();
    private final AtomicInteger successCount = new AtomicInteger(0);
    private final AtomicInteger failureCount = new AtomicInteger(0);

    // ... (all method implementations from above)
    void main() {
        String criticalAlert =
            "URGENT: Database connection pool exhausted - " +
            "immediate attention required";
        log("Running Notification Scenario (awaitAll Policy)");
        log("This demonstrates how awaitAll() processes " +
            "ALL tasks regardless of failures\n");

        try {
            sendCriticalAlert(criticalAlert);  ❶
        } catch (Exception e) {
            log("Caught exception: " + e.getMessage());
        }

        log("\n=================================\n");
        log("--- Running Second Notification Batch ---");

        try {
            sendCriticalAlert(
                "RESOLVED: Database issue fixed - " +
                "all systems operational");  ❷
        } catch (Exception e) {
            log("Caught exception: " + e.getMessage());
        }
    }
}
```

The `main` method demonstrates the resilience of `awaitAll()`:

❶ Sends the first critical alert, allowing us to see how different channels perform

❷ Sends a follow-up alert, demonstrating that the pattern works consistently across multiple batches

> ## Module Import Declaration (JDK 25+)
>
> The `import module java.base;` statement is a module import declaration introduced in JDK 25. It imports, on demand, all public top-level classes and interfaces from:
>
> - The packages exported by the specified module to the current module
> - The packages exported by modules that are transitively read due to reading the specified module
>
> For `import module java.base`, this has the same effect as 54 on-demand package imports (one for each package exported by `java.base`), equivalent to writing `import java.io.*`, `import java.util.*`, `import java.time.*`, `import java.util.concurrent.*`, and so on. This feature eliminates the need for multiple individual package imports when working with fundamental Java APIs, making our code significantly more concise.

Now, let's run the code:

```
java --enable-preview AwaitedAllDemo.java
```

The output would be as follows:

```
04:59:39.852 main         : Running Notification Scenario (awaitAll Policy)
04:59:39.852 main         : This demonstrates how awaitAll() processes ALL tasks regardless of failures

04:59:39.852 main         : Sending critical alert to all notification channels...
04:59:39.853 main         : Alert message: URGENT: Database connection pool exhausted - immediate attention required
04:59:39.857 main         : Waiting for all notification attempts to complete
04:59:39.857 VThread[#38]:   -> Sending push notification...
04:59:39.857 VThread[#36]:   -> Sending SMS notification...
04:59:39.857 VThread[#34]:   -> Sending email notification...
04:59:39.970 VThread[#38]:   <- Push notification sent successfully
04:59:40.088 VThread[#36]:   <- SMS failed: Carrier gateway timeout
04:59:40.234 VThread[#34]:   <- Email sent successfully
04:59:40.235 main         : ...All notification attempts completed.
04:59:40.236 main         :
--- Notification Summary ---
04:59:40.237 main         : Total channels attempted: 3
04:59:40.238 main         : Successful deliveries: 2
04:59:40.239 main         : Failed deliveries: 1
04:59:40.239 main         :
Detailed results:
04:59:40.243 main         : ✓ PUSH: Delivered to device
04:59:40.244 main         : ✗ SMS: Carrier gateway timeout
04:59:40.244 main         : ✓ EMAIL: Delivered to inbox
```

```
04:59:40.244 main          :
⊚ Alert successfully delivered through 2 channel(s)
```

When we analyze the output, we can clearly see the resilient behavior of the `await All()` policy.

In this scenario, all three notification tasks are forked onto virtual threads and run concurrently. Even though the SMS notification fails with a `Carrier gateway time out` error, the email and push notifications continue running and complete successfully. The main thread waits at `join()` until all tasks finish, regardless of their individual outcomes. The side effects (notification results) are collected and summarized, showing that two out of three channels successfully delivered the alert.

The key observation is that unlike `allSuccessfulOrThrow()`, failed tasks never cancel other running tasks. Each notification channel gets a fair chance to deliver the message, maximizing our reach. This behavior is crucial for critical alerting systems where partial delivery is infinitely better than no delivery at all. The policy ensures that temporary issues with one channel don't prevent successful delivery through other available channels.

Resilient concurrent server

Another compelling use case for `awaitAll()` is building resilient concurrent servers. In such servers, you want to ensure that every client connection is handled and allowed to complete, even if one specific connection handler encounters an error. The `awaitAll()` policy prevents one failing client from crashing or prematurely stopping the server's ability to handle other active connections. Unlike `allSuccessfulOr Throw()`, which would cancel all active connections when one fails, `awaitAll()` ensures that each client connection runs to completion independently.

The key advantage is fault isolation. When individual connection handlers encounter errors (network timeouts, malformed requests, client disconnections), these failures remain isolated and don't propagate to other active connections. This makes `await All()` the ideal choice for server applications where uptime and reliability are paramount.

Let's examine a resilient echo server that demonstrates this pattern. We'll start with the main server infrastructure and connection tracking:

```
import module java.base;
import static ca.bazlur.mcj.chap4.rewrite.Utils.log;
import static java.util.concurrent.StructuredTaskScope.open;

public class ResilientServer {

    private final AtomicInteger connectionCount = new AtomicInteger(0);
    private final AtomicInteger activeConnections = new AtomicInteger(0);
}
```

These atomic counters will allow us to safely track both the total number of connections received and the number of currently active connections across multiple threads.

Now let's write the core server method that demonstrates how `awaitAll()` manages multiple concurrent connections:

```
public void serve(ServerSocket serverSocket)
        throws IOException, InterruptedException {
    log("Server starting on port: " +
        serverSocket.getLocalPort());

    try (var scope = open(StructuredTaskScope.Joiner.
            <Void>awaitAll())) {

        serverSocket.setSoTimeout(1000);

        while (!Thread.currentThread().isInterrupted()) {
            try {
                Socket socket = serverSocket.accept();
                int connId = connectionCount.incrementAndGet();
                activeConnections.incrementAndGet();

                log("Accepted connection #" + connId);

                // Fork a task to handle this connection
                scope.fork(() -> {
                    handleConnection(socket, connId);
                    return null;
                });

            } catch (SocketTimeoutException e) {
                continue; // Check for interruption
            }
        }

        log("Server stopping, waiting for " +
            "connections to finish...");
        scope.join(); // Wait for all connections to complete

    } finally {
        if (!serverSocket.isClosed()) {
            serverSocket.close();
        }
        log("Server shutdown complete. Total connections: " +
            connectionCount.get());
    }
}
```

The connection handler demonstrates error isolation:

```
private void handleConnection(Socket socket, int connectionId) {
    try (socket;
```

Understanding the API | 161

```java
          var reader = new BufferedReader(
              new InputStreamReader(socket.getInputStream()));
          var writer = new PrintWriter(
              socket.getOutputStream(), true)) {

      log("  [Conn-" + connectionId + "] Started");
      writer.println("Welcome to Echo Server! " +
          "Type 'quit' to exit.");

      String line;
      while ((line = reader.readLine()) != null) {
        log("  [Conn-" + connectionId + "] Received: " + line);

        if ("quit".equalsIgnoreCase(line.trim())) {
          writer.println("Goodbye!");
          break;
        }

        // Echo back the message
        writer.println("Echo: " + line);
      }

      log("  [Conn-" + connectionId + "] Completed successfully");
    } catch (IOException e) {
      log("  [Conn-" + connectionId + "] Error: " +
          e.getMessage());
    } finally {
      activeConnections.decrementAndGet();
      log("  [Conn-" + connectionId + "] Finished. Active: " +
          activeConnections.get());
    }
  }
}
```

Each client connection is handled in its own forked task. When one connection encounters an error, it only affects that specific connection—other active connections continue processing normally. `IOException` in one connection handler doesn't cancel other running connections. Each connection completes at its own pace.

Each connection handler properly closes its resources in the `finally` block, preventing resource leaks even when errors occur.

Let's run the server and observe its resilient behavior:

```
java --enable-preview ResilientServer.java
```

Now connect this server from two different terminals:

Terminal # 1

```
telnet   localhost 8080
Trying   ::1...
Connected  to localhost.
Escape   character is '^]'.
Welcome   to Echo Server! Type 'quit' to exit.
hello
Echo:   hello
```

Terminal # 2

```
telnet   localhost 8080
Trying   ::1...
Connected  to localhost.
Escape   character is '^]'.
Welcome   to Echo Server! Type 'quit' to exit.
hello
Echo:   hello
```

The output of the server would look as follows:

```
06:16:05.611 main           : Server starting on port: 8080
06:16:10.631 main           : Accepted connection #1
06:16:10.641 VThread[#34]:    [Conn-1] Started
06:16:23.630 VThread[#34]:    [Conn-1] Received: hello
06:16:33.990 main           : Accepted connection #2
06:16:33.991 VThread[#40]:    [Conn-2] Started
06:16:35.973 VThread[#40]:    [Conn-2] Received: hello
06:16:37.549 VThread[#40]:    [Conn-2] Received: quit
06:16:37.553 VThread[#40]:    [Conn-2] Completed successfully
06:16:37.556 VThread[#40]:    [Conn-2] Finished. Active: 1
06:16:41.799 VThread[#34]:    [Conn-1] Received: quit
06:16:41.801 VThread[#34]:    [Conn-1] Completed successfully
06:16:41.802 VThread[#34]:    [Conn-1] Finished. Active: 0
```

When we analyze this output, we can see how `awaitAll()` allows each connection to complete independently at its own pace. This demonstrates the key benefit of `awaitAll()` for server applications: concurrent connections operate without interfering with each other, making the server both resilient and efficient.

After first success. The `Joiner.allUntil(Predicate<Subtask> isDone)` method lets you define custom stopping conditions. Let's create a backup service that stops as soon as any backup location succeeds.

First, we'll define our result record and shared state:

```
public record BackupResult(String location, boolean success) {}
private final AtomicBoolean hasSuccess = new AtomicBoolean(false);
```

Now let's implement our backup methods:

```
private BackupResult backupToCloud(String data) throws InterruptedException {
  log(" -> Backing up to cloud...");
  Thread.sleep(Duration.ofMillis(500));

  if (new Random().nextBoolean()) { ❶
    log(" <- Cloud backup successful");
    hasSuccess.set(true);
    return new BackupResult("Cloud", true);
  } else {
    log(" <- Cloud backup failed");
    return new BackupResult("Cloud", false);
  }
}

private BackupResult backupToUSB(String data) throws InterruptedException {
  log(" -> Backing up to USB...");
  Thread.sleep(Duration.ofMillis(300));

  if (new Random().nextBoolean()) { ❷
    log(" <- USB backup successful");
    hasSuccess.set(true);
    return new BackupResult("USB", true);
  } else {
    log(" <- USB backup failed");
    return new BackupResult("USB", false);
  }
}

private BackupResult backupToNetwork(String data) throws InterruptedException {
  log(" -> Backing up to network drive...");
  Thread.sleep(Duration.ofMillis(400));

  if (new Random().nextBoolean()) { ❸
    log(" <- Network backup successful");
    hasSuccess.set(true);
    return new BackupResult("Network", true);
  } else {
    log(" <- Network backup failed");
    return new BackupResult("Network", false);
  }
}
```

Each backup method simulates different scenarios:

❶ Cloud backup has a 50% success rate.

❷ USB backup has a 50% success rate.

❸ Network backup has a 50% success rate.

Now let's implement the backup orchestration using `allUntil()`:

```
public void performBackup(String data) throws InterruptedException {
  log("Starting backup to multiple locations...");

  try (var scope = open(Joiner.<BackupResult>allUntil(subtask -> {
    boolean shouldStop = hasSuccess.get(); ❶
    if (shouldStop) {
      log("✅ Backup successful! Canceling other attempts...");
    }
    return shouldStop;
  }))) {

    scope.fork(() -> backupToCloud(data)); ❷
    scope.fork(() -> backupToUSB(data)); ❸
    scope.fork(() -> backupToNetwork(data)); ❹

    scope.join(); ❺

    if (hasSuccess.get()) {
      log("Backup completed successfully!");
    } else {
      log("All backup attempts failed!");
    }
  }
}
```

The backup orchestration illustrates stopping upon the first success:

❶ The predicate stops execution as soon as any backup is successful.

❷ It attempts a cloud backup.

❸ It attempts a USB backup.

❹ It attempts a network backup.

❺ It waits for the first success or for all backups to fail.

Complete demonstration class:

```
import static java.util.concurrent.StructuredTaskScope.*;
public class BackupDemo {
    // ... (methods from above)

    void main() {
        try {
            performBackup("important-data.zip");
        } catch (Exception e) {
            log("Error: " + e.getMessage());
        }
    }
}
```

Exception Handling in StructuredTaskScope

Exception handling in structured concurrency adheres to well-defined patterns that depend on the `Joiner` policy in use. A `StructuredTaskScope` is initiated with a `Joiner` that manages subtask completion and produces the outcome for the `join` method. In certain instances, the outcome will be a result, while in others, it will be an exception.

When the outcome is an exception, the `join` method throws `StructuredTask Scope.FailedException` with the original exception as the cause. For many `Joiner` implementations, this exception will be from a subtask that failed. In the case of `all SuccessfulOrThrow()` and `awaitAllSuccessfulOrThrow()`, for example, the exception is from the first subtask to fail.

Many of the details regarding how exceptions are handled will depend on usage. In some cases, it may be beneficial to add a `catch` block to the `try-with-resources` statement to catch `FailedException`. In other cases, it may be more advantageous to allow `FailedException` to propagate to higher levels for centralized error handling.

Let's explore the different exception-handling strategies through practical examples, starting with the most straightforward approach and building toward more sophisticated patterns.

Basic exception handling

The most common pattern is to wrap your structured concurrency code in a try-catch block that handles `FailedException`. This allows you to examine the underlying cause and decide how to respond.

Consider a user data service that needs to fetch information from multiple sources. If any source fails, we want to provide a meaningful error message rather than exposing internal system details:

```
import module java.base;
import static ca.bazlur.mcj.Utils.log;
import static java.util.concurrent.StructuredTaskScope.*;

public class BasicExceptionHandling {

    public String fetchUserData(String userId) {
        try (var scope = open(Joiner.<String>allSuccessfulOrThrow())) { ❶
            var profileTask = scope.fork(() -> fetchUserProfile(userId));
            var preferencesTask = scope.fork(() ->
                fetchUserPreferences(userId));

            var results = scope.join();

            // Process successful results
```

```
            return results.map(Subtask::get)
                .collect(Collectors.joining(", "));

        } catch (FailedException e) {  ❷
            log("Task failed: " + e.getCause().getMessage());
            return "Error: Unable to fetch user data";
        } catch (InterruptedException e) {  ❸
            Thread.currentThread().interrupt();
            throw new RuntimeException("Operation interrupted", e);
        }
    }

    private String fetchUserProfile(String userId)
            throws InterruptedException {
        Thread.sleep(Duration.ofMillis(200));
        if ("invalid".equals(userId)) {
            throw new IllegalArgumentException("Invalid user ID");
        }
        return "Profile for " + userId;
    }

    private String fetchUserPreferences(String userId)
            throws InterruptedException {
        Thread.sleep(Duration.ofMillis(150));
        if (userId.startsWith("blocked")) {
            throw new SecurityException("User access blocked");
        }
        return "Preferences for " + userId;
    }

    void main() {
        var demo = new BasicExceptionHandling();
        demo.fetchUserData("invalid");
    }
}
```

Let's break down what's in this code:

❶ The `allSuccessfulOrThrow()` joiner ensures that if any subtask fails, the entire operation fails with a `FailedException`.

❷ Use `getCause()` to access the original exception wrapped inside `FailedException` for logging purposes.

❸ Always restore the interrupted status when handling `InterruptedException`.

In this example, we use `allSuccessfulOrThrow()` because we need both the user profile and preferences to provide meaningful data. If either subtask fails, the entire operation should fail, but we want to present a user-friendly error message rather than exposing the technical details.

Pattern matching for sophisticated error handling

When you need to handle different types of exceptions with specific recovery strategies, pattern matching provides an elegant solution. This approach enables you to customize your response according to the type of failure.

Let's consider a real-world example that every developer can relate to: an ecommerce order-processing system. When a customer places an order, several operations must succeed: payment processing, inventory verification, and shipping calculation. Each can fail in different ways, and we want to provide specific, actionable feedback to help customers understand what went wrong.

In traditional exception handling, you might catch a generic exception and return a vague "something went wrong" message. With pattern matching in structured concurrency, we can offer precise, helpful responses that guide customers toward resolution.

Consider the following code snippets:

```
import module java.base;
import static java.util.concurrent.StructuredTaskScope.*;
import static java.util.concurrent.StructuredTaskScope.open;

public class OrderProcessingService {
    public record OrderResult(String orderId,
                              String status,
                              String message,
                              boolean successful) {
    }
    public OrderResult processOrder(String customerId,
                                    String productId, double amount) {
        try (var scope = open(Joiner.<String>allSuccessfulOrThrow())) {  ❶
            var paymentTask = scope.fork(() ->
                processPayment(customerId, amount));
            var inventoryTask = scope.fork(() ->
                checkAndReserveInventory(productId));
            var shippingTask = scope.fork(() ->
                calculateShipping(customerId, productId));
            var results = scope.join()
                .map(Subtask::get)
                .toList();
            String orderId = generateOrderId();
            return new OrderResult(orderId, "CONFIRMED",
                "Order confirmed successfully", true);
        } catch (FailedException e) {
            Throwable cause = e.getCause();  ❷
            return handleOrderProcessingError(cause);
        } catch (InterruptedException e) {
            Thread.currentThread().interrupt();
            throw new RuntimeException("Operation interrupted", e);
        }
```

```
    }
    private static OrderResult handleOrderProcessingError(Throwable cause) {
        return switch (cause) { ❸
            case PaymentDeclinedException pde -> new OrderResult(null,
                "PAYMENT_FAILED",
                """
                Your payment was declined. Please check your
                card details or try a different payment method.""",
                false);
            case InsufficientInventoryException iie ->
                new OrderResult(null, "OUT_OF_STOCK",
                    """
                    Sorry, this item is currently out of stock.
                    We'll notify you when it becomes available.""",
                    false);
            case ShippingNotAvailableException snae ->
                new OrderResult(null, "SHIPPING_UNAVAILABLE",
                    """
                    We can't ship to your address right now.
                    Please contact customer service for
                    alternatives.""", false);
            case NetworkException ne ->
                new OrderResult(null,
                "TEMPORARY_ERROR",
                """
                We're experiencing technical difficulties.
                Please try again in a few minutes.""", false);
            case SecurityException se -> new OrderResult(null,
                "SECURITY_CHECK_FAILED",
                """
                Additional verification required.
                Please contact customer service.""", false);
            default -> ❹
                new OrderResult(null, "SYSTEM_ERROR",
                """
                Something went wrong on our end. \
                Please try again or contact support.""", false);
        };
    }
}
```

Let's examine the key points that make this exception-handling pattern effective:

❶ All three operations must succeed for order processing to complete; if any fails, the entire operation fails with a `FailedException`.

❷ Extracts the original exception from the `FailedException` wrapper to determine the specific failure type.

❸ Pattern matching maps each business exception type to a specific customer-friendly error response.

❹ The default case handles unexpected exceptions with a generic system error message.

The beauty of this approach lies in the `switch` expression that evaluates the cause of the failure. Each case addresses a specific business scenario with appropriate customer communication. Notice how we use `allSuccessfulOrThrow()` because order processing is an all-or-nothing operation—if any step fails, the entire order should fail, but with specific guidance about what went wrong.

Let's integrate the individual operations that make up our order-processing system so we can execute them. While these are merely placeholder methods, we might have similar functionality in a real application:

```java
    private String processPayment(String customerId, double amount)
            throws PaymentDeclinedException, NetworkException,
                              SecurityException, InterruptedException {
      Thread.sleep(Duration.ofMillis(200));
      // Simulate different payment scenarios
      if (amount > 5000.0) {
        throw new SecurityException("High-value transaction requires" +
            "additional verification");
      }
      if (customerId.contains("declined")) {
        throw new PaymentDeclinedException("Insufficient funds");
      }
      if (customerId.contains("network")) {
        throw new NetworkException("Payment gateway timeout");
      }
      return "Payment processed: $" + amount;
    }

    private String checkAndReserveInventory(String productId)
                throws InsufficientInventoryException, NetworkException,
                                  InterruptedException {
      Thread.sleep(Duration.ofMillis(150));
      if (productId.contains("outofstock")) {
        throw new InsufficientInventoryException(
            "Only 0 items available, requested 1");
      }
      if (productId.contains("network")) {
        throw new NetworkException("Inventory service unavailable");
      }
      return "Reserved inventory for " + productId;
    }

    private String calculateShipping(String customerId, String productId)
                throws ShippingNotAvailableException, NetworkException,
```

```java
                                    InterruptedException {
    Thread.sleep(Duration.ofMillis(100));
    if (customerId.contains("remote")) {
      throw new ShippingNotAvailableException(
          "No shipping available to remote location");
    }
    if (productId.contains("hazardous")) {
      throw new ShippingNotAvailableException(
          "Cannot ship hazardous materials to this address");
    }
    if (customerId.contains("network")) {
      throw new NetworkException("Shipping service unavailable");
    }
    return "Shipping calculated: $12.99";
  }

  private String generateOrderId() {
    return "ORD-" + System.currentTimeMillis();
  }
```

Each method simulates real-world scenarios that ecommerce developers face daily. Payment processing may fail due to insufficient funds or security holds. Inventory checks may reveal out-of-stock situations. Shipping calculations may uncover geographical or regulatory restrictions.

We define custom exception types that represent these specific business scenarios:

```java
  public static class PaymentDeclinedException extends Exception {
    public PaymentDeclinedException(String message) {
      super(message);
    }
  }

  public static class InsufficientInventoryException extends Exception {
    public InsufficientInventoryException(String message) {
      super(message);
    }
  }

  public static class ShippingNotAvailableException extends Exception {
    public ShippingNotAvailableException(String message) {
      super(message);
    }
  }

  public static class NetworkException extends Exception {
    public NetworkException(String message) {
      super(message);
    }
  }
```

It's a best practice to create domain-specific exception types that represent business scenarios rather than technical failures. This makes your error handling more meaningful and your code more maintainable.

Now let's have the main method test it out:

```
void main() {
  var demo = new OrderProcessingService();
  var result1 = demo.processOrder("user123", "outofstock", 3500);
  System.out.println("Out of stock scenario: " + result1);
  var result2 = demo.processOrder("declined_user", "laptop", 1200);
  System.out.println("Payment declined scenario: " + result2);
  var result3 = demo.processOrder("remote_customer", "book", 25);
  System.out.println("Shipping unavailable scenario: " + result3);
  var result4 = demo.processOrder("user456", "laptop", 1200);
  System.out.println("Successful order: " + result4);
}
```

When we run this example, we will see how different failure scenarios produce specific, customer-friendly error messages. The `FailedException` gives us access to the underlying cause, and pattern matching allows us to map each business exception to the appropriate customer communication.

Strategic exception propagation

Sometimes, the best strategy is to allow exceptions to propagate to higher levels, where they can be addressed with a broader context. This approach is especially useful when building layered applications that involve different responsibilities at various levels.

Consider a critical data-processing service where any failure should trigger system-wide alerts and fallback procedures:

```
import module java.base;
import static java.util.concurrent.StructuredTaskScope.open;

public class ExceptionPropagationExample {

    // Let exceptions propagate for centralized handling
    public List<String> fetchCriticalData(List<String> sources)
            throws StructuredTaskScope.FailedException,
                    InterruptedException { ❶

        try (var scope = open(StructuredTaskScope.Joiner.
                <String>allSuccessfulOrThrow())) {

            var tasks = sources.stream()
                .map(source -> scope.fork(()
                    -> fetchFromSource(source)))
```

```
                .toList();
            
            // If any source fails, let FailedException propagate
            var results = scope.join();
            
            return results.map(StructuredTaskScope.Subtask::get)
                .toList();
        }
        // No catch block - let FailedException propagate ❷
    }
    
    // Higher-level method with centralized exception handling
    public void processDataWithCentralizedHandling() {
        try {
            var sources = List.of("source1", "source2");
            var data = fetchCriticalData(sources);
            log("Successfully fetched data: " + data);
        } catch (StructuredTaskScope.FailedException e) { ❸
            // Centralized logging and error handling
            log("Critical data fetch failed: " +
                e.getCause().getMessage());
            
            // Could trigger alerts, fallback procedures, etc.
            handleCriticalSystemFailure(e);
            
        } catch (InterruptedException e) {
            Thread.currentThread().interrupt();
            log("Operation was interrupted");
        }
    }
    
    private String fetchFromSource(String source)
        throws InterruptedException {
        // Stub method
    return "Data from " + source;
    }
    
    private void handleCriticalSystemFailure(FailedException e) {
    Throwable cause = e.getCause();
    // Stub methods, feel free to add your own implementations
    }
}
```

Here's how the exception propagation strategy works in this example:

❶ The method signature explicitly declares that it throws both `FailedException` and `InterruptedException`, signaling to callers that they must handle these exceptions.

❷ Deliberately omitting a `catch` block allows exceptions to propagate up the call stack to where they can be handled with more context.

❸ The higher-level method provides centralized exception handling that can implement comprehensive error responses like logging, alerting, and fallback procedures.

By allowing `FailedException` to propagate from `fetchCriticalData()`, we enable the calling method to implement comprehensive error handling that might include logging, alerting, and triggering fallback systems.

Best Practice: Use exception propagation when lower-level methods don't have sufficient context to handle failures appropriately. Let exceptions bubble up to components that can make informed decisions about recovery strategies.

When propagating checked exceptions, ensure that intermediate layers properly declare thrown exceptions in their method signatures to maintain compile-time safety.

Handling exceptions within subtasks

For cases where specific exceptions should trigger default results rather than failing the entire operation, it's often better to handle exceptions within the subtask itself. This pattern is particularly useful for optional data sources where partial failure shouldn't prevent the entire operation from succeeding.

Imagine a dashboard service that gathers data from multiple optional services. If some services are unavailable, we still want to display the dashboard with whatever data we can gather:

```
import module java.base;
import static ca.bazlur.mcj.chap4.Utils.log;
import static java.util.concurrent.StructuredTaskScope.*;

public class SubtaskExceptionHandling {
    public record ServiceResponse(String service, String data,
                                  boolean successful) {
    }
    public List<ServiceResponse> gatherOptionalData(List<String> services)
            throws InterruptedException {
        try (var scope
                = open(Joiner.<ServiceResponse>allSuccessfulOrThrow())) {  ❶
            var tasks = services.stream()
                    .map(service -> scope.fork(() ->
                            fetchWithDefaults(service)))  ❷
                    .toList();

            var results = scope.join();
            return results.map(Subtask::get)
                    .toList();
```

```
            } catch (FailedException e) { ❸
                // This should rarely happen since we handle
                // exceptions in subtasks
                log("Unexpected failure: " + e.getCause().getMessage());
                throw new RuntimeException("System error", e);
            }
        }

        // Handle exceptions within the subtask to provide defaults
        private ServiceResponse fetchWithDefaults(String service) { ❹
            try {
                String data = fetchServiceData(service);
                return new ServiceResponse(service, data, true);
            } catch (IOException e) {
                log("Network error for " + service + ": " + e.getMessage());
                return new ServiceResponse(service, "Default data", false);
            } catch (TimeoutException e) {
                log("Timeout for " + service + ": " + e.getMessage());
                return new ServiceResponse(service, "Cached data", false);
            } catch (Exception e) {
                log("Unexpected error for " + service + ": " +
                    e.getMessage());
                return new ServiceResponse(service, "Error", false);
            }
        }

        private String fetchServiceData(String service)
                throws IOException, TimeoutException, InterruptedException {
            Thread.sleep(Duration.ofMillis(100));
            return "Data from " + service;
        }
    }
```

Let's examine how this exception-handling strategy enables graceful degradation:

❶ Using `allSuccessfulOrThrow()` with subtasks that handle their own exceptions means this will rarely throw `FailedException`.

❷ Each service is fetched in a separate subtask that internally handles exceptions and provides fallback responses.

❸ The `catch` block handles truly unexpected failures, since individual service failures are handled within subtasks.

❹ Exception handling within the subtask converts failures into successful responses with default data, preventing individual service failures from cascading.

By handling exceptions within `fetchWithDefaults()`, we ensure that network failures or timeouts for individual services don't prevent the entire dashboard from loading. Each service attempt either succeeds with real data or fails gracefully with default or cached data.

Best Practice: Handle exceptions within subtasks when you want to implement graceful degradation. This pattern works well for optional operations where partial success is acceptable.

When subtasks handle their own exceptions, the outer `FailedException` catch block should rarely execute. Consider logging when it does, as this may indicate an unexpected system issue.

Understanding how different joiners handle exceptions

The choice of joiner has a significant impact on how exceptions are handled. Let's compare the behavior of `allSuccessfulOrThrow()` and `awaitAll()` when dealing with failures.

The `allSuccessfulOrThrow()` joiner implements a fail-fast strategy where any single failure causes the entire operation to fail immediately:

```
private void demonstrateAllSuccessfulOrThrow() {
    try (var scope = open(StructuredTaskScope.Joiner.
            <String>allSuccessfulOrThrow())) { ❶
        scope.fork(() -> successfulTask("Task1"));
        scope.fork(() -> failingTask("Task2")); ❷
        scope.fork(() -> successfulTask("Task3"));
        var results = scope.join(); ❸
        log("All tasks completed successfully");
    } catch (StructuredTaskScope.FailedException e) { ❹
        log("Failed due to: " + e.getCause().getMessage());
        log("Remaining tasks were canceled");
    } catch (InterruptedException e) {
        Thread.currentThread().interrupt();
    }
}
```

Here are the key characteristics of the `allSuccessfulOrThrow()` approach:

❶ Creates a scope that requires all tasks to succeed or the entire operation fails.

❷ When this task throws an exception, it triggers the fail-fast behavior.

❸ The `join()` call will throw `FailedException` because `Task2` failed, and `Task3` may be canceled.

❹ Exception handling catches the failure and logs that the remaining tasks were canceled.

The `awaitAll()` joiner takes a different approach, allowing all tasks to complete regardless of individual failures:

```
private void demonstrateAwaitAll() {
    try (var scope = open(StructuredTaskScope.Joiner.
            <Void>awaitAll())) { ❶
        scope.fork(() -> successfulTask("Task1"));
        scope.fork(() -> failingTask("Task2")); ❷
        scope.fork(() -> successfulTask("Task3"));
        scope.join(); ❸
        log("All tasks were allowed to complete");
    } catch (InterruptedException e) {
        Thread.currentThread().interrupt();
    }
}
```

Here are the key characteristics of the `awaitAll()` approach:

❶ The `awaitAll()` joiner waits for all tasks to complete, regardless of individual failures.

❷ `Task2` will still throw an exception, but it won't prevent other tasks from completing.

❸ The `join()` method never throws `FailedException` with `awaitAll()`—it waits for all tasks to finish, even if some fail.

The `allSuccessfulOrThrow()` joiner implements a fail-fast strategy: when `Task2` fails, it immediately cancels the remaining tasks and throws `FailedException`. In contrast, `awaitAll()` allows all tasks to complete regardless of individual failures, requiring us to handle exceptions within each subtask if we want to collect both successes and failures.

General exceptions

Unless otherwise specified, passing a `null` argument to a method in this class will cause a `NullPointerException` to be thrown. This consistent behavior helps catch programming errors early and makes the API more predictable.

Beyond the `null` pointer checks, the API throws specific exceptions for different error conditions, making it easier to handle problems appropriately.

Consider the following example:

```
import java.util.concurrent.Callable;
import java.util.concurrent.StructuredTaskScope;
import static ca.bazlur.mcj.chap4.Utils.log;
import static java.util.concurrent.StructuredTaskScope.open;
```

Understanding the API | 177

```java
public class ExceptionBehaviorDemo {
  public void demonstrateCommonExceptions() {
    try {
      log("Testing null joiner...");
      try (var scope = open(null)) { ❶
        log("This should not be reached");
      }
    } catch (NullPointerException e) {
      log("NullPointerException caught for null joiner");
    }

    try {
      Callable<? extends String> nullCallable = null; ❷
      try (var scope = open(StructuredTaskScope.Joiner.
          <String>allSuccessfulOrThrow())) {
        scope.fork(nullCallable); ❸
      }
    } catch (NullPointerException e) {
      log("NullPointerException caught for null callable");
    }

    try {
      var scope = open(StructuredTaskScope.Joiner.
          <String>allSuccessfulOrThrow());
      scope.close(); ❹
      scope.fork(() -> "This should fail"); ❺
    } catch (IllegalStateException e) {
      log("IllegalStateException caught for closed scope operation");
    }
  }

  void main() {
    var demo = new ExceptionBehaviorDemo();
    demo.demonstrateCommonExceptions();
  }
}
```

Let's examine each exception scenario:

❶ Attempting to open a scope with a null joiner immediately throws NullPointer Exception, preventing the scope from being created with an invalid configuration.

❷ Creates a null callable variable to demonstrate what happens when null tasks are submitted to the scope.

❸ Calling fork() with a null callable throws NullPointerException, ensuring that only valid tasks can be submitted for execution.

❹ Manually closes the scope before the try-with-resources block completes, putting the scope into a closed state.

❺ Attempting to fork a task on a closed scope throws IllegalStateException, preventing operations on invalid scope instances.

Let's run the preceding program:

```
java --enable-preview ExceptionBehaviorDemo.java
```

The output would be as follows:

```
23:14:21.314 main      : NullPointerException caught for null joiner
23:14:21.317 main      : NullPointerException caught for null callable
23:14:21.317 main      : IllegalStateException caught for closed scope operation
```

Configuration

While the default configuration of StructuredTaskScope works well for many scenarios, real-world applications often require more control over how concurrent tasks are executed. Configuration allows you to customize thread creation, add monitoring capabilities, and implement timeout policies that align with your application's requirements.

Understanding Configuration

When we create a StructuredTaskScope using the simple open() or open(Joiner) methods, we get a sensible default configuration:

- ThreadFactory: Creates unnamed virtual threads
- Monitoring name: No name assigned (anonymous scope)
- Timeout: No timeout (tasks run until completion or cancellation)

```
// Uses default configuration
try (var scope = open(Joiner.allSuccessfulOrThrow())) { ❶
    // Virtual threads created with the default settings
    scope.fork(() -> doWork());
    scope.join();
}
```

❶ This default configuration creates anonymous virtual threads with no timeout.

For production applications, we will often need more sophisticated control. The Configuration API provides an overloaded open method that accepts a configuration function:

```
static <T, R> StructuredTaskScope<T, R>
        open(Joiner<? super T, ? extends R> joiner,
```

```
                Function<Configuration, Configuration> configFunction) {
    return StructuredTaskScopeImpl.open(joiner, configFunction);
}
```

The `Configuration` interface is a sealed interface that provides three configuration methods, each returning a new `Configuration` object with the specified modification:

```
sealed interface Configuration {
    Configuration withThreadFactory(ThreadFactory threadFactory);
    Configuration withName(String name);
    Configuration withTimeout(Duration timeout);
}
```

The configuration follows an immutable builder pattern—each method returns a new `Configuration` object rather than modifying the existing one. This allows you to chain multiple configuration calls together in a fluent style.

The key insight is that the configuration function transforms the default configuration by applying one or more modifications.

Here's the basic pattern:

```
try (var scope = open(Joiner.allSuccessfulOrThrow(),
        cf -> cf.withTimeout(Duration.ofSeconds(10)))) {
}
ThreadFactory factory = Thread.ofVirtual()
    .name("user-processor-", 0)
    .factory();
try (var scope = open(Joiner.allSuccessfulOrThrow(), cf -> cf
    .withThreadFactory(factory)
    .withTimeout(Duration.ofSeconds(30))
    .withName("my-scope"))) {
  // Continue with your code
}
```

Named threads

The most common customization is creating named threads to improve debugging and monitoring. Named threads make it much easier to identify which threads are doing which work in thread dumps and profiling tools.

Consider the following code snippets:

```
import module java.base;
import static java.util.concurrent.StructuredTaskScope.*;

public class NamedThreadExample {
  public void processUserRequests(List<String> userIds) {
    ThreadFactory factory = Thread.ofVirtual()
        .name("user-processor-", 0)
        .factory();
```

```
    try (var scope = open(Joiner.<String>allSuccessfulOrThrow(),
        cf -> cf.withThreadFactory(factory))) {
      var tasks = userIds.stream()
          .map(userId -> scope.fork(() -> processUser(userId)))
          .toList();
      var results = scope.join()
          .map(Subtask::get)
          .toList();
      System.out.println("Processed users: " + results);
    } catch (FailedException | InterruptedException e) {
      System.out.println("Processing failed: " + e.getMessage());
    }
  }

  private String processUser(String userId)
      throws InterruptedException {
    System.out.println("Processing user " + userId +
        " on thread: " + Thread.currentThread().getName());
    Thread.sleep(Duration.ofMillis(100));
    return "User " + userId + " processed";
  }

  void main() {
    processUserRequests(List.of("user1", "user2", "user3"));
  }
}
```

When we run this code, we'll see output like:

```
Processing user user2 on thread: user-processor-1
Processing user user3 on thread: user-processor-2
Processing user user1 on thread: user-processor-0
```

Timeout configuration

Timeouts are crucial for building resilient applications. They prevent operations from hanging indefinitely and allow your application to fail fast when services are unresponsive.

Consider the following code snippets:

```
import module java.base;
import static java.util.concurrent.StructuredTaskScope.*;

public class TimeoutExample {
  public List<String> fetchDataWithTimeout(List<String> sources)
      throws TimeoutException,
      FailedException,
      InterruptedException {
    Duration timeout = Duration.ofSeconds(5); ❶
    try (var scope = open(Joiner.<String>allSuccessfulOrThrow(),
        cf -> cf.withTimeout(timeout))) { ❷
```

```
            var tasks = sources.stream()
                .map(source -> scope.fork(() -> fetchFromSource(source)))
                .toList();
            // If timeout expires before join() completes,
            // TimeoutException is thrown
            return scope.join() ❸
                    .map(Subtask::get)
                    .toList();
        }
    }

    private String fetchFromSource(String source) throws InterruptedException {
        int delay = switch (source) {
            case "fast_source" -> 1000;
            case "slow_source" -> 3000;
            case "very_slow_source" -> 8000; ❹
            default -> 2000;
        };
        Thread.sleep(Duration.ofMillis(delay));
        return "Data from " + source;
    }

    void main() {
        var sources = List.of("fast_source", "slow_source", "very_slow_source");
        try {
            var results = fetchDataWithTimeout(sources);
            System.out.println("Success: " + results);
        } catch (TimeoutException e) { ❺
            System.out.println("Operation timed out after 5 seconds");
            System.out.println("Some sources were too slow to respond");
        } catch (FailedException e) {
            System.out.println("Task failed: " + e.getCause().getMessage());
        } catch (InterruptedException e) {
            Thread.currentThread().interrupt();
            System.out.println("Operation interrupted");
        }
    }
}
```

Let's examine how the timeout mechanism works in this example:

❶ Sets a five-second timeout duration for the entire operation.

❷ Configures the scope with the timeout—the countdown begins when the scope opens.

❸ If any subtask hasn't completed within five seconds, join() throws Timeout Exception.

❹ This source takes eight seconds, which exceeds our five-second timeout and will trigger the timeout.

❺ Catches and handles the timeout exception with user-friendly error messages.

If we run the preceding code, the output would be something like this:

```
Operation timed out after 5 seconds
Some sources were too slow to respond
```

The timeout starts counting from the moment the scope is opened, not when join() is called. This means the timeout covers the entire lifecycle of the scope.

This demonstrates how timeouts provide fail-fast behavior when some operations take longer than expected, preventing your application from hanging indefinitely.

Combining configuration options

The most powerful aspect of configuration is the ability to combine various options to precisely construct the execution environment your application needs.

Consider the following code snippets:

```
import module java.base;

import static java.util.concurrent.StructuredTaskScope.*;

public class ComprehensiveConfigurationExample {

  public void main() {
    ThreadFactory factory = Thread.ofVirtual() ❶
        .name("api-client-", 0) ❷
        .factory(); ❸

    Duration timeout = Duration.ofSeconds(15); ❹

    try (var scope = open(Joiner.<String>allSuccessfulOrThrow(),
        cf -> cf.withThreadFactory(factory) ❺
            .withTimeout(timeout) ❻
            .withName("api-integration-scope"))) { ❼

      System.out.println("Starting comprehensive API integration");
      System.out.println("Timeout: " + timeout.getSeconds() + " seconds");

      // Fork multiple API calls
      var userTask = scope.fork(this::callUserAPI);
      var profileTask = scope.fork(this::callProfileAPI);
```

```java
      var preferencesTask = scope.fork(this::callPreferencesAPI);

      var results = scope.join()
          .map(Subtask::get)
          .toList();

      System.out.println("All API calls completed: " + results);

    } catch (StructuredTaskScope.TimeoutException e) {
      System.out.println("API integration timed out - some services too slow");

    } catch (StructuredTaskScope.FailedException e) {
      System.out.println("API integration failed: " + e.getCause().getMessage());

    } catch (InterruptedException e) {
      Thread.currentThread().interrupt();
      System.out.println("API integration interrupted");
    }
  }

  private String callUserAPI() throws InterruptedException {
    Thread.sleep(Duration.ofSeconds(3));
    IO.println(Thread.currentThread().getName()
        + " : " + "User data retrieved");
    return "User data";
  }

  private String callProfileAPI() throws InterruptedException {
    Thread.sleep(Duration.ofSeconds(2));
    IO.println(Thread.currentThread().getName()
        + " : " + "Profile data retrieved");
    return "Profile data";
  }

  private String callPreferencesAPI() throws InterruptedException {
    Thread.sleep(Duration.ofSeconds(4));
    IO.println(Thread.currentThread().getName()
        + " : " + "Preferences data retrieved");
    return "Preferences data";
  }
}
```

Let's examine this configuration step by step:

❶ Creates a builder for virtual threads, which are lightweight and ideal for I/O-bound operations like API calls

❷ Sets up a naming pattern where threads will be named `api-client-0`, `api-client-1`, `api-client-2`, etc., making them easily identifiable in debugging tools

❸ Converts the configured thread builder into a ThreadFactory that the scope can use to create threads

❹ Sets a 15-second timeout to ensure the operation fails fast if any API becomes unresponsive

❺ Configures the scope to use our custom ThreadFactory for creating worker threads

❻ Applies the timeout to the scope, starting the countdown when the scope is opened

❼ Assigns a descriptive name to the scope for monitoring and management purposes, making it easier to identify in production logs and monitoring tools

Custom Joiners

While the built-in joiners like allSuccessfulOrThrow() and awaitAll() offer a solid foundation for task coordination and result management, structured concurrency doesn't stop there. It allows developers to create custom joiners to meet specific application needs. This flexibility unlocks a whole new realm of possibilities for orchestrating concurrent workflows with precise control over how subtasks are managed and results are collected.

Custom joiners can be created by implementing the StructuredTask Scope .Joiner<T, R> interface. This interface provides methods to handle subtask completion events and determine when the scope should complete and what result it should produce.

Every joiner implements the StructuredTaskScope.Joiner<T, R> interface, where T is the type of values produced by subtasks and R is the type of the final result. The interface defines three key methods:

onFork(Subtask<? extends T> subtask)
    Called each time a subtask is forked, before the thread is created to run it

onComplete(Subtask<? extends T> subtask)
    Called each time a subtask completes, allowing you to process the result and decide whether to continue or complete early

result()
    Called when the scope is ready to produce its final result

Let's explore several practical examples that demonstrate the power and flexibility of custom joiners.

Collecting all results and exceptions

Let's consider a scenario where we want to gather the results of all subtasks, whether they succeed or fail, and collect any exceptions that occur. This pattern is helpful for batch processing, where we want maximum information about what succeeded and what failed:

```
import module java.base;

public class CollectingJoiner<T>
        implements StructuredTaskScope.Joiner<T, CollectingJoiner.Result<T>> {
    private final Queue<T> results = new ConcurrentLinkedQueue<>();
    private final Queue<Throwable> exceptions = new ConcurrentLinkedQueue<>();

    @Override
    public Result<T> result() {
        return new Result<>(
                results.stream().toList(),
                exceptions.stream().toList()
        );
    }

    @Override
    public boolean onComplete(StructuredTaskScope.Subtask<? extends T> subtask) {
        switch (subtask.state()) {
            case SUCCESS -> results.add(subtask.get()); ❶
            case FAILED -> exceptions.add(subtask.exception()); ❷
            case UNAVAILABLE -> { ❸
                // Task was canceled, treat as failure
                exceptions.add(new RuntimeException("Task was canceled"));
            }
        }
        return false; ❹
    }

    public record Result<T>(List<T> successes, List<Throwable> failures) {
        public boolean hasFailures() {
            return !failures.isEmpty();
        }
        public int totalTasks() {
            return successes.size() + failures.size();
        }
    }
}
```

Let's examine how this joiner handles different subtask outcomes:

❶ When a subtask completes successfully, we add its result to the results queue for later retrieval.

❷ When a subtask fails with an exception, we collect the exception for analysis rather than immediately failing the entire operation.

❸ Tasks in the UNAVAILABLE state were canceled before completion. We treat cancellation as a failure and create a descriptive exception.

❹ Returning false allows all remaining subtasks to continue running until they naturally complete.

Now let's use this joiner to build a service that fetches headlines from various online sources, collecting as many as possible, even if some sources fail:

```
import module java.base;
import static ca.bazlur.mcj.chap4.Utils.log;
import static java.util.concurrent.StructuredTaskScope.open;

public class NewsAggregator {
  public CollectingJoiner.Result<String> fetchAllHeadlines()
      throws InterruptedException {
    var newsSources = List.of(
        "TechCrunch",
        "InfoWorld",
        "InfoQ",
        "FailingSource"
    );

    try (var scope = open(new CollectingJoiner<String>())) {
      for (String source : newsSources) {
        scope.fork(() -> fetchHeadlines(source));  ❶
      }
      var result = scope.join();  ❷
      log("Successfully fetched from " + result.successes().size() +
          " sources");
      log("Failed to fetch from " + result.failures().size() +
          " sources");
      return result;  ❸
    }
  }

  private String fetchHeadlines(String source) throws InterruptedException {
    log("Fetching headlines from " + source);
    Thread.sleep(Duration.ofMillis(200 + new Random().nextInt(300)));
    if (source.equals("FailingSource")) {  ❹
      throw new RuntimeException("Network timeout for " + source);
    }
    return "Headlines from " + source + ": Breaking news, Tech updates";
  }

  void main() {
    var aggregator = new NewsAggregator();
```

```
    try {
      var result = aggregator.fetchAllHeadlines();
      log("\n=== Results ===");
      result.successes() ❺
          .forEach(headline -> log(headline));
      if (result.hasFailures()) { ❻
        log("\n=== Failures ===");
        result.failures()
            .forEach(error ->
                log(error.getMessage()));
      }
    } catch (InterruptedException e) {
      Thread.currentThread().interrupt();
      log("Operation interrupted");
    }
  }
}
```

This example demonstrates the power of collecting both successes and failures:

❶ Launches a subtask for each news source simultaneously, allowing them to run in parallel.

❷ The `CollectingJoiner` waits for all subtasks to complete, collecting both successful headlines and any failures that occur.

❸ Returns a result that contains both the successful data and information about what failed.

❹ One source is designed to fail, demonstrating how the joiner handles mixed outcomes.

❺ Displays all successfully fetched headlines, giving users the maximum available information.

❻ Reports on failures without letting them prevent the display of successful results.

When we run this example, we'll see output as follows:

```
00:53:44.291 VThread[#34]: Fetching headlines from TechCrunch
00:53:44.291 VThread[#42]: Fetching headlines from FailingSource
00:53:44.291 VThread[#39]: Fetching headlines from InfoQ
00:53:44.291 VThread[#36]: Fetching headlines from InfoWorld
00:53:44.773 main         : Successfully fetched from 3 sources
00:53:44.773 main         : Failed to fetch from 1 sources
00:53:44.773 main         :
=== Results ===
01:43:17.431 main         : Headlines from InfoWorld: Breaking news, Tech updates
01:43:17.431 main         : Headlines from TechCrunch: Breaking news, Tech updates
```

```
01:43:17.431 main        : Headlines from InfoQ: Breaking news, Tech updates
01:43:17.431 main        :
=== Failures ===
01:43:17.431 main        : Network timeout for FailingSource
```

Quorum-based completion

Let's implement a joiner inspired by distributed systems that completes when a quorum of subtasks succeeds. This is useful for scenarios where you need a certain number of confirmations before proceeding:

```
import java.util.concurrent.StructuredTaskScope;
import java.util.concurrent.atomic.AtomicInteger;

public class QuorumJoiner<T> implements StructuredTaskScope.Joiner<T, Boolean> {
  private final int requiredSuccesses;
  private final AtomicInteger successCount = new AtomicInteger(0); ❶
  private final AtomicInteger totalCount = new AtomicInteger(0); ❷
  private volatile boolean quorumReached = false; ❸

  public QuorumJoiner(int requiredSuccesses) {
    this.requiredSuccesses = requiredSuccesses;
  }

  @Override
  public Boolean result() {
    return quorumReached; ❹
  }

  @Override
  public boolean onFork(StructuredTaskScope.Subtask<? extends T> subtask) {
    totalCount.incrementAndGet(); ❺
    return false;  // Allow all tasks to proceed ❻
  }

  @Override
  public boolean onComplete(StructuredTaskScope.Subtask<? extends T> subtask) {
    if (subtask.state() == StructuredTaskScope.Subtask.State.SUCCESS) {
      int currentSuccess = successCount.incrementAndGet(); ❼
      if (currentSuccess >= requiredSuccesses) { ❽
        quorumReached = true;
        return true; ❾
      }
    }
    return false; ❿
  }

  public int getSuccessCount() {
    return successCount.get();
  }

  public int getTotalCount() {
```

Understanding the API | 189

```
        return totalCount.get();
    }
}
```

Let's examine how this quorum-based joiner manages consensus:

❶ Tracks the number of subtasks that have completed successfully using an atomic counter for thread safety.

❷ Keeps track of how many subtasks have been forked, useful for calculating completion percentages or remaining tasks.

❸ A volatile boolean that indicates whether the required quorum has been reached, ensuring visibility across threads.

❹ Returns whether the quorum was successfully achieved by the time the scope was completed.

❺ Increments the total count each time a subtask is forked, giving us visibility into the total number of tasks.

❻ Returns `false` to allow all subtasks to be created; we don't want to prevent task creation at fork time.

❼ When a subtask succeeds, atomically increments the success counter and captures the new count.

❽ Tests whether we've reached the required number of successes for our quorum.

❾ Once we have enough successes, sets the flag and returns `true` to cancel remaining tasks and complete the scope.

❿ If we don't have enough successes yet, returns `false` to let other tasks continue running.

Here's how to use the quorum joiner for a distributed database write operation:

```
import java.time.Duration;
import java.util.List;
import java.util.Random;
import static ca.bazlur.mcj.chap4.Utils.log;
import static java.util.concurrent.StructuredTaskScope.open;

public class DistributedDatabase {
  private final List<String> nodes = List.of(
      "node-1", "node-2", "node-3", "node-4", "node-5" ❶
  );
```

```
    private final int quorumSize = 3; // Need 3 out of 5 nodes  ❷

    public boolean writeData(String key, String value)
        throws InterruptedException {
      log("Writing data to distributed database:\n " + key + "=" + value);
      try (var scope = open(new QuorumJoiner<Boolean>(quorumSize))) {  ❸
        for (String node : nodes) {
          scope.fork(() -> writeToNode(node, key, value));  ❹
        }
        boolean success = scope.join();  ❺
        log("Write operation " + (success ? "succeeded" : "failed"));
        log("Required quorum: " + quorumSize + " nodes");
        return success;
      }
    }

    private Boolean writeToNode(String node, String key, String value)
        throws InterruptedException {
      log("Writing to " + node);
      Thread.sleep(Duration.ofMillis(100 + new Random().nextInt(200)));  ❻
      // Simulate occasional node failures
      if (new Random().nextDouble() < 0.2) {  ❼
        log(node + " write failed");
        throw new RuntimeException("Write failed on " + node);
      }
      log(node + " write succeeded");
      return true;
    }

    void main() {
      var database = new DistributedDatabase();
      try {
        boolean result = database.writeData("user:123", "John Doe");  ❽
        log("\nFinal result: " + (result ? "SUCCESS" : "FAILURE"));
      } catch (InterruptedException e) {
        Thread.currentThread().interrupt();
        log("Database operation interrupted");
      }
    }
}
```

Let's examine how this works:

❶ Defines a cluster of five database nodes. In a real system, these would be different physical servers or containers.

❷ Sets quorum size to three out of five nodes. This provides fault tolerance while maintaining availability; the system can survive up to two node failures.

❸ Creates a `StructuredTaskScope` with a custom `QuorumJoiner` that completes when the required number of successful operations is reached, rather than waiting for all tasks.

❹ Forks a separate virtual thread for each node write operation. All writes execute concurrently, maximizing parallelism and reducing total latency.

❺ Blocks until quorum is achieved or determined impossible. The `QuorumJoiner` returns `true` if enough writes succeed, `false` if too many fail to reach quorum.

❻ Simulates realistic network latency with random delays between 100 and 300ms, representing typical database write times across a network.

❼ Introduces a 20% failure rate to simulate real-world distributed system challenges like network partitions, disk failures, or node crashes.

❽ The high-level API abstracts away all the complexity of distributed coordination, presenting a simple synchronous interface to callers.

If we now run the preceding program, we will get the following output:

```
21:11:24.267 main         : Writing data to distributed database:
 user:123=John Doe
01:18:38.141 VThread[#34]: Writing to node-1
01:18:38.142 VThread[#36]: Writing to node-2
01:18:38.141 VThread[#44]: Writing to node-5
01:18:38.142 VThread[#42]: Writing to node-4
01:18:38.142 VThread[#39]: Writing to node-3
01:18:38.252 VThread[#42]: node-4 write succeeded
01:18:38.285 VThread[#34]: node-1 write succeeded
01:18:38.364 VThread[#39]: node-3 write failed
01:18:38.376 VThread[#36]: node-2 write succeeded
01:18:38.378 main         : Write operation succeeded
01:18:38.378 main         : Required quorum: 3 nodes
01:18:38.379 main         :
Final result: SUCCESS
```

Adaptive completion

Sometimes we may want a completion logic that adapts based on the results we're seeing. Let's create a joiner that completes early if it sees too many failures:

```
import module java.base;

public class AdaptiveJoiner<T>
    implements StructuredTaskScope.Joiner<T, CollectingJoiner.Result<T>> {
  private final int minSampleSize;
  private final double maxFailureRate;
```

```
    private final Queue<T> successes = new ConcurrentLinkedQueue<>();
    private final Queue<Throwable> failures = new ConcurrentLinkedQueue<>();

    public AdaptiveJoiner(double maxFailureRate, int minSampleSize) {
      this.maxFailureRate = maxFailureRate;
      this.minSampleSize = minSampleSize;
    }

    @Override
    public CollectingJoiner.Result<T> result() {
      return new CollectingJoiner.Result<>(
          successes.stream().toList(),
          failures.stream().toList()
      );
    }

    @Override
    public boolean onComplete(StructuredTaskScope.Subtask<? extends T> subtask) {
      switch (subtask.state()) {
        case SUCCESS -> successes.add(subtask.get());       ❶
        case FAILED -> failures.add(subtask.exception());   ❶
        case UNAVAILABLE -> failures.add(
            new RuntimeException("Task canceled"));
      }
      int total = successes.size() + failures.size();
      // Only check failure rate after minimum sample size
      if (total >= minSampleSize) {  ❷
        double failureRate = (double) failures.size() / total;
        return failureRate > maxFailureRate;  ❸
      }
      return false;  // Continue processing  ❹
    }
  }
```

Now let's explain how it works:

❶ Collects both successes and failures as they occur.

❷ Only evaluates the failure rate after we have enough data points to make a meaningful decision.

❸ If the failure rate exceeds our threshold, complete early to avoid wasting resources on a likely failing operation.

❹ If the failure rate is acceptable or we don't have enough data yet, continue processing.

Let's now use it in an example:

```
import module java.base;
import static ca.bazlur.mcj.chap4.rewrite.Utils.log;
```

```java
import static java.util.concurrent.StructuredTaskScope.open;

public class WebCrawlerWithCircuitBreaker {
  private final List<String> urls = List.of(
      "https://api.service1.com/data", ❶
      "https://api.service2.com/data",
      "https://api.service3.com/data",
      "https://api.service4.com/data",
      "https://api.service5.com/data"
  );
  private final Random random = new Random();
  private double systemFailureRate = 0.1; // Start with 10% failure rate

  public CollectingJoiner.Result<String> crawlWithCircuitBreaker()
      throws InterruptedException {
    log("Starting web crawl with circuit breaker protection");
    log("Max failure rate: 30%, Min sample size: 5");
    // Create adaptive joiner that stops if >30% fail after 5 samples
    try (var scope = open(new AdaptiveJoiner<String>(0.30, 5))) { ❷
      for (String url : urls) {
        scope.fork(() -> fetchUrl(url)); ❸
      }
      var result = scope.join(); ❹
      log("\n=== FINAL RESULTS ===");
      log("Successful fetches: " + result.successes().size());
      log("Failed fetches: " + result.failures().size());
      log("Total processed: " + (result.successes().size()
          + result.failures().size()));
      log("Remaining URLs (not processed): " +
          (urls.size() - result.successes().size() - result.failures().size()));
      return result;
    }
  }

  private String fetchUrl(String url) throws InterruptedException {
    log("Fetching: " + url);
    // Simulate network delay
    Thread.sleep(Duration.ofMillis(200 + random.nextInt(300))); ❺
    // Simulate system degradation over time
    if (random.nextDouble() < systemFailureRate) { ❻
      systemFailureRate += 0.05; // Failures increase over time
      throw new RuntimeException("Network timeout for " + url);
    }
    log("✓ Successfully fetched: " + url);
    return "Data from " + url;
  }

  public void demonstrateScenarios() throws InterruptedException {
    log("=== SCENARIO 1: Normal Operation ===");
    systemFailureRate = 0.1; // Low failure rate
    crawlWithCircuitBreaker();
    Thread.sleep(1000);
```

```
    log("\n=== SCENARIO 2: System Under Stress ===");
    systemFailureRate = 0.4; // High initial failure rate
    crawlWithCircuitBreaker();
    Thread.sleep(1000);
    log("\n=== SCENARIO 3: Cascading Failures ===");
    systemFailureRate = 0.6; // Very high failure rate
    crawlWithCircuitBreaker();
  }

  void main() {
    var crawler = new WebCrawlerWithCircuitBreaker();
    try {
      crawler.demonstrateScenarios();
    } catch (InterruptedException e) {
      Thread.currentThread().interrupt();
      log("Crawling interrupted");
    }
  }
}
```

Now let's see what's going on in the preceding code:

❶ Defines a list of API endpoints to crawl. In a real system, this might be thousands of URLs from a web crawler queue or API discovery service.

❷ Configures the adaptive joiner with failure tolerance settings. A 30% max failure rate with five minimum samples provides a good balance between responsiveness and stability.

❸ Forks concurrent HTTP requests for each URL. All requests execute in parallel using virtual threads, maximizing throughput while the system is healthy.

❹ Blocks until completion or circuit breaker activation. The adaptive joiner will return early if too many failures occur, saving time and resources.

❺ Simulates realistic network conditions with variable latency. Real HTTP requests have unpredictable response times due to network conditions and server load.

❻ Models system degradation where failures compound over time. This simulates real-world scenarios like cascading failures, memory leaks, or infrastructure problems that worsen under load.

Now, if we run this and get the output, it will be as follows:

```
01:55:50.225 main         : === SCENARIO 1: Normal Operation ===
01:55:50.226 main         : Starting web crawl with circuit breaker protection
01:55:50.226 main         : Max failure rate: 30%, Min sample size: 5
01:55:50.269 VThread[#42]: Fetching: https://api.service4.com/data
01:55:50.270 VThread[#45]: Fetching: https://api.service5.com/data
```

```
... [3 more fetch operations] ...
01:55:50.473 VThread[#39]: ✓ Successfully fetched: https://api.service3.com/data
... [3 more successful fetches] ...
01:55:50.753 main           : === FINAL RESULTS ===
01:55:50.753 main           : Successful fetches: 4, Failed fetches: 1

01:55:51.759 main           : === SCENARIO 2: System Under Stress ===
... [initialization and fetch operations] ...
01:55:52.182 main           : Successful fetches: 3, Failed fetches: 2

01:55:53.188 main           : === SCENARIO 3: Cascading Failures ===
... [initialization and fetch operations] ...
01:55:53.653 main           : Successful fetches: 0, Failed fetches: 5
=== FINAL RESULTS ===
01:55:53.653 main           : Successful fetches: 0
01:55:53.653 main           : Failed fetches: 5
01:55:53.653 main           : Total processed: 5
01:55:53.653 main           : Remaining URLs (not processed): 0
```

Rate-limited joiner

Sometimes we need to control the rate at which subtasks are executed to avoid overwhelming external services. Let's create a joiner that implements rate limiting using Semaphore:

```
import module java.base;

public class RateLimitedJoiner<T>
    implements StructuredTaskScope.Joiner<T, List<T>> {
  private final Semaphore semaphore;                                       ❶
  private final Queue<T> results = new ConcurrentLinkedQueue<>();
  private final Queue<Throwable> failures = new ConcurrentLinkedQueue<>();

  public RateLimitedJoiner(int maxConcurrentTasks) {
    this.semaphore = new Semaphore(maxConcurrentTasks);                    ❷
  }

  @Override
  public boolean onFork(StructuredTaskScope.Subtask<? extends T> subtask) {
    try {
      semaphore.acquire();                                                 ❸
    } catch (InterruptedException e) {
      Thread.currentThread().interrupt();
    }
    return false;                                                          ❹
  }

  @Override
  public boolean onComplete(StructuredTaskScope.Subtask<? extends T> subtask) {
    switch (subtask.state()) {
      case SUCCESS -> results.add(subtask.get());                          ❺
      case FAILED -> failures.add(subtask.exception());                    ❻
```

```
      case UNAVAILABLE -> failures.add(new RuntimeException("Task canceled"));
    }
    semaphore.release(); ❼
    return false; ❽
  }

  @Override
  public List<T> result() {
    return results.stream().toList();
  }
}
```

Let's examine how this semaphore-based rate limiting works:

❶ Uses a `Semaphore` to control the number of concurrent executions allowed.

❷ Creates the `Semaphore` with the maximum number of concurrent tasks allowed.

❸ Acquires a permit before the task starts execution. If no permits are available, this call blocks until one becomes available, effectively controlling the rate of task execution.

❹ Returns `false` to allow the subtask to be created and start execution (now that we have a permit).

❺ Collects successful results when tasks are completed successfully.

❻ Collects failures to maintain visibility into what went wrong.

❼ Always releases the semaphore permit when a task completes, regardless of success or failure, making it available for other waiting tasks.

❽ Allows all tasks to complete rather than stopping early.

Let's demonstrate the rate-limited joiner with a batch API-calling scenario:

```
import module java.base;
import static ca.bazlur.mcj.chap4.Utils.log;
import static java.util.concurrent.StructuredTaskScope.open;

public class RateLimitedAPIService {
  public List<String> fetchDataWithRateLimit() throws InterruptedException {
    var endpoints = List.of(
        "api/users", "api/orders", "api/products",
        "api/analytics", "api/reports", "api/logs"
    );
    // Allow maximum 3 concurrent API calls
    var rateLimitedJoiner = new RateLimitedJoiner<String>(3);
    try (var scope = open(rateLimitedJoiner)) {
```

```java
      for (String endpoint : endpoints) {
        scope.fork(() -> callAPI(endpoint));  ❶
      }
      var results = scope.join();  ❷
      log("Completed " + results.size() +
          " API calls with rate limiting");
      return results;
    }
  }

  private String callAPI(String endpoint) throws InterruptedException {
    log("Starting API call: " + endpoint );
    Thread.sleep(Duration.ofMillis(500 + new Random().nextInt(1000)));
    log("Completed API call: " + endpoint);
    return "Response from " + endpoint;
  }

  void main() {
    var service = new RateLimitedAPIService();
    try {
      var results = service.fetchDataWithRateLimit();
      log("All results: " + results);
    } catch (InterruptedException e) {
      Thread.currentThread().interrupt();
      log("Service interrupted");
    }
  }
}
```

Let's see how it works:

❶ Each `fork()` call will acquire a semaphore permit before the task starts executing, ensuring only three tasks run concurrently.

❷ Waits for all API calls to complete, with the semaphore automatically managing the concurrency.

When we run this example with six endpoints but a limit of three concurrent tasks, we'll see output as follows:

```
02:28:43.648 VThread[#38]: Starting API call: api/products
02:28:43.648 VThread[#36]: Starting API call: api/orders
02:28:43.648 VThread[#34]: Starting API call: api/users
02:28:44.266 VThread[#34]: Completed API call: api/users
02:28:44.268 VThread[#44]: Starting API call: api/analytics
02:28:44.499 VThread[#38]: Completed API call: api/products
02:28:44.501 VThread[#46]: Starting API call: api/reports
02:28:45.021 VThread[#36]: Completed API call: api/orders
02:28:45.022 VThread[#47]: Starting API call: api/logs
02:28:45.381 VThread[#44]: Completed API call: api/analytics
02:28:45.849 VThread[#47]: Completed API call: api/logs
02:28:45.974 VThread[#46]: Completed API call: api/reports
```

```
02:28:45.975 main         : Completed 6 API calls with rate limiting
02:28:45.975 main         : All results: [Response from api/users, Response from
api/products, Response from api/orders, Response from api/analytics, Response
from api/logs, Response from api/reports]
```

Conditional joiners

The onFork method can also be used to implement conditional execution based on runtime state. For example, a generic joiner that accepts any condition for deciding when to stop new tasks.

Let's implement this idea:

```
import module java.base;

public class ConditionalJoiner<T>
    implements StructuredTaskScope.Joiner<T, List<T>> {
  private final Supplier<Boolean> shouldContinue;  ❶
  private final Queue<T> results = new ConcurrentLinkedQueue<>();
  private final Queue<Throwable> failures = new ConcurrentLinkedQueue<>();

  public ConditionalJoiner(Supplier<Boolean> shouldContinue) {
    this.shouldContinue = shouldContinue;  ❷
  }

  @Override
  public boolean onFork(StructuredTaskScope.Subtask<? extends T> subtask) {
    if (!shouldContinue.get()) {  ❸
      System.out.println("Condition failed, stopping new tasks");
      return true;   // Cancel scope to prevent new work  ❹
    }
    return false;    // Condition satisfied, allow task  ❺
  }

  @Override
  public boolean onComplete(StructuredTaskScope.Subtask<? extends T> subtask) {
    switch (subtask.state()) {
      case SUCCESS -> results.add(subtask.get());  ❻
      case FAILED -> failures.add(subtask.exception());  ❼
      case UNAVAILABLE -> failures.add(new RuntimeException("Task canceled"));
    }
    return false;  // Continue processing existing tasks  ❽
  }

  @Override
  public List<T> result() {
    return results.stream().toList();
  }

  public List<Throwable> getFailures() {
    return failures.stream().toList();
```

```
    }
}
```

Let's examine how this joiner handles different subtask outcomes:

❶ Accepts any condition as a `Supplier<Boolean>` that determines whether to continue processing

❷ Stores the condition supplier for evaluation during task forking

❸ Checks the condition each time a new task wants to start

❹ If condition fails, stop the scope to prevent new tasks from starting

❺ When condition passes, allow tasks to proceed normally

❻ Collects successful results as usual

❼ Keeps track of failures for analysis

❽ Allows already-running tasks to complete

Now let's apply this to a simple example:

```
package ca.bazlur.modern.concurrency.c04;


import java.time.Duration;
import java.util.List;
import java.util.Random;
import java.util.concurrent.StructuredTaskScope;
import java.util.concurrent.atomic.AtomicInteger;

import static java.util.concurrent.StructuredTaskScope.open;

public class SystemHealthCheckDemo {

  void main() throws InterruptedException {
    var results = new SystemHealthCheckDemo()
        .processWithSystemHealthCheck();
    results.forEach(System.out::println);
  }

  public List<String> processWithSystemHealthCheck()
      throws InterruptedException {
    var healthChecker = new SystemHealthChecker();
    var joiner = new ConditionalJoiner<String>(healthChecker::isSystemHealthy);

    try (var scope = open(joiner)) {
      for (int i = 0; i < 10; i++) {
```

```
            int id = i;
            scope.fork(() -> processTask("health-task-" + id));
        }
        return scope.join();
    }
}

private String processTask(String taskName)
    throws InterruptedException {
  Thread.sleep(Duration.ofMillis(200
      + new Random().nextInt(300)));

  if (taskName.contains("error-task")
      && new Random().nextDouble() < 0.4)
    throw new RuntimeException("Task failed: " + taskName);

  return "Completed: " + taskName;
  }
}
```

In the preceding code, we check an external system's health and stop if dependencies become unavailable.

The simple `SystemHealthChecker` class looks as follows:

```
private static class SystemHealthChecker {
    private final AtomicInteger checkCount
        = new AtomicInteger(0);

    public boolean isSystemHealthy() {
      checkCount.incrementAndGet();
      try {
        Thread.sleep(100);
      } catch (InterruptedException e) {
        throw new RuntimeException(e);
      }
      return checkCount.get() < 7;
    }
}
```

Custom joiners represent one of the most powerful aspects of structured concurrency in Java. They transform `StructuredTaskScope` from a simple parallel execution tool into a sophisticated coordination platform that can adapt to virtually any concurrent programming challenge.

The beauty of the joiner pattern lies in its simplicity and flexibility. With just three methods, `onFork`, `onComplete`, and `result`, we can implement arbitrarily complex coordination logic while maintaining the safety guarantees and clean structure that make structured concurrency so powerful.

The examples we've explored are just the beginning. The real power emerges when you start designing joiners that capture the unique coordination patterns in your own domain, creating reusable components that make concurrent programming not just safer, but genuinely elegant.

Memory Consistency Effects

StructuredTaskScope provides well-defined memory consistency guarantees that make it easier to reason about the visibility of shared data across threads.

Actions in the owner thread of a StructuredTaskScope prior to the forking of a subtask happen before any actions taken by that subtask, which in turn happen before (*https://oreil.ly/QRQkV*) the subtask result is retrieved. This *happens-before* relationship ensures that any data modifications made in the owner thread before calling fork() are visible to the subtask, and any changes made by the subtask are visible when retrieving its result.

> ### Memory Consistency Properties
>
> StructuredTaskScope's memory consistency guarantees rest on Java's fundamental happens-before relationships, as defined in the Java Language Specification (Chapter 17) (*https://oreil.ly/TUOvw*). These rules ensure that memory operations across threads occur in a predictable, safe manner.
>
> Java provides several built-in happens-before relationships that make concurrent programming safe:
>
> - Actions within a single thread execute in program order.
> - Synchronized blocks create ordering between threads through monitor operations.
> - Volatile variables provide visibility guarantees without locking.
> - Thread creation and joining establish clear memory boundaries.
>
> The java.util.concurrent package builds upon these foundation rules to provide higher-level guarantees. Operations like submitting tasks to executors, placing items in concurrent collections, and retrieving Future results all establish happens-before relationships that ensure thread safety.

Let's see this guarantee in action with a realistic example. Let's imagine we are building a configuration service that needs to validate settings across multiple systems simultaneously:

```
import module java.base;
import java.util.concurrent.ConcurrentHashMap;
import java.util.concurrent.atomic.AtomicInteger;
import static ca.bazlur.mcj.chap4.Utils.log;
```

```java
import static java.util.concurrent.StructuredTaskScope.open;

public class MemoryConsistencyDemo {
  private String configuration = "default";
  private final Map<String, String> cache = new ConcurrentHashMap<>();

  public void demonstrateMemoryConsistency() throws InterruptedException {
    // Owner thread sets up a shared state before forking
    configuration = "production-config"; ❶
    cache.put("database-url", "prod.example.com"); ❶
    cache.put("api-key", "secret-key-123"); ❶
    log("Owner thread prepared: " + configuration);
    try (var scope = open(StructuredTaskScope.Joiner.
        <String>allSuccessfulOrThrow())) {
      // Fork subtasks that read owner thread's data
      var configTask = scope.fork(() -> { ❷
        log("Subtask sees: " + configuration); ❸
        return "Config: " + configuration;
      });
      var cacheTask = scope.fork(() -> { ❷
        String url = cache.get("database-url"); ❸
        log("Subtask found URL: " + url);
        return "Connected to: " + url;
      });
      var results = scope.join() ❹
          .map(StructuredTaskScope.Subtask::get)
          .toList();
      log("Owner received: " + results); ❺
    }
  }
}
```

Let's trace through what happens:

❶ Before creating any subtasks, the owner thread prepares the shared state. It updates the configuration string and populates the cache with essential connection details.

❷ When we call fork(), something important happens under the hood. The structured concurrency framework establishes a happens-before relationship, ensuring that all the preparations we made in steps 1, 2, and 3 become visible to the subtasks.

❸ Here's where the magic happens. Without any additional synchronization on our part, both subtasks can reliably see the updated configuration and cache contents. The configuration variable shows production-config (not default), and the cache contains all the entries we added.

❹ The `join()` operation creates another happens-before edge, this time from the subtasks back to the owner thread.

❺ The owner thread now sees all the results from the subtasks, guaranteed to be up to date and consistent.

The happens-before guarantee works in both directions. When subtasks modify shared state, those changes become visible to the owner thread after the join operation completes.

Let's examine another snippet:

```
public void demonstrateSubtaskUpdates() throws InterruptedException {
  var results = new ConcurrentHashMap<String, String>(); ❶
  var counter = new AtomicInteger(0); ❶
  log("Initial count: " + counter.get());

  try (var scope = open(StructuredTaskScope.Joiner.
    <String>allSuccessfulOrThrow())) {
    var worker1 = scope.fork(() -> { ❷
      results.put("task1", "completed"); ❸
      int count = counter.incrementAndGet(); ❹
      log("Worker1 incremented to: " + count);
      return "Worker1 done";
    });
    var worker2 = scope.fork(() -> { ❷
      results.put("task2", "completed"); ❸
      int count = counter.incrementAndGet(); ❹
      log("Worker2 incremented to: " + count);
      return "Worker2 done";
    });
    scope.join(); ❺
    // Owner thread sees all subtask updates
    log("Final count: " + counter.get()); ❻
    log("Final results: " + results); ❻
  }
}
```

This example shows how multiple subtasks can safely update shared state:

❶ We start by creating thread-safe containers, a `ConcurrentHashMap` for collecting results and an `AtomicInteger` for counting operations.

❷ We launch two workers that will run simultaneously. They might execute in any order, but both will safely update our shared containers.

❸ Each worker adds an entry to the results map. Because we're using `Concurrent HashMap`, these operations are thread-safe even when happening concurrently.

❹ The atomic counter ensures that increments from different threads don't interfere with each other, preventing the classic "lost update" problem.

❺ The join() operation ensures that all worker modifications are visible to the owner thread.

❻ After the join completes, the owner thread sees the final state of both the counter and the results map, with all updates from both workers properly reflected.

As we can see, StructuredTaskScope leverages these proven mechanisms to provide its guarantees. When we fork a subtask, it's similar to starting a thread, creating a happens-before edge that makes all prior owner thread actions visible to the subtask. When we join, it's like calling Thread.join(), establishing a happens-before relationship that makes all subtask actions visible to the owner thread.

The concurrent collections from java.util.concurrent extend these guarantees further, ensuring that operations like putting items into a ConcurrentHashMap or incrementing an AtomicInteger are safely visible across threads.

This automatic memory consistency is one of the key advantages of structured concurrency. We can focus on the business logic of our concurrent operations, confident that the memory consistency details are handled correctly. The fork and join operations provide clear synchronization points where we know all necessary memory barriers are in place. However, this doesn't mean we can ignore thread safety entirely. We still need to use appropriate concurrent collections and atomic operations when multiple subtasks modify shared state.

Nested Scopes

We've explored how to create custom joiners and manage concurrent tasks within a single scope, but the power of structured concurrency extends further. Just as we can nest code blocks within methods, we can nest StructuredTaskScope instances to create sophisticated, multilevel hierarchies of concurrent tasks.

Nested scopes are invaluable for managing complex workflows where tasks naturally break down into multiple levels of subtasks. Each nested scope is self-contained, encapsulating its subtasks' lifecycle and error handling.

When a subtask creates its own nested StructuredTaskScope, a parent-child relationship is established, forming a tree structure. The parent scope becomes responsible for the child scope's lifecycle, including shutdown and completion of its subtasks.

This hierarchical structure (Figure 4-3) propagates errors and cancellations upward. If a subtask in a nested scope fails, the error is first handled by its immediate parent scope, then propagated up the chain until it's handled or reaches the top-level scope.

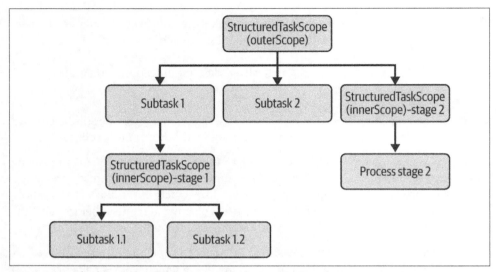

Figure 4-3. The hierarchical structure of tasks in structured concurrency

Let's examine a document processor that gathers content from multiple sources and then performs analysis:

```
public class DocumentProcessor {

    public DocumentReport processDocument(String documentId)
                        throws InterruptedException {

        try (var gatheringScope = open(StructuredTaskScope.Joiner.
                <String>allSuccessfulOrThrow())) { ❶
            var headerTask = gatheringScope.fork(() ->
                            fetchHeader(documentId)); ❷
            var bodyTask = gatheringScope.fork(() -> fetchBody(documentId)); ❷
            var metadataTask = gatheringScope.fork(() ->
fetchMetadata(documentId)); ❷

            gatheringScope.join(); ❸

            return analyzeContent(headerTask.get(),
bodyTask.get(),
metadataTask.get()); ❹
        } catch (StructuredTaskScope.FailedException e) {
            throw new RuntimeException("Failed to gather document content", e);
        }
    }
}
```

In the preceding code, what really happens is:

❶ Creates the top-level scope to gather all document components concurrently

❷ Launches concurrent tasks to fetch header, body, and metadata from different sources

❸ Waits for all content gathering to complete before proceeding to analysis

❹ Moves to the analysis phase with all required content available

Now let's examine the nested analysis scope:

```
private DocumentReport analyzeContent(String header,
                                      String body,
                                      String metadata)
    throws InterruptedException {

  try (var analysisScope = open(StructuredTaskScope.Joiner.
      allSuccessfulOrThrow()))  { ❶
    var wordCountTask = analysisScope.fork(() ->
        countWords(body)); ❷
    var sentimentTask = analysisScope.fork(() ->
        analyzeSentiment(body)); ❷
    var summaryTask = analysisScope.fork(() ->
        generateSummary(header, body, metadata)); ❷
    analysisScope.join(); ❸
    return new DocumentReport(
        wordCountTask.get(),
        sentimentTask.get(),
        summaryTask.get()
    );
  } catch (StructuredTaskScope.FailedException e) {
    throw new RuntimeException("Failed to analyze document content", e);
  }
}
```

In the preceding code snippets, we have:

❶ Creates a second-level scope specifically for performing analysis on the gathered content

❷ Launches concurrent analysis tasks for word counting, sentiment analysis, and summary generation

❸ Waits for all analysis to complete and constructs the final report

This creates a clean two-level hierarchy:

```
Document Processing (Level 1)
├── Header Fetching (Level 2)
├── Body Fetching (Level 2)
├── Metadata Fetching (Level 2)
└── Content Analysis (Level 2)
```

```
├── Word Counting (Level 3)
├── Sentiment Analysis (Level 3)
└── Summary Generation (Level 3)
```

Here are the supporting methods that complete our example:

```java
private String fetchHeader(String documentId)
    throws InterruptedException {
  Thread.sleep(Duration.ofMillis(100));
  return "Header for document " + documentId;
}

private String fetchBody(String documentId)
    throws InterruptedException {
  Thread.sleep(Duration.ofMillis(200));
  return "This is the main content of document " + documentId +
      " with multiple sentences and important information.";
}

private String fetchMetadata(String documentId)
    throws InterruptedException {
  Thread.sleep(Duration.ofMillis(150));
  return "Created: 2024-01-01, Author: John Doe";
}

private Integer countWords(String content)
    throws InterruptedException {
  Thread.sleep(Duration.ofMillis(100));
  return content.split("\\s+").length;
}

private String analyzeSentiment(String content)
    throws InterruptedException {
  Thread.sleep(Duration.ofMillis(200));
  return content.toLowerCase().contains("important") ? "Positive" : "Neutral";
}

private String generateSummary(String header, String body, String metadata)
    throws InterruptedException {
  Thread.sleep(Duration.ofMillis(150));
  return header + ": " + body.substring(0, Math.min(50, body.length())) + "...";
}

public record DocumentReport(int wordCount,
                             String sentiment, String summary) {
  @Override
  public String toString() {
    return String.format("Document Report:\n  Words: %d\n  " +
            "Sentiment: %s\n  Summary: %s",
        wordCount, sentiment, summary);
  }
}
```

Now let's use the following main method and run the above code:

```
void main() {
  var processor = new DocumentProcessor();
  try {
    var report = processor.processDocument("DOC-123");
    System.out.println(report);
  } catch (InterruptedException e) {
    Thread.currentThread().interrupt();
    System.out.println("Processing interrupted");
  }
}
```

When we run this, we will see output like:

```
Document Report:
  Words: 14
  Sentiment: Positive
  Summary: Header for document DOC-123: This is the main content of document DOC-
  123 with ...
```

This nested approach demonstrates structured concurrency's elegance. Each scope manages its own lifecycle and resources, creating a clean hierarchy where failures propagate naturally, resources are automatically cleaned up, and cancellation cascades properly from parent to child scopes.

Observability

As we have learned, structured concurrency provides an inherent structure that imposes a clear hierarchical relationship between tasks and their subtasks. This hierarchy mirrors the nested structure of the code, making it much easier to understand and reason about the flow of concurrent execution.

This treelike structure becomes extremely useful for debugging. Traditional thread dumps often present a chaotic jumble of threads with no clear relationships. In contrast, structured thread dumps provide a hierarchical view of our concurrent system, making it easier to identify issues.

We can generate structured thread dumps in JSON format using the `jcmd` tool:

```
jcmd <pid> Thread.dump_to_file -format=json <output_file>
```

These dumps reveal valuable information, including task hierarchy and subtask states.

Let's look at an example using our document processor:

```
import module java.base;
import static java.util.concurrent.StructuredTaskScope.open;

public class DocumentProcessor {
  private final ThreadFactory threadFactory = Thread.ofVirtual()
```

```
            .name("doc-proc", 1)
            .factory();


    public DocumentReport processDocument(String documentId)
            throws InterruptedException {
        try (var gatheringScope = open(
            StructuredTaskScope.Joiner.<String>allSuccessfulOrThrow(),
                conf -> conf.withThreadFactory(threadFactory)
                            .withName("doc-gathering-scope"))) { ❶

            var headerTask = gatheringScope.fork(() ->
                fetchHeader(documentId)); ❷
            var bodyTask = gatheringScope.fork(() ->
                fetchBody(documentId)); ❷
            var metadataTask = gatheringScope.fork(() ->
                fetchMetadata(documentId)); ❷

            gatheringScope.join(); ❸

            return analyzeContent(headerTask.get(),
                    bodyTask.get(), metadataTask.get());
        } catch (StructuredTaskScope.FailedException e) {
            throw new RuntimeException("Failed to gather document content", e);
        }
    }

    private String fetchHeader(String documentId) throws InterruptedException {
      Thread.sleep(Duration.ofSeconds(10)); ❹
      return "Header for document " + documentId;
    }

    private String fetchBody(String documentId) throws InterruptedException {
      Thread.sleep(Duration.ofSeconds(10));
      return "This is the main content of document " + documentId;
    }

    private String fetchMetadata(String documentId) throws InterruptedException {
      Thread.sleep(Duration.ofSeconds(10));
      return "Created: 2024-01-01, Author: John Doe";
    }
}
```

We have slightly changed our program to demonstrate the thread dump:

❶ We give the scope a descriptive name and use a custom `ThreadFactory` with named threads to make identification easier in thread dumps.

❷ Launches parallel tasks for fetching different parts of the document.

❸ Waits for all gathering operations to complete.

❹ We simulate slow operations that would show up clearly in a thread dump.

If we run this code and generate a thread dump while the operations are in progress, we get a beautifully structured view:

```
{
  "threadDump": {
    "processId": "10259",
    "time": "2025-06-10T00:49:22.146091Z",
    "runtimeVersion": "25-ea+25-3096",
    "threadContainers": [
      {
        "container": "<root>",
        "parent": null,
        "owner": null,
        "threads": [
          {
            "tid": "3",
            "name": "main",
            "stack": [
              "java.base/jdk.internal.misc.Unsafe.park(Native Method)",
              "java.base/java.util.concurrent.locks.LockSupport.park(LockSupport.java:369)",
              "java.base/jdk.internal.misc.ThreadFlock.awaitAll(ThreadFlock.java:305)",
              "java.base/java.util.concurrent.StructuredTaskScopeImpl.join(StructuredTaskScopeImpl.java:243)",
              "ca.bazlur.mcj.chap4.DocumentProcessor.processDocument(DocumentProcessor.java:23)"
            ]
          }
        ],
        "threadCount": "8"
      },
      {
        "container": "doc-gathering-scope/jdk.internal.misc.ThreadFlock$ThreadContainerImpl@78fd3572",
        "parent": "<root>",
        "owner": "3",
        "threads": [
          {
            "tid": "36",
            "name": "doc-proc2",
            "stack": [
              "java.base/java.lang.Thread.sleep(Thread.java:574)",
              "ca.bazlur.mcj.chap4.DocumentProcessor.fetchBody(DocumentProcessor.java:69)",
              "ca.bazlur.mcj.chap4.DocumentProcessor.lambda$processDocument$2(DocumentProcessor.java:20)"
            ]
          },
          {
```

```
          "tid": "38",
          "name": "doc-proc3",
          "stack": [
            "java.base/java.lang.Thread.sleep(Thread.java:574)",
            "ca.bazlur.mcj.chap4.DocumentProcessor.fetchMetadata(DocumentProces
            sor.java:76)",
            "ca.bazlur.mcj.chap4.DocumentProcessor.lambda$processDocument$3(Doc
            umentProcessor.java:21)"
          ]
        },
        {
          "tid": "26",
          "name": "doc-proc1",
          "stack": [
            "java.base/java.lang.Thread.sleep(Thread.java:574)",
            "ca.bazlur.mcj.chap4.DocumentProcessor.fetchHeader(DocumentProcesso
            r.java:63)",
            "ca.bazlur.mcj.chap4.DocumentProcessor.lambda$processDocument$1(Doc
            umentProcessor.java:19)"
          ]
        }
      ],
      "threadCount": "3"
    }
  ]
}
}
```

The thread dump reveals several key insights:

- We can clearly see our named scope `doc-gathering-scope` as a separate container with its parent being `<root>` and owner being thread 3 (the main thread).

- All three subtasks (`doc-proc1`, `doc-proc2`, `doc-proc3`) are clearly grouped under our document-gathering scope, making it easy to understand which threads belong to which logical operation.

- Each thread's stack trace shows exactly what operation it's performing—`fetchHeader`, `fetchBody`, and `fetchMetadata`—making debugging straightforward.

- The `owner: 3` field shows that the main thread (`tid 3`) owns this scope, establishing the clear parent-child relationship.

Tools can now analyze these structured thread dumps to reveal even more insights. For example, the simple tool Threadly (*https://oreil.ly/oTZEH*) can parse the JSON thread dump and visualize the tree structure of structured concurrency, making it even easier to understand the hierarchical relationships and debug complex concurrent applications.

While the `jcmd` tool offers a convenient way to generate structured thread dumps, there might be situations where we need more control or want to automate the process. The `HotSpotDiagnosticMXBean` comes in handy here. We can use it to trigger thread dumps programmatically whenever a specific condition arises, such as an exception within a `StructuredTaskScope`.

Here's an example of how we might use it:

```
public void processWithErrorHandling(String documentId) {
  try (var scope = open(StructuredTaskScope.Joiner.
        <String>allSuccessfulOrThrow(),
      cf -> cf.withName("error-prone-scope"))) {
    scope.fork(() -> {
      if (new Random().nextBoolean()) { ❶
        throw new RuntimeException("Simulated failure");
      }
      return fetchHeader(documentId);
    });
    scope.join();
  } catch (StructuredTaskScope.FailedException e) {
    HotSpotDiagnosticMXBean bean = ManagementFactory
        .getPlatformMXBean(HotSpotDiagnosticMXBean.class); ❷
    try {
      Path path = Path.of("./structured-concurrency-error.json");
      bean.dumpThreads(path.toAbsolutePath().toString(),
          HotSpotDiagnosticMXBean.ThreadDumpFormat.JSON); ❸
      System.out.println("Thread dump captured: " + path);
    } catch (IOException ex) {
      throw new RuntimeException("Failed to generate thread dump", ex);
    }
    throw new RuntimeException("Processing failed", e);
  } catch (InterruptedException e) {
    Thread.currentThread().interrupt();
    throw new RuntimeException("Processing interrupted", e);
  }
}
```

We have done a few things in this code:

❶ We randomly introduce failures to trigger the error handling and thread dump generation.

❷ We obtain a reference to the `HotSpotDiagnosticMXBean` for programmatic thread dump generation.

❸ When an error occurs, we automatically generate a JSON thread dump for later analysis.

So we can conclude that structured concurrency not only simplifies concurrent programming but also enhances debugging and maintenance, providing a clearer view of task execution and relationships.

In Closing

Structured concurrency represents a significant advancement in concurrent programming for Java. By embracing the principle of tying subtask lifecycles to their parent tasks, we've unlocked a new level of reliability, maintainability, and observability in our concurrent applications.

Throughout this chapter, we've seen how structured concurrency addresses fundamental challenges in concurrent programming. Clear resource management ensures automatic cleanup of subtasks, preventing the resource leaks and zombie threads that plagued traditional concurrent code. Hierarchical error handling allows failures to propagate naturally through the task hierarchy, making error handling predictable and comprehensive. Enhanced debugging capabilities provide structured thread dumps with clear visibility into task relationships, transforming debugging from guesswork into systematic analysis. Custom joiners enable sophisticated coordination strategies while maintaining the safety guarantees of structured concurrency. Perhaps most importantly, the nested structure mirrors business logic, making concurrent code as readable and maintainable as sequential code.

A common question that arises is whether structured concurrency can be used with both virtual and platform threads. The answer is yes, structured concurrency is compatible with both, offering flexibility to developers. We can easily configure `StructuredTaskScope` with platform threads by providing a custom `ThreadFactory`:

```java
public void demonstratePlatformThreads() throws InterruptedException {
    ThreadFactory platformFactory = Thread.ofPlatform()
        .name("platform-worker-", 0)
        .factory();

    try (var scope = open(Joiner.allSuccessfulOrThrow(),
                    cf -> cf.withThreadFactory(platformFactory))) {

        scope.fork(() -> performTask("Task 1"));
        scope.fork(() -> performTask("Task 2"));

        scope.join();
    }
}
```

However, this brings us back to the original problem: the scarcity of platform threads. We must be mindful of the potential scalability and resource constraints associated with platform threads in high-concurrency scenarios. Virtual threads remain the preferred choice for most structured concurrency applications, offering the scalability benefits that make this programming model truly powerful.

Whether you're managing incoming server requests, coordinating microservice calls, or dealing with complex multistage workflows, structured concurrency provides a powerful and intuitive framework for navigating the complexities of concurrent programming. By adopting this paradigm, you can write code that is not only more efficient and robust but also easier to understand and ultimately more enjoyable to work with.

CHAPTER 5
Scoped Values

He who does not place things in their proper place has committed injustice.
—Ali ibn Abi Talib (may God be pleased with him)

In this chapter, we will explore `ScopedValue`, a powerful addition to Java that was finalized in JDK 25. It provides a structured way to bind values to a specific scope while remaining accessible and consistent with the context. Unlike traditional `Thread Local` variables, which can be cumbersome and prone to memory leaks, this offers a cleaner and more efficient approach when dealing with multithreaded applications. In this chapter, we will examine why `ScopedValue` is a better replacement for `Thread Local` and its API and then walk through practical use cases.

Let's begin.

The Burden of Passing Context

There are often scenarios in which we need to share data among various parts of the code where simply using method arguments isn't feasible. This is especially common when our application depends on a framework. To illustrate the idea, let's consider an example.

Imagine a job-scheduling framework in which user code registers tasks that the framework will execute. Whenever the framework runs a job, it creates a `JobContext` object containing metadata such as the job's name, priority, and scheduling constraints. This context is essential for framework operations but is largely irrelevant to user code.

The following example demonstrates a typical job-scheduling framework that suffers from what we call the "parameter passing problem":

```java
import java.time.Instant;
import java.util.HashMap;
import java.util.Map;

interface Job {
    void execute(JobContext context);
}

enum Priority { LOW, MEDIUM, HIGH }

public record JobContext(String jobName, Priority priority,
                         Map<String, Object> metadata) {
    public JobContext(String jobName, Priority priority) {
        this(jobName, priority, new HashMap<>());
        metadata.put("jobName", jobName);
        metadata.put("priority", priority);
        metadata.put("creationTime", Instant.now());
    }

    public Object getMetadataValue(String key) {
        return metadata.get(key);
    }
}
```

The framework's core scheduling logic creates and manages the job context:

```java
// Framework code
public class JobScheduler {
    public void schedule(Job job, String jobName, Priority priority) { ❶
        JobContext context = new JobContext(jobName, priority);
        runJob(job, context);
    }

    private void runJob(Job job, JobContext context) { ❷
        // The framework calls user code here, passing the context
        job.execute(context);
    }

    public Object getJobMetadata(String key, JobContext context) { ❸
        if (context == null) {
            return null;
        }
        return context.getMetadataValue(key);
    }
}
```

To use this framework, we must implement the Job interface and work with the framework's context object:

```java
public class UserJob implements Job {
    private final JobScheduler jobScheduler;

    public UserJob(JobScheduler jobScheduler) {
```

```
            this.jobScheduler = jobScheduler;
    }

    @Override
    public void execute(JobContext context) { ❹
        System.out.println("User job is running!");

        // User code calls back into the framework to retrieve metadata
        Object creationTime
            = jobScheduler.getJobMetadata("creationTime", context); ❺
        System.out.println("Job creation time: " + creationTime);

        // Any helper methods also need the context parameter
        processJobData(context); ❻
    }

    private void processJobData(JobContext context) { ❼
        // Even though this method might not directly use context,
        // it needs the parameter to pass to other framework methods
        Object priority = jobScheduler.getJobMetadata("priority", context);
        System.out.println("Processing job with priority: " + priority);
    }
}
```

❶ The framework creates a `JobContext` containing metadata needed throughout the job's lifecycle.

❷ The `context` must be passed down to user code, even though users shouldn't need to understand framework internals.

❸ Framework methods require the `context` parameter to access metadata, forcing it back up the call chain.

❹ User implementations must accept the `JobContext` parameter in their `execute()` method.

❺ When user code needs framework services, it must pass the `context` back to the framework.

❻ Helper methods in user code become contaminated with framework parameters.

❼ Every method in the user's call chain needs the `context` parameter, even if it doesn't directly use it.

While this approach functions correctly, it introduces several architectural problems that become more pronounced as applications scale.

Parameter Pollution

The `JobContext` is primarily a framework construct that developers using the framework shouldn't need to understand. However, because the framework must manage its internal context across the call chain, from `schedule()` down into user code in `execute()`, and then back into the framework inside `getJobMetadata()`, user code is forced to carry around `JobContext` parameters.

Every method that participates in the job execution flow must declare this parameter, even if the method itself doesn't use any context information. This pollutes method signatures with framework-specific details that have no business meaning to the application logic.

Interface Brittleness

Consider what happens when the framework evolves. If you later expand `JobContext` with additional data, say, a new `job category` field, a distributed tracing context, or a logging reference, you might need to modify every method signature in user code that passes context around. While the `JobContext` class itself maintains backward compatibility, the requirement to thread it through user code means that any expansion of the framework's needs ripples through the entire user codebase.

Coupling and Testability

User code becomes tightly coupled to framework implementation details. Testing individual methods becomes more complex because you must always provide a valid `JobContext`, even for tests that focus on business logic unrelated to the framework.

This coupling also makes it more difficult to migrate between different frameworks or to extract business logic for reuse in various contexts.

Introducing ThreadLocal

To circumvent this problem, the framework code can be designed intelligently using `ThreadLocal`, a tool commonly used in such code.

Let's reimplement the preceding code using `ThreadLocal`:

```
public class JobScheduler {
    private static final ThreadLocal<JobContext> jobContextHolder =
        new ThreadLocal<>(); ❶

    public void schedule(Job job, String jobName, Priority priority) {
        JobContext context = new JobContext(jobName, priority);
        try {
            jobContextHolder.set(context); ❷
            runJob(job);
```

```
        } finally {
            jobContextHolder.remove();  ❸
        }
    }

    private void runJob(Job job) {  ❹
        job.execute();
    }

    public Object getJobMetadata(String key) {
        JobContext context = jobContextHolder.get();  ❺
        return (context != null) ? context.getMetadataValue(key) : null;
    }
}
```

❶ Creates a ThreadLocal variable to hold the JobContext for each thread.

❷ Sets the context in the current thread before executing the job.

❸ Always remove the context in a finally block to prevent memory leaks.

❹ The runJob method no longer needs context parameters.

❺ Framework methods can retrieve context from ThreadLocal whenever needed.

Now the user code becomes much cleaner, with no need to handle framework context:

```
public class UserJob implements Job {
    private final JobScheduler jobScheduler;

    public UserJob(JobScheduler jobScheduler) {
        this.jobScheduler = jobScheduler;
    }

    @Override
    public void execute() {  ❶
        System.out.println("User job is running!");
        // No context parameter needed - framework handles it internally
        Object creationTime = jobScheduler.getJobMetadata("creationTime");  ❷
        System.out.println("Job creation time: " + creationTime);
        // Helper methods are now clean
        processJobData();
    }

    private void processJobData() {  ❸
        // Clean method signature - no framework parameters
        Object priority = jobScheduler.getJobMetadata("priority");
        System.out.println("Processing job with priority: " + priority);
```

        }
    }

❶ User code is completely freed from framework context concerns.

❷ Framework services are accessible without any context parameters.

❸ Helper methods have clean signatures focused on business logic.

This approach solves the parameter-passing problem effectively. User code no longer needs framework-specific parameters; we can now focus on our own business logic. The framework's internal context management is now completely hidden from user code.

This pattern is so effective that virtually all modern frameworks use some form of `ThreadLocal` for context management. Spring Framework, for example, uses `ThreadLocal` extensively for security contexts, transaction contexts, and request contexts.

Limitations of ThreadLocal Variables

Although having `ThreadLocal` in code seems intelligent and useful, `ThreadLocal` variables have many inherent design flaws. Let's discuss them.

First, `ThreadLocal` offers unconstrained mutability. Any code that can call the `get()` method of a `ThreadLocal` variable can also call `set()`, allowing data to change at any time. This makes it difficult to track when and where data is modified.

Consider the following code:

```
public class MutableLoggingContext {
  // A ThreadLocal holding the current log level
  private static final ThreadLocal<String> LOG_LEVEL = new ThreadLocal<>(); ❶

  public static void setLogLevel(String level) {
    LOG_LEVEL.set(level); ❷
  }

  public static String getLogLevel() {
    return LOG_LEVEL.get();
  }

  public static void log(String message) {
    System.out.println("[" + getLogLevel() + "] " + message);
  }

  public static void main(String[] args) throws InterruptedException {
    setLogLevel("INFO");
    log("Starting process..."); ❸
    Thread thread = new Thread(() -> {
      setLogLevel("DEBUG"); ❹
```

```
      log("Thread-specific debug mode enabled");
    });
    thread.start();
    Thread.sleep(100); // Give the other thread time to run
    log("Main thread still at INFO level"); ❺
  }
}
```

In this example:

❶ Any code can access this static `ThreadLocal`.

❷ The log level can be changed from anywhere in the codebase.

❸ The main thread sets its log level to `INFO`.

❹ The child thread independently sets its own log level to `DEBUG`.

❺ The main thread's log level remains `INFO` (thread-local isolation).

As you can see, setting the log level can be done anywhere, leading to confusion about where it was set.

Second, it offers an unbounded lifetime. Once a thread-local variable is set, it remains for the life of that thread unless explicitly removed. This may not be a problem in regular threads, but we now use a thread pool where the same threads are reused repeatedly. This can lead to a data leak from one task to another if `remove()` is forgotten. It can cause memory leaks or even security vulnerabilities if sensitive data persists unintentionally.

Let's examine the following example:

```
import java.util.concurrent.ExecutorService;
import java.util.concurrent.Executors;

public class ThreadLocalLeakExample {
  private static final ThreadLocal<String> currentUser = new ThreadLocal<>();

  public static void main(String[] args) throws InterruptedException {
    try (ExecutorService executor = Executors.newFixedThreadPool(1)) { ❶
      // The first task sets the current user
      executor.submit(() -> {
        currentUser.set("Alice"); ❷
        System.out.println("Task 1: currentUser = " + currentUser.get());
        // Forgot to call currentUser.remove()! ❸
      });
      Thread.sleep(100); // Ensure task 1 completes
      // The second task reuses the same thread
      executor.submit(() -> {
        System.out.println("Task 2: Leaked value = " + currentUser.get()); ❹
```

Introducing ThreadLocal | 223

```
        currentUser.set("Bob");
        System.out.println("Task 2: currentUser = " + currentUser.get());
        currentUser.remove(); //
      });
    }
  }
}
```

This example demonstrates the following:

❶ Single-thread pool ensures the same thread handles both tasks.

❷ First task sets a thread-local value.

❸ Missing cleanup allows the value to persist.

❹ Second task sees the leaked value from the first task.

This can cause memory leaks when objects remain referenced longer than intended, security vulnerabilities when sensitive data like authentication tokens or user contexts leaks between unrelated requests, and incorrect behavior when tasks operate with stale or incorrect context.

When using `InheritableThreadLocal`, child threads automatically inherit values from their parent thread. While this can be convenient, it becomes expensive when creating many child threads:

Now let's look at the next example:

```
public class InheritanceOverheadExample {
  private static final InheritableThreadLocal<byte[]> LARGE_DATA =
      new InheritableThreadLocal<>(); ❶

  public static void main(String[] args) {
    // Parent thread sets a large object
    LARGE_DATA.set(new byte[10_000_000]); // 10MB ❷
    // Create multiple child threads
    for (int i = 0; i < 100; i++) {
      new Thread(() -> {
        // Each child thread gets a reference to the parent's data ❸
        byte[] inherited = LARGE_DATA.get();
        System.out.println("Child has access to " +
            inherited.length + " bytes");
      }).start();
    }
  }
}
```

Problems with inheritance:

❶ `InheritableThreadLocal` automatically copies values to child threads.

❷ Large objects are referenced by all child threads.

❸ Even if children never modify the data, they maintain references.

This example clearly demonstrates the downside of using `InheritableThreadLocal` when large objects are stored. Even though the child threads do not explicitly set or alter the local variable, they automatically inherit their own separate copy of the parent's data, resulting in duplicate memory usage.

Now that we understand the problem with the `ThreadLocal` variable, what would be the solution?

Toward Lightweight Sharing

The limitations of `ThreadLocal` become even more apparent with the introduction of virtual threads (JEP 444 (*https://oreil.ly/nXHrR*)). Unlike traditional platform threads, where each thread has its own dedicated OS resource, virtual threads allow a single OS thread to host thousands or even millions of lightweight threads. While it's technically possible for each virtual thread to maintain its own `ThreadLocal` data, the memory overhead quickly becomes unsustainable. Imagine a million virtual threads, each carrying its own chunk of state—the cost would be staggering. Clearly, we need a better approach.

Since virtual threads are short-lived, the problem of long-lived thread locals is less dire, as garbage collection will remove them; still, the memory overhead of so many duplicates remains. Ideally, we want a new mechanism that allows us to store inheritable, per-thread data without incurring numerous copies. If the data is immutable, so much the better: one shared version can be referenced by child threads without additional duplication. We also need a bounded lifetime for this data; once the method sharing the data has wrapped up, any attached thread locals should lose their relevance. After all, they're meant to be a convenient place to hold state for the duration of a task, not a perpetual stash of memory.

That's where the new API `ScopedValue` (*https://oreil.ly/Bb5W2*) comes into the picture. Let's break it down.

Core Components of ScopedValue

A `ScopedValue` acts as an implicit method parameter, allowing data to be passed through a sequence of method calls without explicitly declaring it in each method's signature. This facilitates cleaner and more maintainable code, especially when dealing with deeply nested method calls or callback structures.

It has three main characteristics:

Immutability
  Once a `ScopedValue` is bound to a value within a specific scope, it cannot be altered, ensuring consistent and predictable behavior throughout its lifespan.

Thread-scoped binding
  Bindings are confined to the current thread, preventing unintended data sharing across threads and enhancing thread safety.

Bounded lifetime
  The binding of a `ScopedValue` is limited to the duration of a specific code block, after which it becomes unbound, aiding in resource management and reducing the risk of memory leaks.

> The `ScopedValue`, explored in this chapter, is available since JDK 25. If you are using an older JDK, you can enable it using the `--enable-preview` flag during compilation and runtime. To compile and run your code in JDK 24, for example, use the following commands:
>
> - With javac: `javac --release 24 --enable-preview Main.java`
> - With java: `java --enable-preview Main`
> - With the source code launcher: `java --enable-preview Main.java`
> - With JShell: `jshell --enable-preview`
>
> We anticipate this feature will be integrated into future JDK releases without requiring any modifications to your code.

To use a scoped value, we first declare it as a static final field. We declare `ScopedValue` the same way we declare `ThreadLocal`:

```
private static final ScopedValue<String> NAME = ScopedValue.newInstance();
```

We don't use the `new` operator to instantiate; rather, we use the factory method to instantiate because its constructors are deliberately set to private.

Then, we can bind a value to the scoped value and execute code within that scope. This is achieved using the `where()` (*https://oreil.ly/2lCFt*) and `run()` (*https://oreil.ly/x73-z*) methods:

```
ScopedValue.where(NAME, "duke").run(() -> doSomething());
```

In this example, the `where()` method associates the `NAME` scoped value with the current user. The `run()` method executes the provided code block (a lambda expression in this case) within the scope of the bound value. The code within the `run()` method can access the scoped value using the `get()` method. In our case, the `doSomething()` method will access the value by calling the `get()` method:

```
NAME.get()
```

If we now want to replace the `JobScheduler` class with `ScopedValue`, we will do as follows:

```
private static final ScopedValue<JobContext> CONTEXT
                                = ScopedValue.newInstance(); ❶

  public void schedule(Job job, String jobName, Priority priority) {
    JobContext context = new JobContext(jobName, priority); ❷
    ScopedValue.where(CONTEXT, context)
        .run(() -> runJob(job)); ❸
  }

  private void runJob(Job job) {
    job.execute(); ❹
  }

  public static JobContext getContext() { ❺
    return CONTEXT.get();
  }

  public static Object getJobMetadata(String key) {
    JobContext context = CONTEXT.get(); ❻
    if (context != null) {
      return context.getMetadataValue(key);
    }
    return null;
  }
}
```

Key aspects of this implementation:

❶ Creates a `ScopedValue` instance using the factory method

❷ Constructs the `context` object to be bound

❸ Binds the `context` and executes the job within that scope

❹ The job executes with access to the scoped `context`

❺ Provides static access to the current `context` (cleaner than the original)

❻ Safely retrieves metadata with `null` checking

Now that we understand how it works, let's take a more in-depth look.

While the previous examples demonstrate the use of run() to execute code within a scope, ScopedValue also provides a call() method when you need to return a value from the scoped execution. The difference is straightforward: run() executes a Runnable (returns void), while call() executes a Callable (returns a value).

Consider the following code snippets:

```
private static final ScopedValue<Double> DISCOUNT_RATE
                                = ScopedValue.newInstance();

public double calculatePrice(double basePrice) {
   // Using call() to return the calculated price from within the scope
   return ScopedValue.where(DISCOUNT_RATE, 0.20)  // 20% discount
       .call(() -> basePrice * (1 - DISCOUNT_RATE.get()));
}

void main() {
   PricingService service = new PricingService();
   double finalPrice = service.calculatePrice(100.0);
   System.out.println("Final price: $" + finalPrice);
   // Output: Final price: $80.00
 }
}
```

In this example, we use call() because we need to return the calculated price. This pattern is particularly useful for computations, transformations, or any operation where you need to retrieve a result while maintaining access to the scoped context.

Running ScopedValue

ScopedValue has a bounded lifetime. We must first set it, and then we can use it.

Consider the following example:

```
public static void main(String[] args) {

   ScopedValue<String> NAME = ScopedValue.newInstance();

   Runnable task = () -> {
       if (NAME.isBound()) {
           System.out.println("Name is bound: " + NAME.get());
       } else {
           System.out.println("Name is not bound");
       }
   };

   task.run();
}
```

If we run this code, it will print `Name is not bound` because we haven't set the value yet. To bind a value and execute code within that scope, we use the `where()` and `run()` methods:

```
public static void main(String[] args) {
 ScopedValue<String> NAME = ScopedValue.newInstance();

 Runnable task = () -> {
     if (NAME.isBound()) {
         System.out.println("Name is bound: " + NAME.get());
     } else {
         System.out.println("Name is not bound");
     }
 };

 ScopedValue.where(NAME, "Bazlur")   ❶
            .run(task);   ❷
}
```

This approach:

❶ Binds the value `Bazlur` to the `NAME` scoped value

❷ Executes the task within the scope of that binding

This code will run in the context of the main thread, as the `main` method starts it. If we run the preceding code, we will see the following output:

```
Name is bound: Bazlur
```

Now, one might ask: after setting the `ScopedValue` using `where().run()`, can we execute the task separately and get the value?

Let's test this:

```
public static void main(String[] args) {
    ScopedValue<String> NAME = ScopedValue.newInstance();
    Runnable task = () -> {
        if (NAME.isBound()) {
            System.out.println("Name is bound: " + NAME.get());
        } else {
            System.out.println("Name is not bound");
        }
    };
    // Execute within scope
    ScopedValue.where(NAME, "Bazlur").run(task);   ❶
    // Try to execute outside scope
    task.run();   ❷
}
```

This demonstrates that:

❶ The first execution runs within the scoped value's bound context.

❷ The second execution runs outside that scope, so the value is no longer bound.

The output of this code will be:

```
Name is bound: Bazlur
Name is not bound
```

The `ScopedValue` only remains bound within the dynamic scope of the `run()` method call. Once that method completes, the binding is automatically removed, ensuring clean scope boundaries and preventing value leakage between unrelated code sections.

The "scope" of a value defines where it exists and where it can be accessed. In Java, this often refers to *lexical scope* (defined by {} blocks) where variables are accessible only within their declared boundaries. However, `ScopedValue` operates on a *dynamic scope*, which is determined by the program's *execution flow*.

Dynamic scope means a value is accessible during the execution of specific methods and the methods they call, directly or indirectly. For example, if a calls b, and b calls c, the scope flows through c but ends when c finishes. `ScopedValue` binds a value to this execution flow, making it available only within the scope of the `run` method that sets it.

This temporary and precise scoping is what makes `ScopedValue` a cleaner and safer alternative to `ThreadLocal`, especially for passing contextual data.

We can ask another question: instead of using the main thread, can we run the task in another thread?

Consider the following code:

```java
public static void main(String[] args) throws InterruptedException {
    ScopedValue<String> NAME = ScopedValue.newInstance();

    Runnable task = () -> {
        if (NAME.isBound()) {
            System.out.println("Name is bound: " + NAME.get());
        } else {
            System.out.println("Name is not bound");
        }
    };
```

```
        Thread thread = Thread.ofPlatform().unstarted(task); ❶
        ScopedValue.where(NAME, "Bazlur")
                   .run(thread::start); ❷

        thread.join();
    }
```

In this code:

❶ Creates an unstarted platform thread with our task

❷ Binds the scoped value and starts the thread within that scope

When we run this code, the output is:

```
Name is not bound
```

The reason we get this result is that scoped values are not automatically inherited by newly created threads. Although `thread::start` executes within the scope where `NAME` is bound, the actual task runs in a separate thread that doesn't inherit the scoped value binding. This behavior is the same for both platform and virtual threads.

Now, instead of creating the `ScopedValue` in the main thread, let's move it to the newly created thread:

```
    public static void main(String[] args) throws InterruptedException {
        ScopedValue<String> NAME = ScopedValue.newInstance();

        Runnable task = () -> {
            if (NAME.isBound()) {
                System.out.println("Name is bound: " + NAME.get());
            } else {
                System.out.println("Name is not bound");
            }
        };

        Thread thread = Thread.ofVirtual().start(() -> { ❶
            ScopedValue.where(NAME, "Bazlur")
                       .run(task); ❷
        });

        thread.join();
    }
```

Now the code works as expected:

❶ Creates and starts a virtual thread

❷ Binds the scoped value and runs the task within the new thread's context

The `ScopedValue` provides a fluent API; using it, we can bind multiple `ScopedValue` chains together.

Let's look at the following example:

```
public class MultiScopedExample {
  private static final ScopedValue<String> USER_ID
                                = ScopedValue.newInstance();
  private static final ScopedValue<String> SESSION_ID
                                = ScopedValue.newInstance();

  public static void main(String[] args) {
    ScopedValue.where(USER_ID, "user123")  ❶
        .where(SESSION_ID, "session456")  ❷
        .run(() -> performTask());  ❸
  }

  public static void performTask() {
    String userId = USER_ID.get();
    String sessionId = SESSION_ID.get();
    System.out.println("Performing task for user: " + userId +
        " in session: " + sessionId);
    logAction();
  }

  public static void logAction() {
    String userId = USER_ID.get();  ❹
    String sessionId = SESSION_ID.get();
    System.out.println("Logging action for user: " + userId +
        " in session: " + sessionId);
  }
}
```

This chaining approach:

❶ Binds the first scoped value

❷ Chains another binding

❸ Executes code with both values bound

❹ Allows both values to remain accessible throughout the call stack

`ScopedValue` has two other convenient methods, `orElse` (*https://oreil.ly/BkL2X*) and `orElseThrow` (*https://oreil.ly/pOT8D*). These two methods are useful when we want to use a default value in case no value is available in the `ScopedValue` or if we want to throw an exception.

Consider the next example:

```
public class ScopedValueDefaultsExample {
  private static final ScopedValue<String> USER_NAME
      = ScopedValue.newInstance();

  public static void main(String[] args) {
    // Using orElse for default values
    String userNameUnbound = USER_NAME.orElse("Guest");   ❶
    System.out.println("No binding -> user name defaults to: "
        + userNameUnbound);
    // Using orElseThrow for validation
    try {
      USER_NAME.orElseThrow(() ->
          new IllegalStateException("No user name bound yet!"));   ❷
    } catch (IllegalStateException e) {
      System.out.println("Caught exception: " + e.getMessage());
    }
    // Within a bound scope
    ScopedValue.where(USER_NAME, "Bazlur").run(() -> {
      String boundUserName = USER_NAME.orElse("Guest");   ❸
      System.out.println("Within binding -> user name is: " + boundUserName);
      // This won't throw since the value is bound
      String validatedName = USER_NAME.orElseThrow(()
          -> new IllegalStateException("No user name bound yet!"));   ❹
      System.out.println("Validated name: " + validatedName);
    });
  }
}
```

These methods:

❶ Provide safe access with a default value when unbound

❷ Allow for validation that throws a custom exception when unbound

❸ Return the bound value (ignoring the default)

❹ Can use the no-argument version when you're certain a value exists

This API design ensures that code can handle both bound and unbound states gracefully, making scoped values robust for various use cases.

Rebinding ScopedValue in nested scopes

One of the powerful features of ScopedValue is its ability to *rebind* within nested scopes. Rebinding allows you to assign a new value to the same ScopedValue for a limited duration, confined to a specific subscope. Once the subscope finishes, the original value is automatically restored, ensuring clean and predictable context management.

This rebinding feature is particularly useful in scenarios such as role-based access control, where a user's role can be temporarily switched during a specific operation. It also enables context-sensitive configurations, for example, allowing settings to be adjusted for a particular execution flow without affecting the broader context. Additionally, it can support task-specific overrides by providing temporary data for a specific task or action.

Now take a look at this example:

```
public class ScopedValueRebindingExample {
  private static final ScopedValue<String> USER_ROLE = ScopedValue.newInstance();
  public static void main(String[] args) {
    // Bind initial value in outer scope
    ScopedValue.where(USER_ROLE, "Admin").run(() -> { ❶
      System.out.println("Outer scope: User role is " + USER_ROLE.get());
      performTask();
      // Rebind in nested scope
      ScopedValue.where(USER_ROLE, "Guest").run(() -> { ❷
        System.out.println("Inner scope: User role is " + USER_ROLE.get());
        performTask();
      }); ❸
      // Original value restored automatically
      System.out.println("Back to outer scope: User role is " + USER_ROLE.get());
      performTask();
    });
  }
  public static void performTask() {
    System.out.println("  Performing task as: " + USER_ROLE.get()); ❹
  }
}
```

Key aspects of this example:

❶ Establishes the initial binding of Admin in the outer scope.

❷ Creates a nested scope that temporarily rebinds the value to Guest.

❸ When this scope exits, the original Admin value is restored.

❹ The same method accesses different values based on the current scope.

If we run this code, we will get the following output:

```
Outer scope: User role is Admin
  Performing task as: Admin
Inner scope: User role is Guest
  Performing task as: Guest
Back to outer scope: User role is Admin
  Performing task as: Admin
```

ScopedValue and Structured Concurrency

ScopedValue is designed to work seamlessly with structured concurrency. As we have seen in the preceding example, ScopedValue isn't inherited by child threads; however, when used within a StructuredTaskScope, ScopedValue bindings are automatically inherited by all child threads created within that scope. This inheritance mechanism facilitates efficient data sharing between parent and child threads without explicitly passing the data as arguments. This is because structured concurrency has well-defined boundaries. When we exit the StructuredTaskScope, all the threads created in the scope are interrupted and then garbage collected; thus, there is no issue with memory leaks.

Let's look at an example:

```java
import java.util.concurrent.StructuredTaskScope;

public class ScopedValueStructuredConcurrencyExample {
    private static final ScopedValue<String>
            USERNAME = ScopedValue.newInstance();

    public static void main(String[] args) {
        ScopedValue.where(USERNAME, "Bazlur").run(() -> {
            doSomething();
        });
    }

    public static void doSomething() {
        try (var scope = StructuredTaskScope.open()) {
            StructuredTaskScope.Subtask<String> task1 = scope.fork(()
                    -> USERNAME.get() + " from task 1");
            StructuredTaskScope.Subtask<String> task2 = scope.fork(()
                    -> USERNAME.get() + " from task 2");
            scope.join();
            String result1 = task1.get();
            String result2 = task2.get();
            System.out.println(result1);
            System.out.println(result2);
        } catch (InterruptedException e) {
            throw new RuntimeException(e);
        }
    }
}
```

In this example, the USERNAME scoped value is bound to the string Bazlur in the main thread. When doSomething() is called, it creates a StructuredTaskScope and forks two child threads. These child threads inherit the USERNAME binding from the parent thread and can access it using USERNAME.get().

Performance Considerations

ScopedValue generally shows better performance compared to ThreadLocal, especially when working with virtual threads. This performance advantage is the result of several factors. First, there is reduced overhead: ThreadLocal variables can introduce significant overhead when each virtual thread needs its own copy, which drives up memory consumption. In contrast, ScopedValue lets us share data among threads within a defined scope, minimizing memory usage and boosting performance. Second, ScopedValue is optimized for virtual threads and structured concurrency. It leverages the lightweight nature of virtual threads to provide efficient data sharing without the usual bottlenecks of traditional thread-local variables. For example, consider a web server that spins up thousands of virtual threads to handle concurrent requests. Each request may need contextual data like user authentication details. By using ScopedValue to share this data within each request's scope, we significantly reduce memory consumption and improve overall throughput compared to using ThreadLocal.

Usability and API Design

Beyond performance, ScopedValue brings several usability advantages that make it a better alternative to ThreadLocal. First, ScopedValue enforces immutability, which means once a value is associated with a ScopedValue within a scope, it cannot be modified. This immutability simplifies reasoning about the code and reduces the risk of errors caused by unintended modifications. In a concurrent environment, immutability is especially useful as it prevents race conditions and data inconsistencies that often arise when multiple threads attempt to modify shared variables.

Second, ScopedValue explicitly defines the lifecycle of shared data through its API design. The run() method clearly marks the scope where the value is accessible. This explicit lifecycle improves code readability and makes it easier to understand how data flows through the program. Unlike the implicit behavior of ThreadLocal, this design ensures a clearer boundary for where the value is valid.

Third, the API of ScopedValue is more concise and intuitive. The where() and run() methods provide a structured way to set and access shared data within a specific scope. Compared to the often verbose and less straightforward methods of Thread Local, ScopedValue's approach feels more natural and easier to work with.

Additionally, ScopedValue acts as a capability object, which allows precise control over who can access the shared data. By declaring the ScopedValue object with access modifiers like private, it becomes possible to restrict access to authorized components only, adding a layer of security and encapsulation to the design.

Finally, `ScopedValue` handles `null` values more explicitly than `ThreadLocal`. With `ThreadLocal`, calling `get()` will return `null` whether the value was explicitly set to `null` or never set at all, which can lead to subtle bugs. In contrast, `ScopedValue` makes a clear distinction. If the value is unbound, calling `get()` throws a `NoSuchElementException`, ensuring any oversight in setting the value is caught early, making the code more robust and predictable.

Migrating to Scoped Values

Scoped values are likely to be useful and preferable in many scenarios where thread-local variables are used today. Beyond serving as hidden method parameters, scoped values can be particularly useful in several areas.

First, sometimes we want to detect recursion, perhaps because a framework is not re-entrant or because recursion must be limited in some way. A scoped value provides a way to detect and handle the recursion.

You can set it up as usual, with `ScopedValue.run()`, and then deep in the call stack, call `ScopedValue.isBound()` to check if it has a binding for the current thread. More elaborately, the scoped value can model a recursion counter by being repeatedly rebounded.

Consider a document-processing system that handles nested templates. Without a recursion limit, a maliciously crafted template with circular reference could crash your application. Let's look at the following code:

```
public class TemplateProcessor {
    private static final ScopedValue<Integer> RECURSION_DEPTH
                                = ScopedValue.newInstance();  ❶

    private static final int MAX_NESTING_LEVEL = 50;

    public String processTemplate(String template) {
        if (!RECURSION_DEPTH.isBound()) {  ❷
            return ScopedValue.where(RECURSION_DEPTH, 0)  ❸
                    .call(() -> processTemplateInternal(template));
        } else {
            return processTemplateInternal(template);
        }
    }
}
```

❶ Creates a `ScopedValue` to track recursion depth across method calls

❷ Uses `isBound()` deep in the call stack to check if it has a binding for the current thread

❸ Sets it up as usual with ScopedValue.run() (note: where() and call() are from the modern API)

The main processing logic handles the template parsing and recursion management. This method is called within the scoped context and has access to the current recursion depth:

```
private String processTemplateInternal(String template) {
    int currentDepth = RECURSION_DEPTH.get(); ❹

    if (currentDepth >= MAX_NESTING_LEVEL) { ❺
      throw new TemplateProcessingException(
          "Template nesting too deep: " + currentDepth + " levels");
    }

    StringBuilder result = new StringBuilder();

    // Simplified template processing logic
    int includeStart = template.indexOf("{{include:");
    if (includeStart >= 0) {
      int includeEnd = template.indexOf("}}", includeStart);
      String includePath = template.substring(includeStart + 10, includeEnd);

      String nestedContent = ScopedValue
          .where(RECURSION_DEPTH, currentDepth + 1) ❻
          .call(() -> processTemplateInternal(loadTemplate(includePath)));

      result.append(template, 0, includeStart);
      result.append(nestedContent);
      result.append(template.substring(includeEnd + 2));
    } else {
      result.append(template);
    }

    return result.toString(); ❼
}
```

❹ Retrieves the current recursion depth within the scope.

❺ Implements a safety check to prevent excessive nesting in non-reentrant frameworks.

❻ The scoped value models a recursion counter by being repeatedly rebounded with incremented values.

❼ When this method returns, the previous depth value is automatically restored.

To complete our implementation, we need supporting methods for template loading and error handling. The `loadTemplate()` method simulates reading templates from a filesystem, including some that create deep nesting for testing:

```
private String loadTemplate(String path) {
    return switch (path) {
      case "header.tpl" -> "<!-- HEADER START -->";
      case "footer.tpl" -> "<!-- FOOTER END -->";
      default -> {
        if (path.startsWith("level")) {
          int level = Integer.parseInt(path.replaceAll("[^0-9]", ""));
          if (level < 10) {
            yield "Level " + level
                + " {{include:level" + (level + 1) + ".tpl}}";
          }
        }
        yield "<!-- Template content from " + path + " -->";
      }
    };
}
```

Let's see how this all works together. The following `main` method demonstrates various usage scenarios, from simple templates to deeply nested ones that trigger our recursion protection:

```
void main() {
        TemplateProcessor processor = new TemplateProcessor();

        // Example 1: Simple template without nesting
        String simpleTemplate = "Hello, this is a simple template!";
        System.out.println("Simple template result:");
        System.out.println(processor.processTemplate(simpleTemplate));
        System.out.println();

        // Example 2: Template with nested includes
        String nestedTemplate = "Header: {{include:header.tpl}} " +
                                "Content goes here {{include:footer.tpl}}";
        System.out.println("Nested template result:");
        System.out.println(processor.processTemplate(nestedTemplate));
        System.out.println();

        // Example 3: Demonstrate recursion depth tracking
        String deeplyNested = "Level 0 {{include:level1.tpl}}";
        System.out.println("Processing deeply nested template...");
        try {
            String result = processor.processTemplate(deeplyNested);
            System.out.println("Result: " + result);
        } catch (TemplateProcessingException e) {
            System.err.println("Error: " + e.getMessage());
        }
    }
```

When we run the preceding code, we get the following result:

```
Simple template result:
Hello, this is a simple template!

Nested template result:
Header: <!-- HEADER START --> Content goes here <!-- FOOTER END -->

Processing deeply nested template...
Result: Level 0 Level 1 Level 2 Level 3 Level 4 Level 5 Level 6 Level 7 Level 8
Level 9 <!-- Template content from level10.tpl -->
```

Second, detecting recursion can also be useful in the case of flattened transactions: any transaction started while a transaction is in progress becomes part of the outermost transaction.

Consider the following simplified example:

```
public class FlattenedTransactionExample {
  private static final ScopedValue<Transaction> CURRENT_TRANSACTION =
      ScopedValue.newInstance();

  public static void main(String[] args) {
    performBusinessOperation();
  }

  private static void performBusinessOperation() {
    // Start outer transaction
    Transaction outerTx = new Transaction("OUTER_TX");
    ScopedValue.where(CURRENT_TRANSACTION, outerTx).run(() -> { ❶
      System.out.println("Starting: " + outerTx.name());
      // Nested operation that might start its own transaction
      performNestedOperation();
      System.out.println("Committing: " + outerTx.name());
    });
  }

  private static void performNestedOperation() {
    if (CURRENT_TRANSACTION.isBound()) { ❷
      // Join existing transaction
      Transaction currentTx = CURRENT_TRANSACTION.get();
      System.out.println("  Joining existing transaction: " + currentTx.name());
      performDatabaseOperation();
    } else {
      // Start new transaction if none exists
      Transaction newTx = new Transaction("NESTED_TX");
      ScopedValue.where(CURRENT_TRANSACTION, newTx).run(() -> {❸
        System.out.println("  Starting new transaction: " + newTx.name());
        performDatabaseOperation();
      });
    }
  }
```

```
    private static void performDatabaseOperation() {
      Transaction tx = CURRENT_TRANSACTION.get();
      System.out.println("    Executing in transaction: " + tx.name()); ❹
    }

    record Transaction(String name) {
    }
}
```

This pattern:

❶ Establishes the outermost transaction

❷ Detects whether a transaction is already active

❸ Only creates a new transaction if none exists

❹ Means all operations participate in the same transaction context

The preceding code uses `ScopedValue` to manage nested transactions. It starts an outer transaction and binds it to a `ScopedValue`. When a nested transaction is attempted, the code checks if a transaction is already bound, effectively joining the outer transaction. This ensures all operations, even nested ones, are part of the same overarching transaction, which simplifies management and maintains data consistency.

If we run this code, we will get the following output:

```
Starting: OUTER_TX
  Joining existing transaction: OUTER_TX
    Executing in transaction: OUTER_TX
Committing: OUTER_TX
```

Another example occurs in graphics, where there is often a drawing context to be shared between parts of the program. `ScopedValues`, because of their automatic cleanup and reentrancy, are better suited to this than thread-local variables.

Consider a typical graphics application where drawing operations, such as colors, line width, and transformations, need to share state. Traditional approaches using thread-local variables require careful manual cleanup and are prone to context leakage. `ScopedValue` would provide a cleaner, safer alternative.

Let's examine how `ScopedValues` can manage drawing context in a component hierarchy:

```
import java.awt.Color;

public class SimpleGraphicsExample {
```

```
// Drawing context as ScopedValues
private static final ScopedValue<Color> DRAW_COLOR
                    = ScopedValue.newInstance();   ❶
private static final ScopedValue<Integer> LINE_WIDTH
                    = ScopedValue.newInstance();

// Simulated drawing methods
static void drawLine(String from, String to) {
    Color color = DRAW_COLOR.isBound() ? DRAW_COLOR.get() : Color.BLACK;  ❷
    int width = LINE_WIDTH.isBound() ? LINE_WIDTH.get() : 1;

    System.out.printf("Drawing line from %s to %s [Color: %s, Width: %d]\n",
        from, to, color.toString(), width);
}

static void drawRectangle(String name) {
    Color color = DRAW_COLOR.isBound() ? DRAW_COLOR.get() : Color.BLACK;
    int width = LINE_WIDTH.isBound() ? LINE_WIDTH.get() : 1;

    System.out.printf("Drawing rectangle '%s' [Color: %s, Width: %d]\n",
        name, color.toString(), width);
}
```

❶ Drawing properties are declared as ScopedValues, providing thread-safe context management.

❷ The isBound() check ensures we have a fallback when no context is established.

Components in a UI hierarchy often need their own drawing styles while inheriting from their parents:

```
// Component that draws itself and its children
    static void drawButton(String label) {
        System.out.println("\n--- Drawing Button: " + label + " ---");

        // Button uses blue color with thick border
        ScopedValue.where(DRAW_COLOR, Color.BLUE)  ❸
            .where(LINE_WIDTH, 3)
            .run(() -> {
                drawRectangle("button-background");

                // Text inside button uses different color
                ScopedValue.where(DRAW_COLOR, Color.WHITE)  ❹
                    .where(LINE_WIDTH, 1)
                    .run(() -> {
                        System.out.println("Drawing text: " + label);
                    });

                // Border automatically uses blue again
                drawRectangle("button-border");  ❺
            });
    }
```

❸ The button creates its own drawing context with blue color and 3-pixel line width.

❹ Text rendering temporarily overrides the color to white, demonstrating safe nesting.

❺ After the text scope ends, the button's blue context is automatically restored.

Containers can establish a drawing context that affects all their children:

```
// Panel that contains multiple components
    static void drawPanel() {
        System.out.println("\n--- Drawing Panel ---");

        // Panel uses gray theme
        ScopedValue.where(DRAW_COLOR, Color.GRAY)
            .where(LINE_WIDTH, 2)
            .run(() -> {
                drawRectangle("panel-background");

                // Draw child components - each with their own style
                drawButton("OK");   ❻
                drawButton("Cancel");

                // Back to panel's gray automatically
                drawLine("divider-start", "divider-end");   ❼
            });
    }
```

❻ Each button maintains its own drawing context, unaffected by the panel's gray theme.

❼ After drawing children, the panel's context remains intact.

Now let's look at our `main` method to complete the example:

```
void main() {
        System.out.println("=== Graphics Context Example ===\n");

        // Set default drawing context
        ScopedValue.where(DRAW_COLOR, Color.BLACK)   ❽
            .where(LINE_WIDTH, 1)
            .run(() -> {
                // Draw with default black color
                drawLine("A", "B");

                // Draw a panel (which has its own colors)
                drawPanel();

                // Automatically back to black after panel
```

```
            System.out.println("\n--- Back to main context ---");
            drawLine("C", "D");  ❾
        });

        // Outside the scope - no context available
        System.out.println("\n--- Outside any context ---");
        drawLine("E", "F");   // Will use defaults  ❿
    }
}
```

❽ Establishes the default drawing context for the entire application.

❾ After the panel completes, the main context is automatically restored without manual intervention.

❿ Operations outside any context fall back to sensible defaults.

Running this example produces the following output, clearly showing context changes:

```
=== Graphics Context Example ===
Drawing line from A to B [Color: java.awt.Color[r=0,g=0,b=0], Width: 1]
--- Drawing Panel ---
Drawing rectangle 'panel-background' [Color: java.awt.Color[r=128,g=128,b=128], Width: 2]
--- Drawing Button: OK ---
Drawing rectangle 'button-background' [Color: java.awt.Color[r=0,g=0,b=255], Width: 3]
Drawing text: OK
Drawing rectangle 'button-border' [Color: java.awt.Color[r=0,g=0,b=255], Width: 3]
--- Drawing Button: Cancel ---
Drawing rectangle 'button-background' [Color: java.awt.Color[r=0,g=0,b=255], Width: 3]
Drawing text: Cancel
Drawing rectangle 'button-border' [Color: java.awt.Color[r=0,g=0,b=255], Width: 3]
Drawing line from divider-start to divider-end [Color: java.awt.Color[r=128,g=128,b=128], Width: 2]
--- Back to main context ---
Drawing line from C to D [Color: java.awt.Color[r=0,g=0,b=0], Width: 1]
--- Outside any context ---
Drawing line from E to F [Color: java.awt.Color[r=0,g=0,b=0], Width: 1]
```

Now that we understand the benefits of `ScopedValue`, let's consider a few important factors before migrating. First, the API is still in preview, so it's a good idea to familiarize yourself with it and explore its capabilities until it becomes available in the JDK without requiring preview flags. This way, you can seamlessly adopt it once it is officially released. Additionally, migrating to a newer JDK should be a key consideration, as `ScopedValue` is only available in the latest JDK. Evaluate any constraints you might face before upgrading to ensure a smooth transition.

When using `ScopedValue`, it's important to ensure that the data we intend to share is immutable, as `ScopedValue` enforces immutability. `ScopedValue` might not be the right fit if our use case requires mutable data. Defining the scope of shared data explicitly with the `where()` and `run()` methods is equally crucial. This ensures the data remains accessible within the intended context, avoiding unintended side effects.

We should also be mindful of the differences in `null` value handling between `Scoped Value` and `ThreadLocal`. `ScopedValue` throws a `NoSuchElementException` when accessing unbound values, whereas `ThreadLocal` returns `null`. This explicit error handling can help catch issues early but requires careful attention during migration.

Finally, it is essential to thoroughly test your application after adopting `ScopedValue` to ensure that concurrency and data consistency are preserved and to address any unforeseen issues that may arise.

In Closing

`ScopedValue` offers a cleaner, safer, and more efficient alternative to `ThreadLocal` for sharing context across a call chain. By being immutable and bounded to a well-defined dynamic scope, it addresses many of `ThreadLocal`'s shortcomings: unconstrained mutability, unbounded lifetime, and memory overhead. Its lightweight nature aligns particularly well with virtual threads and structured concurrency, helping reduce resource usage when spinning up large numbers of concurrent tasks. The explicit syntax of `where()` and `run()` makes it clear when and where a given value is in effect, improving code readability and maintainability.

As of JDK 25, `ScopedValue` has graduated from preview status and is now a stable API, ready for production use. This stabilization marks it as the recommended solution for context propagation in modern Java applications. We can confidently migrate existing `ThreadLocal`-based code to use scoped values without concern about API changes.

CHAPTER 6

The Relevance of Reactive Java in Light of Virtual Threads

I think Loom is going to kill reactive programming.... Reactive programming was a transitional technology.
—Brian Goetz

While I won't comment on the preceding quote—at least not yet—this chapter will introduce an existing alternative that has long been popular among many developers: Reactive Java.

Over the past few chapters, we've explored virtual threads in great detail, understanding how they work, their advantages, and their role in making concurrency in Java more accessible. We recognized that virtual threads are a great innovation in the concurrency landscape. They allow developers to write highly concurrent applications using the familiar imperative programming model while efficiently handling blocking operations.

However, virtual threads are not the only solution for efficiently handling concurrency and blocking I/O. Before virtual threads came into the limelight, many developers turned to reactive programming to build scalable, non-blocking applications. This approach, often associated with Project Reactor, RxJava, Eclipse Vert.x, etc., embraces an entirely different paradigm—one that is event-driven, functional, and inherently asynchronous.

In this chapter, we will explore Reactive Java, examining its execution model, programming style, ease of use and learning curve, challenges, benefits, etc.

Let's begin.

Understanding Reactive Programming in Java

Reactive programming is a declarative paradigm centered on asynchronous data streams and the automatic propagation of change.

Instead of focusing on the step-by-step execution of instructions, developers define the relationships between these streams and how they transform data. These streams can represent anything that changes over time, such as user input, sensor readings, or data from external systems. When a value in a stream changes, the reactive framework automatically propagates that change downstream, updating all dependent components. This allows for efficient handling of asynchronous events and simplifies the development of complex, event-driven applications. Developers can create more maintainable and scalable systems by expressing *what* data transformations and reactions should occur rather than *how* to execute them. Popular reactive programming libraries and frameworks include RxJava, Reactor, and Akka Streams, which provide the tools to create and manipulate these data streams.

In the Java ecosystem, reactive programming is usually associated with *non-blocking, asynchronous operations* and *event-driven architectures*.

> ### Reactive Systems at a Glance
>
> In 2013, the Reactive Manifesto (*https://oreil.ly/Cb14t*) emerged to define what it means to be reactive; it provides a definition of reactive systems and aims to standardize the meaning of *reactive*.
>
> It identifies four key principles:
>
> *Responsive*
> : Reactive systems consistently deliver rapid response times, enhancing user confidence and simplifying error handling.
>
> *Resilient*
> : They maintain responsiveness despite failures by isolating issues, delegating recovery, and using replication for high availability.
>
> *Elastic*
> : They dynamically adapt to varying workloads, efficiently scaling resources up or down to maintain performance.
>
> *Message-Driven*
> : They use asynchronous messaging for loose coupling, isolation, and efficient resource usage, enabling resilience and elasticity.
>
> This essentially comes down to three key aspects: being non-blocking, event-driven, and asynchronous in technical implementation.

Let's unpack these concepts one by one.

Blocking Versus Non-blocking I/O

In the previous chapters, we learned a great deal about blocking operations. Simply put, when an I/O occurs, the caller thread waits until the operation completes. During this time, the thread remains idle, essentially "blocked," until it gets the data it needs. This is what we refer to as a blocking operation.

The alternative approach is non-blocking I/O. In this model, threads are not held up by I/O operations. Instead of waiting, a thread can continue executing other tasks while the I/O happens in the background.

So, how does this work? In a non-blocking system, the operating system takes over the responsibility of handling I/O. When the operation is complete, the OS notifies the application, typically by invoking a callback function. This way, the thread that initiated the request doesn't have to sit idle; it simply gets notified when the data is ready.

To make this idea more concrete, let's walk through an example. Imagine building an HTTP server that needs to handle request pipelining, a critical feature in HTTP/1.1 where clients can send multiple requests without waiting for responses. The server needs to:

- Accept connections from multiple clients
- Process HTTP requests with varying complexity (fast versus slow operations)
- Maintain connection state for keep-alive sessions
- Handle request pipelining correctly
- Scale to handle hundreds or thousands of concurrent connections

That's all there is to it. Now, let's explore how we can implement such a server using both blocking and non-blocking approaches to see the differences in action.

We start with a single-threaded blocking server:

```
public class BlockingHttpServer {
  private static final int PORT = 8080;
  private static final AtomicInteger requestCounter = new AtomicInteger(0);

  public static void main(String[] args) throws IOException {
    System.out.println("Blocking HTTP Server starting on port " + PORT);
    System.out.println("Features: Single-threaded, Request pipelining");
    try (ServerSocket serverSocket = new ServerSocket(PORT)) {
      serverSocket.setReuseAddress(true); ❶
      while (true) {
        Socket clientSocket = serverSocket.accept(); ❷
        handleConnection(clientSocket);
      }
    }
```

```
      }
    }

    private static void handleConnection(Socket socket) {
      System.out.println("New connection from: " +
                    socket.getRemoteSocketAddress());
      try (socket;
          BufferedReader in = new BufferedReader(
              new InputStreamReader(socket.getInputStream()));
          PrintWriter out = new PrintWriter(
              socket.getOutputStream(), true)) {
        socket.setSoTimeout(5000); ❸
        boolean keepAlive = true;
        while (keepAlive) {
          HttpRequest request = parseRequest(in); ❹
          if (request == null) {
            break; // Connection closed
          }
          int requestId = requestCounter.incrementAndGet();
          System.out.println("Request #" + requestId + ": " +
                        request.method + " " + request.path);
          // Check for keep-alive
          keepAlive = "keep-alive".equalsIgnoreCase(
              request.getHeader("Connection"));
          // Process request - this may take time! ❺
          processRequest(request);
          // Send response
          sendResponse(out, request, requestId, keepAlive);
        }
      } catch (SocketTimeoutException e) {
        System.out.println("Connection timeout");
      } catch (IOException e) {
        System.err.println("Connection error: " + e.getMessage());
      }
    }
  }
```

Let's examine the key points in this code:

❶ We enable address reuse to avoid "Address already in use" errors during development.

❷ The `accept()` method blocks until a client connects. This is where our single thread gets stuck waiting for new connections.

❸ We set a socket timeout of five seconds to detect dead connections and prevent the server from hanging indefinitely.

❹ The `parseRequest()` method blocks until a complete HTTP request arrives. While waiting for one client's request, the server cannot accept new connections.

❺ This is a critical limitation: if `processRequest()` takes a long time (such as in the event of a slow database query), the entire server blocks. No other clients can connect or be served.

The server requires several helper methods to handle HTTP communication:

```
private static void sendResponse(PrintWriter out,
                                 HttpRequest request,
                                 int requestId,
                                 boolean keepAlive) {
    // Send HTTP response
    out.println("HTTP/1.1 200 OK");
    out.println("Content-Type: text/plain");
    out.println("Connection: " + (keepAlive ? "keep-alive" : "close"));
    String body = String.format(
        "Request #%d processed\nPath: %s\nTime: %s\n",
        requestId, request.path, Instant.now());
    out.println("Content-Length: " + body.length());
    out.println(); // Empty line between headers and body
    out.print(body);
    out.flush(); ❻
}
```

❻ Ensures immediate delivery of the HTTP response by forcing any buffered data to be sent to the client, preventing delays in response transmission.

To clearly demonstrate the blocking behavior, we'll simulate different processing times:

```
static void processRequest(HttpRequest request)
      throws IOException {
    try {
      if (request.path.startsWith("/slow")) {
        Thread.sleep(Duration.of(30, ChronoUnit.SECONDS)); ❼
        System.out.println("  Slow request processed");
      } else if (request.path.startsWith("/medium")) {
        Thread.sleep(Duration.of(500, ChronoUnit.MILLIS));
        System.out.println("  Medium request processed");
      } else {
        Thread.sleep(Duration.of(100, ChronoUnit.MILLIS));
        System.out.println("  Fast request processed");
      }
    } catch (InterruptedException e) {
      Thread.currentThread().interrupt();
    }
  }
```

❼ A slow request blocks the entire server for 30 seconds. During this time, no new connections can be accepted, and no other requests can be processed. This is added to simulate the slowness of the API call.

Our simple `HttpRequest` class captures the essential elements needed for processing:

```java
static class HttpRequest {
  String method;
  String path;
  String version;
  Map<String, String> headers = new HashMap<>();
  String remainingBuffer; // For non-blocking server
  String getHeader(String name) {
    return headers.get(name.toLowerCase());
  }
}
```

And here is the helper method that parses the request.

```java
static HttpRequest parseRequest(BufferedReader in)
    throws IOException {
  // Read request line
  String requestLine = in.readLine(); //
  if (requestLine == null || requestLine.isEmpty()) {
    return null;
  }
  String[] parts = requestLine.split(" ");
  if (parts.length != 3) {
    throw new IOException("Invalid request line");
  }
  HttpRequest request = new HttpRequest();
  request.method = parts[0];
  request.path = parts[1];
  request.version = parts[2];
  // Read headers
  String headerLine;
  while ((headerLine = in.readLine()) != null) { //
    if (headerLine.isEmpty()) {
      break; // End of headers
    }
    int colonPos = headerLine.indexOf(':');
    if (colonPos > 0) {
      String name = headerLine.substring(0, colonPos).trim();
      String value = headerLine.substring(colonPos + 1).trim();
      request.headers.put(name.toLowerCase(), value);
    }
  }
  return request;
}
```

In this implementation, we created a ServerSocket (*https://oreil.ly/pqjiz*) that listens on port 8080. A Socket (*https://oreil.ly/uEj8h*) represents a single endpoint in a two-way communication link between programs running on a network. On the other hand, a ServerSocket continuously listens for incoming connections and processes client requests accordingly.

Here's how it works in our case:

- The server waits for a client to connect.
- Once a connection is established, the server hands it off to the `handleConnection()` method, which takes care of the interaction.
- This method processes HTTP requests, handling keep-alive connections and request pipelining. The specifics of HTTP processing showcase how blocking I/O impacts server performance.

However, there's a catch. When the server handles a client, the calling thread is blocked until the client disconnects. If the client stops sending data but remains connected, the server stays stuck, waiting for input. Because it's a single-threaded server, no other clients can connect until the current session ends.

To test this server and observe its blocking behavior, we can use curl. Let's run a few experiments:

Terminal 1: Start the server
```
$ java BlockingHttpServer.java
Single-threaded HTTP Server with Pipelining starting on port 8080
Features: Request pipelining, Keep-alive connections
```

The server is now running and waiting for connections. Let's send a simple request:

Terminal 2: Send a single fast request
```
$ curl -v http://localhost:8080/fast
* Host localhost:8080 was resolved.
* IPv6: ::1
* IPv4: 127.0.0.1
*   Trying [::1]:8080...
* Connected to localhost (::1) port 8080
> GET /fast HTTP/1.1
> Host: localhost:8080
> User-Agent: curl/8.7.1
> Accept: */*
>
* Request completely sent off
< HTTP/1.1 200 OK
< Content-Type: text/plain
< Connection: close
< Content-Length: 67
<
Request #1 processed
Path: /fast
Time: 2025-06-14T09:27:02.235713Z
* Closing connection
```

This fast request completes immediately. The server processes it and closes the connection. Now let's demonstrate the blocking problem:

Terminal 3: Test blocking behavior—first send a slow request
```
$ curl -v http://localhost:8080/slow
* Host localhost:8080 was resolved.
* IPv6: ::1
* IPv4: 127.0.0.1
*   Trying [::1]:8080...
* Connected to localhost (::1) port 8080
> GET /slow HTTP/1.1
> Host: localhost:8080
> User-Agent: curl/8.7.1
> Accept: */*
>
* Request completely sent off
< HTTP/1.1 200 OK
< Content-Type: text/plain
< Connection: close
< Content-Length: 67
<
Request #2 processed
Path: /slow
Time: 2025-06-14T09:28:16.218432Z
* Closing connection
```

While this slow request is processing, let's try to connect with another client:

Terminal 4: While the slow request is processing, try a fast request
```
$ curl -v --max-time 5 http://localhost:8080/fast
* Host localhost:8080 was resolved.
* IPv6: ::1
* IPv4: 127.0.0.1
*   Trying [::1]:8080...
* Connected to localhost (::1) port 8080
> GET /fast HTTP/1.1
> Host: localhost:8080
> User-Agent: curl/8.7.1
> Accept: */*
>
* Request completely sent off
* Operation timed out after 5006 milliseconds with 0 bytes received
* Closing connection
curl: (28) Operation timed out after 5006 milliseconds with 0 bytes received
```

Notice how the second client successfully establishes a TCP connection (the OS handles this), but the server doesn't accept it because it's still blocked while processing the slow request. This is the fundamental limitation of our single-threaded design.

The most revealing test is to use curl's timing features to measure the blocking effect:

```
# Send three pipelined requests: fast, slow, fast
$ time curl -s -Z http://localhost:8080/fast \
            http://localhost:8080/slow \
            http://localhost:8080/fast
Request #11 processed
Path: /fast
Time: 2025-06-14T09:34:49.986347Z
Request #12 processed
Path: /slow
Time: 2025-06-14T09:35:19.989656Z
Request #13 processed
Path: /fast
Time: 2025-06-14T09:35:20.094539Z
curl -s -Z http://localhost:8080/fast http://localhost:8080/slow    0.01s user
0.01s system 0% cpu 47.811 total
```

Although two of the three requests are fast, the total time exceeds 30 seconds because all requests must be processed sequentially. The slow request in the middle blocks everything.

If you attempt to connect to the server from another client while an existing client session is active, you'll notice that the connection is blocked. The server can only handle one client at a time. This is because our implementation is single-threaded—it waits for the current client to disconnect before accepting a new one.

An easy solution to this problem is multithreading. By spawning a new thread for each client, we allow multiple connections to be handled concurrently. Let's modify our code to introduce multithreaded support:

```java
    public class MultithreadedHttpServer {
      private static final int PORT = 8080;
      private static final AtomicInteger requestCounter = new AtomicInteger(0);
      private static final int CONNECTION_THREADS = 10;

      public static void main(String[] args) throws IOException {
        System.out.println("Multi-threaded HTTP Server starting on port " + PORT);
        System.out.println("Features: Concurrent connections, Request pipelining");
        System.out.println("Connection pool size: " + CONNECTION_THREADS);

        try (ServerSocket serverSocket = new ServerSocket(PORT);
            ExecutorService connectionExecutor =
               Executors.newFixedThreadPool(CONNECTION_THREADS)) { ❶
          serverSocket.setReuseAddress(true);
          while (true) {
            Socket clientSocket = serverSocket.accept(); ❷
            System.out.println("New connection from: " +
                        clientSocket.getRemoteSocketAddress());
```

```
      // Handle each connection in a separate thread
      connectionExecutor.submit(() -> handleConnection(clientSocket));  ❸
    }
  }
}

private static void handleConnection(Socket socket) {
  String clientAddr = socket.getRemoteSocketAddress().toString();
  System.out.println("Thread " + Thread.currentThread().getName() +
                     " handling connection from: " + clientAddr);
  // Same request processing logic as BlockingHttpServer
  // but running in a separate thread  ❹
  try (socket;
      BufferedReader in = new BufferedReader(
          new InputStreamReader(socket.getInputStream()));
      PrintWriter out = new PrintWriter(
          socket.getOutputStream(), true)) {
    socket.setSoTimeout(5000);
    boolean keepAlive = true;
    while (keepAlive) {
      HttpRequest request = parseRequest(in);
      if (request == null) break;
      int requestId = requestCounter.incrementAndGet();
      System.out.println("Thread " + Thread.currentThread().getName() +
                         " - Request #" + requestId + ": " +
                         request.method + " " + request.path);
      keepAlive = "keep-alive".equalsIgnoreCase(
          request.getHeader("Connection"));
      processRequest(request);
      sendResponse(out, request, requestId, keepAlive);
    }
  } catch (Exception e) {
    System.err.println("Connection error from " + clientAddr +
                       ": " + e.getMessage());
  }
}
```

Key improvements in the multithreaded version:

❶ We create a fixed thread pool with 10 threads to handle connections.

❷ The main thread can immediately return to accepting new connections.

❸ Each connection runs in its thread, allowing concurrent processing.

❹ Individual connections still process requests sequentially (maintaining proper pipelining), but multiple connections can be served simultaneously.

In our multithreaded implementation, we created a fixed thread pool with 10 threads, allowing up to 10 clients to connect simultaneously. We could increase the thread count to handle more clients, but before the advent of virtual threads, this approach had inherent limitations. Platform threads are expensive, and increasing their number beyond a certain point would not yield any better results, as we discussed in Chapter 2.

With virtual threads, however, scaling becomes as simple as changing one line of code:

```
try (ServerSocket serverSocket = new ServerSocket(PORT);
    ExecutorService executor = Executors.newVirtualThreadPerTaskExecutor();
) {}
```

This would allow the server to handle a massive number of concurrent connections with minimal overhead. But that's not our focus right now. Instead, let's explore what alternatives existed before virtual threads.

One powerful approach was new input/output (NIO), which enables high throughput using a minimal number of threads.

Java NIO is a readiness-based, non-blocking API introduced in JDK 1.4 that replaces stream-oriented java.io with buffer-oriented channels (`SocketChannel`, `FileChannel`, etc.) and a `Selector` event loop. Instead of a thread blocking until an operation completes, a non-blocking `read()` or `write()` call returns immediately, often with zero bytes transferred. At the same time, the channel is registered with the selector. The selector sleeps inside `select()` until the operating system reports that one or more channels are ready for I/O; the thread then processes only those channels, enabling thousands of concurrent connections to be serviced by a handful of threads. Combined with direct or memory-mapped buffers, which allow zero-copy data transfers between user and kernel space, NIO delivers high throughput and scalability without the per-connection thread and stack overhead of the classic thread-per-socket model.

Java I/O Versus NIO: A Quick Comparison

Java offers two distinct approaches to handling I/O: the traditional java.io package and the more modern java.nio (new input/output). The key difference lies in their approach. Java I/O is stream-based and generally blocking, meaning a thread must wait for operations to complete. On the other hand, Java NIO is buffer-based and non-blocking, allowing greater scalability for handling large data transfers and high-performance applications.

For instance, consider reading a file using Java I/O:

```
try (BufferedReader reader
        = new BufferedReader(
            new FileReader("input.txt"))) {
    String line;
```

```
      while ((line = reader.readLine()) != null) {
        System.out.println(line);
      }
    } catch (IOException e) {
      e.printStackTrace();
    }
```

BufferedReader (*https://oreil.ly/kMKl7*) reads text from an input stream, line by line, making it efficient and easy to use for sequential file reading.

Now, contrast that with Java NIO's `FileChannel`:

```
try (FileChannel channel = FileChannel.open(
        Path.of("input.txt"),
        StandardOpenOption.READ)) {
    ByteBuffer buffer = ByteBuffer.allocate(1024);
    while (channel.read(buffer) > 0) {
        buffer.flip();
        while (buffer.hasRemaining()) {
            System.out.print((char) buffer.get());
        }
        buffer.clear();
    }
} catch (IOException e) {
    e.printStackTrace();
}
```

This version is buffer-driven, meaning data is first loaded into a `ByteBuffer`, manipulated in memory, and only then processed.

Instead of using `ServerSocket`, NIO introduces `ServerSocketChannel` (*https://oreil.ly/-nprM*). Similarly, `Socket` is replaced by `SocketChannel` (*https://oreil.ly/OsyaE*). Rather than relying on `InputStream` (*https://oreil.ly/VG-g_*) and `OutputStream` (*https://oreil.ly/YfUM5*), NIO uses buffers (*https://oreil.ly/WdXHC*). A buffer acts as a temporary storage area, holding a fixed amount of data before it's sent to its destination. This shift in design provides greater flexibility and efficiency when handling I/O operations.

Buffers in Java NIO improve performance by minimizing direct interactions with the operating system and enabling efficient data transfer. Unlike traditional I/O, which reads and writes data byte by byte, buffers allow batch processing, which reduces the number of system calls. This is particularly useful in high-performance applications like network servers and file handling.

One of the key efficiency boosters is zero-copy mechanisms, where ByteBuffer (*https://oreil.ly/zr3wz*) can work with memory-mapped files or direct buffers (off-heap memory). This eliminates unnecessary copying of data between user space and kernel space, significantly speeding up large file transfers. Additionally, non-blocking I/O with buffers enables scalable, event-driven applications by allowing a single thread to manage multiple connections efficiently.

Another critical component in NIO is the Selector (*https://oreil.ly/QjWUJ*), which plays a vital role in managing multiple channels, such as ServerSocketChannel and SocketChannel, with a single thread. Think of it as an intelligent traffic controller that listens for various I/O events and directs operations accordingly. For instance, when a new client connection is ready to be accepted, the selector signals an OP_ACCEPT event (*https://oreil.ly/zDSSz*). When data is available to be read from a SocketChannel, it triggers an OP_READ event (*https://oreil.ly/pyHhL*). Similarly, when a channel is ready to accept outgoing data, the OP_WRITE event (*https://oreil.ly/L1SPh*) is fired, and in client mode, a successful connection attempt results in an OP_CONNECT event (*https://oreil.ly/1NnVA*).

The underlying implementation of selectors is system-dependent. On macOS, for example, KQueueSelectorImpl (*https://oreil.ly/XmP4Y*) leverages the queue (*https://oreil.ly/xI-UN*) system call. A more general-purpose implementation, PollSelector Impl (*https://oreil.ly/N72Qw*), is based on the poll system call. The specific mechanism varies depending on the operating system, but the concept remains the same: efficiently managing multiple channels with minimal thread overhead.

Let's examine some code to see how these components work together in practice:

```
public class NonBlockingHttpServer {
    private static final int PORT = 8080;
    private static final AtomicInteger requestCounter = new AtomicInteger(0);
    private final ConcurrentLinkedQueue<PendingUpdate> pendingUpdates
                                  = new ConcurrentLinkedQueue<>();

    public static void main(String[] args) {
        System.out.println("Starting non-blocking NIO server...");
        System.out.println("Features: Single-threaded event loop, " +
                    "Non-blocking I/O, High concurrency");
        try {
            new NonBlockingHttpServer().start();
```

```
            } catch (IOException e) {
                System.err.println("Server failed to start: " + e.getMessage());
            }
        }

        private void start() throws IOException {
            try (Selector selector = Selector.open();
                 ServerSocketChannel serverChannel = ServerSocketChannel.open()) {
                serverChannel.bind(new InetSocketAddress(PORT));
                serverChannel.configureBlocking(false); ❶
                serverChannel.register(selector, SelectionKey.OP_ACCEPT);
                System.out.println("Non-blocking HTTP server on port " + PORT);
                // Single-threaded event loop ❷
                while (true) {
                    // Process pending updates from async threads
                    processPendingUpdates(); ❸

                    selector.select(100); ❹
                    Set<SelectionKey> selectedKeys = selector.selectedKeys();
                    Iterator<SelectionKey> iterator = selectedKeys.iterator();
                    while (iterator.hasNext()) {
                        SelectionKey key = iterator.next();
                        iterator.remove();
                        try {
                            if (key.isAcceptable()) {
                                handleAccept(key, selector); ❺
                            } else if (key.isReadable()) {
                                handleRead(key); ❻
                            } else if (key.isWritable()) {
                                handleWrite(key); ❼
                            }
                        } catch (IOException e) {
                            System.err.println("Error handling key: "
                                                        + e.getMessage());
                            key.cancel();
                            if (key.channel() != null) {
                                key.channel().close();
                            }
                        }
                    }
                    // Process any pending requests
                    processAllPendingRequests(selector);
                }
            }
        }
    }
```

Key improvements in the non-blocking version:

❶ We configure the server channel as non-blocking, essential for NIO operation.

❷ A single thread handles all I/O events through an event loop.

❸ Before processing events, we handle any selector updates queued by async threads. This crucial step prevents race conditions that could crash the server.

❹ The `selector` uses a timeout (100ms) instead of blocking indefinitely. This ensures pending updates from async threads are processed promptly, even if no I/O events occur.

❺ New connections are accepted without blocking the thread.

❻ Data reading is non-blocking; partial reads are handled gracefully.

❼ Data writing is non-blocking; partial writes are queued for later completion.

In the preceding code, we start by creating a `Selector` using `Selector.open()`. Instead of using a traditional constructor, it offers a static factory method, which is the preferred approach. This `Selector` is the core of our server, allowing it to manage multiple client connections efficiently with just a single thread.

Next, we create a `ServerSocketChannel` and bind it to a specific address. It is crucial to configure the channel as non-blocking using `serverSocketChannel.configureBlocking(false)`. Without this, the server would block on every operation, defeating the purpose of using NIO.

Once the `ServerSocketChannel` is set up, we register it with the `Selector`, specifying that we are interested in accept events. This means the server will be notified when a new client attempts to connect.

We also created all the handlers here. These classes take responsibility for each event, and we have just separated them.

Inside the main loop, we first call `processPendingUpdates()`, which handles a critical synchronization challenge. Since `SelectionKey` objects are not thread-safe, we cannot modify them directly from async processing threads. Instead, we use a thread-safe queue to communicate between threads:

```
private void processPendingUpdates() {
    PendingUpdate update;
    while ((update = pendingUpdates.poll()) != null) {
        try {
            if (update.key.isValid()) {
                update.key.interestOps(update.key.interestOps()
                        | SelectionKey.OP_WRITE);
            }
        } catch (Exception e) {
            System.err.println("Error updating key: " + e.getMessage());
        }
    }
}
```

```
    }

    static class PendingUpdate {
        final SelectionKey key;

        PendingUpdate(SelectionKey key) {
            this.key = key;
        }
    }
```

After processing updates, we call the `selector.select(100)`, which blocks for up to 100 milliseconds. The timeout is important: without it, the selector might block indefinitely, preventing timely processing of updates from async threads. As soon as an event is detected or the timeout expires, `select()` returns, allowing the server to process events or pending updates accordingly.

Once an event is detected, we retrieve the selection keys from the selector. Each key represents a specific event for a registered channel. Since multiple events can occur, the server processes them sequentially within a loop. After handling a key, it is removed from the set to prevent reprocessing.

When `key.isAcceptable()` returns `true`, it indicates that a new client is attempting to connect. At this point, we invoke the `handleAccept(key, selector)` method to handle the accept event.

Let's look at the code of the accept handler now:

```
    private void handleAccept(SelectionKey key, Selector selector)
            throws IOException {
        ServerSocketChannel serverChannel = (ServerSocketChannel) key.channel();
        SocketChannel clientChannel = serverChannel.accept();  ❶

        if (clientChannel != null) {
            clientChannel.configureBlocking(false);
            clientChannel.register(selector, SelectionKey.OP_READ,
                            new ClientState());  ❷

            System.out.println("Accepted connection from: " +
                            clientChannel.getRemoteAddress());
        }
    }

    static class ClientState {
        ByteBuffer readBuffer = ByteBuffer.allocate(8192);
        StringBuilder requestBuilder = new StringBuilder();
        ConcurrentLinkedQueue<String> responseQueue =
                            new ConcurrentLinkedQueue<>();  ❸
        Queue<HttpRequest> pendingRequests = new LinkedList<>();
        boolean keepAlive = true;
        boolean isProcessing = false;  ❹
    }
```

The accept handler manages new client connections:

❶ The `accept()` call is non-blocking and may return `null` if no connection is ready.

❷ Each client gets a `ClientState` object to track its connection state and partial data.

❸ The response queue uses `ConcurrentLinkedQueue` instead of a regular `LinkedList`. This is crucial because responses will be added from async processing threads, and we need thread-safe operations without explicit synchronization.

❹ The `isProcessing` flag prevents duplicate processing of requests from the same client, avoiding race conditions when multiple events trigger in quick succession.

In the handle method, we first grab hold of the `ServerSocketChannel`. In this case, we can be certain that `key.channel()` will return a `ServerSocketChannel`, which is why we can safely cast it without worrying about a `ClassCastException`. The connection is accepted using `serverChannel.accept()`, and as always, we configure it to be non-blocking.

Once the connection is established, we create a `ClientState` object for the client and register the client's channel with the `Selector` for read operations using `SelectionKey.OP_READ`. To make things more manageable, the `ClientState` is attached to the `SelectionKey` as an attachment, allowing us to retrieve it later when needed.

The `ClientState` class plays a crucial role in managing the state of each connected client. It holds the `SocketChannel` for the client, buffers for reading and writing data (`readBuffer` and `responseQueue`), and maintains a `StringBuilder` (`requestBuilder`) to accumulate incoming HTTP request data. This structured per-client state management is essential for handling multiple clients efficiently, ensuring that each connection maintains its own context without interfering with others.

When `key.isReadable()` is true, it means a client has sent data. In this case, we invoke the `handleRead(key)` method.

Let's see what we have in the read handler:

```
private void handleRead(SelectionKey key) throws IOException {
    SocketChannel channel = (SocketChannel) key.channel();
    ClientState state = (ClientState) key.attachment();

    int bytesRead = channel.read(state.readBuffer); ❶
    if (bytesRead == -1) {
        // Client disconnected
        channel.close();
        return;
    }
```

Understanding Reactive Programming in Java | 263

```
        if (bytesRead > 0) {
            state.readBuffer.flip();
            byte[] data = new byte[state.readBuffer.remaining()];
            state.readBuffer.get(data);
            state.requestBuilder.append(new String(data, StandardCharsets.UTF_8));
            state.readBuffer.clear();

            // Process complete requests
            processCompleteRequests(state, key); ❷
        }
    }

    private void processCompleteRequests(ClientState state, SelectionKey key) {
        String buffer = state.requestBuilder.toString();
        while (true) {
            HttpRequest request = parseHttpRequest(buffer); ❸
            if (request == null) {
                break; // No complete request found
            }
            state.pendingRequests.offer(request);
            buffer = request.remainingBuffer;
            // Check keep-alive based on HTTP version and headers
            String connection = request.getHeader("Connection");
            if (request.version.equals("HTTP/1.0")) {
                // HTTP/1.0 defaults to close unless keep-alive is explicit
                state.keepAlive = "keep-alive".equalsIgnoreCase(connection);
            } else {
                // HTTP/1.1 defaults to keep-alive unless close is explicit
                state.keepAlive = !"close".equalsIgnoreCase(connection);
            }
        }
        state.requestBuilder = new StringBuilder(buffer);
        if (!state.responseQueue.isEmpty()) {
            key.interestOps(key.interestOps() | SelectionKey.OP_WRITE); ❹
        }
    }
```

The read handler processes incoming data with several important characteristics:

❶ Reading is non-blocking and may return partial data.

❷ We process complete HTTP requests as they arrive, handling partial requests gracefully.

❸ The keep-alive logic now correctly handles both HTTP/1.0 and HTTP/1.1 protocols. HTTP/1.0 defaults to closing connections unless the client explicitly requests keep-alive, while HTTP/1.1 defaults to keeping connections alive unless the client requests closure. This distinction is crucial for compatibility with tools like Apache Bench.

❹ We register interest in writing events only when we have data to send.

The handler reads data from the client's channel and puts it into the readBuffer. Once the bytes are received, they are decoded into characters using UTF-8 and appended to the requestBuilder. The system processes HTTP requests by looking for the standard HTTP request terminator ("\r\n\r\n"). When a complete request is detected, the server parses it and processes it asynchronously, ensuring the event loop is never blocked.

When key.isWritable() is true, it signals that the client's channel is ready to receive data. At this point, the handleWrite(key) method takes over, ensuring that any pending responses in the queue are written back to the client efficiently.

Let's look at the code:

```
private void handleWrite(SelectionKey key) throws IOException {
    SocketChannel channel = (SocketChannel) key.channel();
    ClientState state = (ClientState) key.attachment();

    while (!state.responseQueue.isEmpty()) {
        String response = state.responseQueue.peek();
        ByteBuffer buffer
            = ByteBuffer.wrap(response.getBytes(StandardCharsets.UTF_8));

        int written = channel.write(buffer);
        if (buffer.hasRemaining()) {
            // Socket buffer is full, try again later
            break;
        }

        // Response fully written, remove from queue
        state.responseQueue.poll();
    }

    if (state.responseQueue.isEmpty()) {
        // No more data to write, stop watching for write events
        key.interestOps(key.interestOps() & ~SelectionKey.OP_WRITE);

        if (!state.keepAlive && state.pendingRequests.isEmpty()) {
            // Close connection if not keep-alive and no pending requests
            System.out.println("Closing connection: "
                    + channel.getRemoteAddress());
            channel.close();
            key.cancel();
        }
    }
}
```

The handler iterates through the client's responseQueue, writing each enqueued HTTP response to the client's channel using non-blocking writes. If the socket's buffer becomes full, the writing process pauses, waiting for the next `OP_WRITE` event before resuming. Once all responses are successfully written and the `responseQueue` is empty, the server removes the `OP_WRITE` interest from the `Selector` for that client, ensuring that no unnecessary write events are triggered when there's nothing left to send. The thread-safe `ConcurrentLinkedQueue` ensures that responses added by async threads don't cause race conditions during this process.

After handling all the selected keys, we process any pending requests that were parsed:

```java
private void processAllPendingRequests(Selector selector) {
    for (SelectionKey key : selector.keys()) {
        if (!key.isValid() || key.attachment() == null)
            continue;
        ClientState state = (ClientState) key.attachment();

        if (state.isProcessing || state.pendingRequests.isEmpty())
            continue;

        state.isProcessing = true; ❶
        while (!state.pendingRequests.isEmpty()) {
            HttpRequest request = state.pendingRequests.poll();
            int requestId = requestCounter.incrementAndGet();
            System.out.println("Request #" + requestId + ": "
                    + request.method + " " + request.path);
            // Simulate async processing
            CompletableFuture.runAsync(() -> { ❷
                String response;
                try {
                    // Process request (simulate the work)
                    if (request.path.equals("/slow")) {
                        Thread.sleep(2000); // Simulate slow operation
                        System.out.println("  Slow request processed");
                    } else {
                        System.out.println("  Fast request processed");
                    }
                    response = buildHttpResponse(request, requestId,
                                                 state.keepAlive);
                } catch (Exception e) {
                    System.err.println("Error processing request #" + requestId
                            + ": " + e.getMessage());
                    response = buildErrorResponse(request, requestId, e);
                }
                state.responseQueue.offer(response); ❸

                // Queue the update for the selector thread
                pendingUpdates.offer(new PendingUpdate(key)); ❹
                selector.wakeup();
            });
        }
```

```
            state.isProcessing = false;
        }
    }
```

The power of asynchronous processing becomes evident here:

❶ The processing flag ensures we don't start processing the same client's requests multiple times if events trigger in quick succession.

❷ Slow operations are handled asynchronously without blocking the event loop.

❸ Responses are safely added to the concurrent queue from the async thread.

❹ Instead of modifying the `SelectionKey` directly from the async thread (which would cause race conditions), we queue an update that the main selector thread will process. This is a critical pattern for thread safety in NIO applications.

A common misconception arises from the Java documentation stating that "Selection keys are safe for use by multiple concurrent threads." This leads many developers to believe they can modify `interestOps` from any thread. In reality, this statement only means that reading key properties won't cause memory corruption. It does not mean that operations like `interestOps()` are atomic or safe for concurrent modification.

Modifying a `SelectionKey`'s `interestOps` while `selector.select()` is executing can lead to:

- Race conditions where `interestOps` changes are lost
- Missed I/O events
- `CancelledKeyException` errors
- Inconsistent behavior that often only appears under high load

Always modify `SelectionKey`'s `interestOps` from the same thread that runs the selector loop. This is why we use the `pendingUpdates` queue pattern; it ensures all modifications happen safely in the selector thread.

Next, we will discuss the helper methods that complete the non-blocking HTTP server implementation.

The `buildHttpResponse` method constructs a properly formatted HTTP response with headers and body:

```
    private String buildHttpResponse(HttpRequest request,
                                     int requestId, boolean keepAlive) {
```

```
    StringBuilder response = new StringBuilder();
    // Match the request's HTTP version
    response.append(request.version).append(" 200 OK\r\n");
    // Headers
    response.append("Content-Type: text/plain\r\n");
    response.append("Server: NonBlockingHttpServer/1.0\r\n");
    response.append("Date: ").append(Instant.now()).append("\r\n");
    // Handle connection header properly
    if (request.version.equals("HTTP/1.0") && keepAlive) {
      response.append("Connection: keep-alive\r\n");

      return null;
    } else if (request.version.equals("HTTP/1.1") && !keepAlive) {
      response.append("Connection: close\r\n");
    }
    // For HTTP/1.1 with keep-alive, no Connection header needed (it's defaulted)
    String body = String.format(
        "Request #%d processed\nPath: %s\nMethod: %s\nTime: %s\nThread: %s\n",
        requestId,
        request.path,
        request.method,
        Instant.now(),
        Thread.currentThread().getName());
    response.append("Content-Length: ").append(body.length()).append("\r\n");
    response.append("\r\n"); // Empty line between headers and body
    response.append(body);
    return response.toString();
}
```

A crucial thing to note here is that the response now echoes the client's HTTP version instead of always returning HTTP/1.1. This ensures compatibility with HTTP/1.0 clients like Apache Bench. The Connection header is also handled correctly based on the protocol version and keep-alive status.

The heart of request handling is parsing the raw HTTP data. The parseHttpRequest method extracts HTTP requests from the byte stream, handling partial data gracefully:

```
private HttpRequest parseHttpRequest(String buffer) {
    int requestEndIndex = buffer.indexOf("\r\n\r\n");
    if (requestEndIndex == -1) {
      requestEndIndex = buffer.indexOf("\n\n");
      if (requestEndIndex == -1) {
        return null; // No complete request yet
      }
    }

    String requestText = buffer.substring(0, requestEndIndex);
    String[] lines = requestText.split("\r\n|\n");
    if (lines.length == 0) return null;

    // Parse request line
```

```java
    String[] requestLineParts = lines[0].split(" ");
    if (requestLineParts.length != 3) return null;
    HttpRequest request = new HttpRequest();
    request.method = requestLineParts[0];
    request.path = requestLineParts[1];
    request.version = requestLineParts[2];

    for (int i = 1; i < lines.length; i++) {
      String line = lines[i];
      int colonPos = line.indexOf(':');
      if (colonPos > 0) {
        String name = line.substring(0, colonPos).trim();
        String value = line.substring(colonPos + 1).trim();
        request.headers.put(name.toLowerCase(), value);
      }
    }

    // Store remaining buffer for next request
    request.remainingBuffer = buffer.substring(
        requestEndIndex
            + (buffer.substring(requestEndIndex)
                  .startsWith("\r\n\r\n") ? 4 : 2));
    return request;
}
```

When request processing fails, we need a specialized error response. The buildError Response method creates an appropriate HTTP 500 error response:

```java
private String buildErrorResponse(HttpRequest request,
                                  int requestId, Exception error) {
    StringBuilder response = new StringBuilder();
    // Match the request's HTTP version
    response.append(request.version).append(" 500 Internal Server Error\r\n");

    // Headers
    response.append("Content-Type: text/plain\r\n");
    response.append("Server: NonBlockingHttpServer/1.0\r\n");
    response.append("Date: ").append(Instant.now()).append("\r\n");
    // Always close connection on error
    response.append("Connection: close\r\n");

    // Body
    String body = String.format(
        "Request #%d failed\nPath: %s\nError: %s\nTime: %s",
        requestId,
        request.path,
        error.getMessage() != null
            ? error.getMessage()
            : error.getClass().getSimpleName(),
        Instant.now());

    response.append("Content-Length: ")
        .append(body.length()).append("\r\n")
```

```
        .append("\r\n") // Empty line between headers and body
        .append(body);

    return response.toString();
}
```

The `HttpRequest` class remains exactly the same as in our previous example, so we won't repeat it here. It contains the HTTP method, path, version, headers map, and the remaining buffer for handling partial requests in our non-blocking server.

If we run the Java program now, even though it operates with a single thread, it can handle multiple connections simultaneously. This is the power of NIO: it can efficiently manage numerous clients without spawning a separate thread for each connection.

To test its scalability, let's create a simple multiclient application that can send thousands of connection requests to this server, pushing it to handle a large volume of concurrent connections and observing how it performs under load:

```
import java.io.BufferedReader;
import java.io.IOException;
import java.io.InputStreamReader;
import java.io.PrintWriter;
import java.net.Socket;
import java.util.ArrayList;
import java.util.List;

public class PipeliningLoadTest {
  public static void main(String[] args) throws Exception {
    int numConnections = 10;
    int requestsPerConnection = 100;
    long startTime = System.currentTimeMillis();
    List<Thread> threads = new ArrayList<>();
    for (int i = 0; i < numConnections; i++) {
      Thread t = Thread.ofVirtual().start(() -> {  ❶
        try {
          testPipelining(requestsPerConnection);
        } catch (Exception e) {
          e.printStackTrace();
        }
      });
      threads.add(t);
    }
    for (Thread t : threads) {
      t.join();
    }
    long elapsed = System.currentTimeMillis() - startTime;
    System.out.println("Total time: " + elapsed + "ms");
    System.out.println("Requests per second: " +
        (numConnections * requestsPerConnection * 1000.0 / elapsed));
}
```

```java
    private static void testPipelining(int numRequests)
        throws Exception {
      Socket socket = new Socket("localhost", 8080);
      PrintWriter out = new PrintWriter(
          socket.getOutputStream(), true);
      BufferedReader in = new BufferedReader(
          new InputStreamReader(socket.getInputStream()));
      for (int i = 0; i < numRequests; i++) {
        String path = (i % 10 == 0) ? "/slow" : "/fast"; ❷
        out.println("GET " + path + " HTTP/1.1");
        out.println("Host: localhost");
        out.println("Connection: " +
            (i == numRequests - 1 ? "close" : "keep-alive")); ❸
        out.println();
      }
      for (int i = 0; i < numRequests; i++) {
        readResponse(in); ❹
      }
      socket.close();
    }

    static void readResponse(BufferedReader in)
        throws IOException {
      // Read status line and headers
      String line;
      int contentLength = 0;
      while ((line = in.readLine()) != null) {
        System.out.println(line);
        if (line.startsWith("Content-Length: ")) {
          contentLength = Integer.parseInt(
              line.substring("Content-Length: ".length()));
        }
        if (line.isEmpty()) {
          break; // End of headers
        }
      }
      // Read body
      char[] body = new char[contentLength];
      in.read(body);
      System.out.println(new String(body));
    }
  }
```

This load test demonstrates several important aspects of HTTP pipelining and concurrent connection handling:

❶ We use virtual threads to efficiently create 10 concurrent connections. Each virtual thread handles one connection with 100 pipelined requests.

❷ Every tenth request is slow (two-second delay) to simulate a realistic workload mix.

❸ The last request on each connection uses "Connection: close" to properly terminate the keep-alive session.

❹ After sending all requests, we read all responses in order—this is the essence of true HTTP/1.1 pipelining.

The load test spins up 10 virtual-thread clients, each opening a single persistent connection to the server and pipelining 100 HTTP/1.1 requests down that socket (1,000 requests total). Every tenth request targets the /slow path, pausing for two seconds to simulate heavy work; the other nine hit /fast and return immediately. After dispatching all requests, each client reads the responses in order, preserving pipeline semantics. When all threads join, the harness prints the total wall-clock time and calculates the throughput in requests per second. Because only 10 OS sockets are active and the server's selector handles readiness events in one thread, the test stresses connection concurrency and pipelining efficiency rather than raw socket count. This makes it ideal for highlighting NIO's ability to keep throughput high even when individual requests vary widely in latency.

Event-Driven Architecture

While our simple guessing game scales well and serves its purpose, real-world applications are far more complex. They involve much more than just handling a few guesses from a client. So, how do we structure our code in a way that supports larger, more dynamic systems?

Fortunately, many frameworks have been built on top of the event-driven paradigm, making it easier to efficiently handle concurrency and scalability. Frameworks like Netty (*https://netty.io*) and Vert.x (*https://vertx.io*) are great examples of this approach.

If we were to rewrite our guessing game using Vert.x, the implementation would look something like this:

```
import io.vertx.core.AbstractVerticle;
import io.vertx.core.Promise;
import io.vertx.core.Vertx;
import io.vertx.core.json.JsonObject;
import io.vertx.ext.web.Router;
import io.vertx.ext.web.RoutingContext;
import java.util.concurrent.atomic.AtomicLong;

public class VertxHttpServer extends AbstractVerticle {
  private static final int PORT = 8080;
  private final AtomicLong requestCounter = new AtomicLong(0); ❶
  private long startTime;

  @Override
```

```java
    public void start(Promise<Void> startPromise) {
      startTime = System.currentTimeMillis();
      Router router = Router.router(vertx);  ❷
      router.get("/fast").handler(this::handleFastRequest);
      router.get("/slow").handler(this::handleSlowRequest);
      router.get("/stats").handler(this::handleStats);
      vertx.createHttpServer()
          .requestHandler(router)
          .listen(PORT, "localhost");  ❸
    }

    private void handleFastRequest(RoutingContext ctx) {
      long requestId = requestCounter.incrementAndGet();
      ctx.response()
          .putHeader("content-type", "text/plain")
          .end("Request #" + requestId + ": Fast request processed");  ❹
    }

    private void handleSlowRequest(RoutingContext ctx) {
      long requestId = requestCounter.incrementAndGet();
      vertx.setTimer(2000, id -> {  ❺
        ctx.response()
            .putHeader("content-type", "text/plain")
            .end("Request #" + requestId + ": Slow request processed");
      });
    }

    private void handleStats(RoutingContext ctx) {
      long uptimeMillis = System.currentTimeMillis() - startTime;
      JsonObject stats = new JsonObject()
              .put("totalRequests", requestCounter.get())
              .put("uptimeMillis", uptimeMillis)
              .put("currentThread", Thread.currentThread().getName())
              .put("isEventLoopThread", Vertx.currentContext()
                                  .isEventLoopContext());  ❻
      ctx.response()
          .putHeader("content-type", "application/json")
          .end(stats.encodePrettily());
    }

    public static void main(String[] args) {
      Vertx vertx = Vertx.vertx();
      vertx.deployVerticle(new VertxHttpServer());  ❼
    }
  }
```

This Vert.x implementation showcases several key principles of event-driven architecture:

❶ We use `AtomicLong` for thread-safe request counting, since multiple event loop threads might increment it concurrently.

❷ The `Router` handles HTTP routing declaratively; each route is mapped to a handler method.

❸ The server starts asynchronously on the event loop without blocking the main thread.

❹ Fast requests complete immediately on the event loop thread, demonstrating non-blocking I/O.

❺ The crucial difference: `vertx.setTimer()` schedules the response after two seconds *without* blocking the event loop thread. This is the key to maintaining high concurrency.

❻ The `stats` endpoint reveals which thread is handling the request, helping us verify that all requests run on event loop threads.

❼ Deploying a `verticle` starts the event-driven server with Vert.x managing the event loops automatically.

To run this Vert.x server, you'll need to add the following dependencies to your Maven project. Create a Maven project, then add these dependencies and run it:

```
<dependency>
    <groupId>io.vertx</groupId>
    <artifactId>vertx-core</artifactId>
    <version>5.0.0</version>
</dependency>
<dependency>
    <groupId>io.vertx</groupId>
    <artifactId>vertx-web</artifactId>
    <version>5.0.0</version>
</dependency>
```

This gives us HTTP endpoints where we can test with curl:

```
curl -X GET http://localhost:8080/fast
curl -X GET http://localhost:8080/slow
curl -X GET http://localhost:8080/stats
```

Let's focus on the high-level concept rather than diving into the intricate details of how Vert.x is implemented under the hood. At its core, Vert.x is built on a multicore reactor pattern, leveraging an event-loop concurrency model. It uses a lightweight set of event loop threads that continuously listen for I/O events via non-blocking operations such as NIO. Whenever an event occurs, such as an incoming request, a short, non-blocking callback is executed within the event loop, ensuring responsiveness.

However, not all tasks can be handled in an event loop. Some operations are inherently blocking or long-running, such as database queries or filesystem access. Vert.x intelligently offloads them to a separate worker thread pool to prevent these tasks from slowing down the event loop. This design ensures that the event loop remains free to handle new requests without unnecessary delays.

One of the key strengths of Vert.x is its event bus (*https://oreil.ly/9Fs7I*), which allows different components of an application to communicate asynchronously. This approach keeps the system loosely coupled while ensuring seamless coordination between different parts of the application (Figure 6-1).

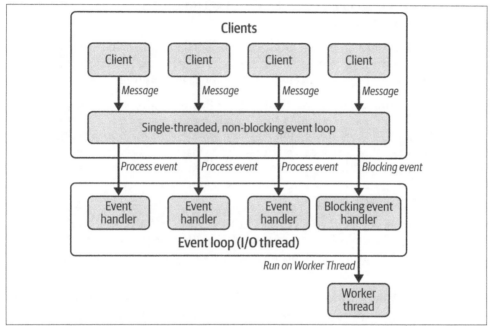

Figure 6-1. Overview of event loop of event-driven architecture in Vert.x

In Figure 6-1, we get a glimpse of how a framework like Vert.x operates with the event loop at its core. This framework is responsible for managing client connections, handling outbound requests, and writing responses—all in a non-blocking manner. Typically, a reactive framework sits on top of this, providing a higher-level API that simplifies network operations. We'll explore these in more detail soon. Instead of dealing with raw, non-blocking I/O directly, developers work with intuitive abstractions, such as HTTP requests, responses, and Kafka messages, making the development experience far more streamlined.

Our application code sits at the highest layer. Our code doesn't interact directly with the event loop; instead, it works through event handlers. For example, in our earlier code snippet, we created handlers like `handleFastRequest` and `handleSlowRequest` to process specific HTTP routes.

So far, everything seems great. However, here's the critical piece: the event handlers in your application are executed using the event loop thread—essentially an I/O thread. If our code blocks this thread, no other concurrent events can be processed. The result is a complete breakdown in responsiveness and concurrency that would be catastrophic for a system designed to be highly reactive.

Notice how in our Vert.x example, the slow request handler uses `vertx.setTimer()` instead of `Thread.sleep()`. This is crucial—the timer schedules a callback to run after two seconds without blocking the event loop thread. The thread is immediately free to handle other requests while waiting.

The solution is simple: your code must be non-blocking. It should never, under any circumstance, block the I/O threads. If it does, the entire event loop comes to a standstill, dragging down the responsiveness of your application as well.

There are workarounds, of course. You could offload blocking operations to a separate worker thread pool—something Vert.x itself does to some extent. But this should never be the norm. In fact, relying too much on worker threads defeats the purpose of a reactive system. Why? Because every time you switch execution from an I/O thread to a worker thread and back, you introduce context switches. These add overhead, slowing down response times and chipping away at the efficiency gains you set out to achieve in the first place.

So, how do you ensure your application code remains non-blocking? It's one thing to say, "write non-blocking code," but as we've seen, that's easier said than done. The reality is that writing truly non-blocking code isn't always straightforward; it requires a shift in mindset.

That's where we can really focus on reactive frameworks. They provide asynchronous APIs specifically to help us avoid blocking operations while still handling complex workflows efficiently. Instead of waiting for a task to complete, we register callbacks, use promises, or leverage reactive streams to orchestrate execution without ever stalling the event loop.

But what exactly are these asynchronous APIs, and how do they work? Let's explore.

Asynchronous APIs

Most of us are familiar with synchronous APIs, but let's take a moment to revisit the concept. Consider the following simple Java method:

```
public class AiService {
    public String chat(String message) {
        return "Echo: " + message.toUpperCase();
    }
}
```

This method takes a string as input, processes it, and returns a response. We can invoke it like this:

```
String result = aiService.chat("What is the meaning of life?");
```

In this case, the caller thread executes the chat method and blocks execution until it receives a response. This is a classic example of a *synchronous API*—the caller has to wait.

Now, what if we want to make this API asynchronous? That is, instead of waiting for the result, we let the method return immediately, and once the response is ready, a callback function handles it. Let's modify our method accordingly:

```
public void chat(String message, Consumer<String> consumer) {
    Thread.startVirtualThread(() -> {
        try {
            String response = "Echo: " + message.toUpperCase();
            consumer.accept(response);
        } catch (Exception e) {
            consumer.accept("Error during chat: " + e.getMessage());
        }
    });
}
```

This version of the method now takes two parameters:

1. The message itself
2. A callback function (of type `Consumer<String>`) that will be invoked when the response is ready

Now, let's see how we can use this asynchronous API:

```
aiService.chat("Hello, how are you?", response -> {
    System.out.println("Response 1: " + response);
});
aiService.chat("What is your name?", response -> {
    System.out.println("Response 2: " + response);
});
```

Here's what happens: the first chat call is made, but unlike before, the main thread does *not* wait for the result. Instead, it immediately moves to execute the second chat call. Meanwhile, the responses will be processed asynchronously when they become available. This is the essence of asynchronous programming—freeing up the main thread to perform other tasks while waiting for results.

However, the callback has some inherent issues. It doesn't integrate well. What if we want to pass the result from the first callback to another chat method? Let's try to do so:

```
aiService.chat("What is the meaning of life?", response -> {
    aiService.chat(response, response2 -> {
```

```
            aiService.chat(response2, response3 -> {
                aiService.chat(response3, response4 -> {
                    System.out.println(response4);
                });
            });
        });
    });
```

As we can see here, using callbacks for asynchronous execution can quickly become unmanageable. The more callbacks we introduce, the harder it becomes to read and maintain our code, leading to what's often called callback hell.

So, what's the alternative?

Java provides a much cleaner solution: `CompletableFuture`. It allows us to write asynchronous code that remains readable, structured, and composable. Let's modify our chat method to return a `CompletableFuture<String>` instead:

```
public CompletableFuture<String> chat(String message) {
    return CompletableFuture.supplyAsync(() -> {
        try {
            return "Echo: " + message.toUpperCase();
        } catch (Exception e) {
            return "Error during chat: " + e.getMessage();
        }
    });
}
```

Now, instead of relying on callbacks, we can chain multiple asynchronous calls together in a more structured way:

```
aiService.chat("What is the meaning of life?")
        .thenCompose(aiService::chat)
        .thenCompose(aiService::chat)
        .thenCompose(aiService::chat)
        .thenAccept(System.out::println);
```

This makes composing asynchronous methods much easier than dealing with nested callbacks. We haven't touched on error handling yet, but `CompletableFuture` provides a rich API for gracefully managing failures.

So, does this mean we've solved the problem of blocking I/O threads? Well, while `CompletableFuture` does a great job of handling single asynchronous results, there's something we haven't considered yet: streams of data. `CompletableFuture` works beautifully for methods that return a single value, but what happens when we need to deal with sequences of results—a continuous flow of data rather than a one-time response?

That's where things get a little more interesting. In fact, that's where the reactive framework shines best.

Reactive Programming in Java

Reactive programming in Java is a paradigm centered around asynchronous, nonblocking, and event-driven applications. A core concept is the *reactive stream*, a standard (defined by the Reactive Streams Specification (*https://oreil.ly/HhQ9M*)) for managing asynchronous data flows with *backpressure*.

Let's discuss what a reactive stream is and then talk about backpressure, one by one.

Understanding Reactive Streams

In reactive programming, we organize our code around streams, creating chains of transformations known as pipelines. In this paradigm, everything can be viewed as a stream of events flowing from producers to consumers through a series of transformations.

Events can be anything: user clicks, sensor readings, incoming messages, etc. They travel from an upstream source to a downstream Subscriber, passing through operators that transform or filter the data (Figure 6-2).

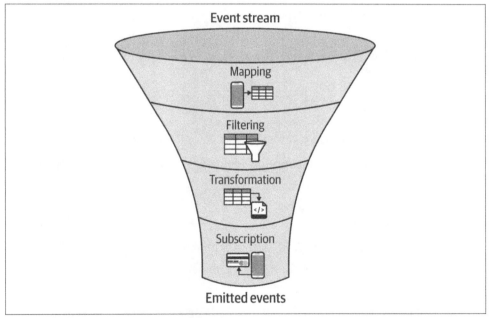

Figure 6-2. Reactive programming data flow

Each operator observes its upstream and produces a new stream. However, streams are lazy by default—they don't start processing until there's a Subscriber. We don't know *when* an event will arrive (asynchronous), so we set up "observers" to react when it does.

In reactive programming, we work with four fundamental components:

Publisher
    The source that emits data items asynchronously. Think of it as a data producer that can emit zero or more items over time.

Subscriber
    The consumer that receives and processes emitted items. Subscribers express interest in receiving data and define how it should be handled.

Subscription
    The link between a Publisher and a Subscriber, managing the flow of data and enabling backpressure control.

Processor
    A component that acts as both Subscriber and Publisher, transforming data as it flows through the stream.

A reactive stream can emit three types of signals:

Data items
    The actual values flowing through the stream

Error signal
    Indicates that an unrecoverable error occurred, terminating the stream

Completion signal
    Indicates successful stream completion with no more items to emit

There are several reactive programming libraries in Java. The most notable ones include:

Project Reactor (https://oreil.ly/rKyko)
    Provides the core types:

- `Flux<T>` (*https://oreil.ly/5Xb9z*) (0 to N items)
- `Mono<T>` (*https://oreil.ly/2fKjm*) (0 to 1 items)

RxJava (https://oreil.ly/hrj2a)
    A reactive extension for Java. It provides the types:

- `Observable<T>` (*https://oreil.ly/HY8sm*) (0 to N items)
- `Single<T>` (*https://oreil.ly/UlIwi*) (exactly 1 item)
- `Maybe<T>` (*https://oreil.ly/Or-Vx*) (0 to 1 items)

Let's explore reactive programming with Project Reactor through a series of examples:

```
public class ReactiveExample {
    public static void main(String[] args) {
        // Create a Flux emitting integers 1 to 5
        Flux<Integer> numbers = Flux.just(1, 2, 3, 4, 5); ❶
        // Process the stream: filter even numbers and convert to strings
        numbers
            .filter(n -> n % 2 == 0) ❷ // Keep even numbers
            .map(n -> "Value: " + n) ❸ // Transform to strings
            .subscribe(
                System.out::println, ❹ // onNext: print each value
                error -> System.err.println("Error: " + error), ❺ // onError
                () -> System.out.println("Done!") ❻ // onComplete
            );
    }
}
```

This code demonstrates the basic reactive stream pipeline:

❶ Creates a cold stream with five integer values. The stream won't emit any values until a Subscriber subscribes.

❷ The `filter` operator creates a new stream containing only elements that match the predicate, in this case, even numbers.

❸ The `map` operator transforms each element, converting integers to formatted strings.

❹ The `subscribe` method triggers the pipeline execution and defines how to handle each emitted value.

❺ The error-handling callback executes if any operator in the pipeline throws an exception.

❻ The completion callback executes when the stream completes all emissions.

The output would be:

```
Value: 2
Value: 4
Done!
```

Now that we have a basic idea of what it looks like, let's explore reactive programming through a practical example: building a cryptocurrency price-monitoring system.

Imagine we're building a system that monitors cryptocurrency prices from multiple exchanges in real time. This scenario perfectly illustrates the strengths of reactive programming, which include handling multiple asynchronous data sources, transforming data streams, and reacting to specific conditions.

First, let's define our data model:

```
public record PriceData(String exchange, String symbol, double price,
                    Instant timestamp) {}

public record PriceAlert(String symbol, String message, AlertType type) {}

enum AlertType {THRESHOLD_CROSSED, RAPID_CHANGE, ANOMALY}
```

Now, let's create a simple reactive price-monitoring system:

```
import reactor.core.publisher.Flux;
import java.time.Duration;
import java.time.Instant;

public class SimplePriceMonitor {
    public static void main(String[] args) throws InterruptedException {
        // Create a stream of price updates ❶
        Flux<PriceData> priceStream = Flux.interval(Duration.ofSeconds(1))
            .map(i -> new PriceData(
                "Binance",
                "BTC/USD",
                50000 + (Math.random() - 0.5) * 1000, ❷
                Instant.now()
            ));

        // Process the stream ❸
        priceStream
            .filter(price -> price.price() > 50200) ❹
            .map(price -> String.format("BTC price $%.2f exceeds threshold!",
                                price.price())) ❺
            .subscribe(
                alert -> System.out.println(alert), ❻
                error -> System.err.println("Error: " + error),
                () -> System.out.println("Monitoring complete")
            );

        // Keep the main thread alive
        Thread.sleep(10000);
    }
}
```

Let's examine what's happening in this code:

❶ Creates a cold stream that emits a value every second. The `interval` operator uses a daemon thread, so we need to keep the main thread alive. The stream doesn't start emitting until a Subscriber subscribes to it.

❷ Generates simulated price data with random fluctuations around a $50,000 base price.

❸ Begins the stream-processing pipeline. Each operator creates a new stream that observes the previous one.

❹ Filters the stream to only include prices above $50,200, demonstrating selective processing.

❺ Transforms the price data into alert messages, showing how data can be reshaped as it flows.

❻ Subscribes to the stream, triggering the entire pipeline to start processing.

Real-world applications require more sophisticated stream processing. Let's build a comprehensive price monitoring system that handles multiple exchanges and symbols:

```java
public class CryptoPriceMonitor {
    private static final List<String> EXCHANGES =
        List.of("Binance", "Coinbase", "Kraken");
    private static final List<String> SYMBOLS =
        List.of("BTC/USD", "ETH/USD", "SOL/USD");

    // Sinks for broadcasting alerts to multiple Subscribers ❶
    private static final Sinks.Many<PriceAlert> alertSink =
        Sinks.many().multicast().onBackpressureBuffer();

    public static void main(String[] args) throws InterruptedException {
        // Create merged stream from multiple exchanges ❷
        Flux<PriceData> priceStream = Flux.merge(
            EXCHANGES.stream()
                .map(CryptoPriceMonitor::createExchangeFeed)
                .toList()
        );

        // Group prices by symbol for parallel processing ❸
        priceStream
            .groupBy(PriceData::symbol)
            .subscribe(symbolFlux -> {
                String symbol = symbolFlux.key();

                // Calculate 5-second moving average ❹
                symbolFlux
                    .window(Duration.ofSeconds(5))
                    .flatMap(window -> calculateMovingAverage(window, symbol))
                    .subscribe(avg -> System.out.printf(
                        " %s Moving Avg: $%.2f%n", symbol, avg));

                // Detect rapid price changes ❺
                symbolFlux
                  .buffer(2, 1)
```

```
            .filter(buffer -> buffer.size() == 2)
            .map(buffer -> detectRapidChange(buffer.get(0), buffer.get(1)))
            .filter(Optional::isPresent)
            .map(Optional::get)
            .subscribe(alertSink::tryEmitNext);
        });

    // Subscribe to alerts ❻
    alertSink.asFlux()
        .subscribe(alert -> System.out.printf(" [%s] %s: %s%n",
            alert.type(), alert.symbol(), alert.message()));

    Thread.sleep(30000);
}

private static Flux<PriceData> createExchangeFeed(String exchange) {
    return Flux.interval(Duration.ofMillis(
            100 + (int) (Math.random() * 400))) ❼
        .map(i -> {
            String symbol = SYMBOLS.get(
                (int) (Math.random() * SYMBOLS.size()));
            double basePrice = getBasePrice(symbol);
            double variation = (Math.random() - 0.5) * 0.01;
            double price = basePrice * (1 + variation);

            return new PriceData(exchange, symbol, price,
                                 Instant.now());
        })
        .doOnNext(price -> System.out.printf(
            "%s [%s]: $%.2f%n", ❽
            price.exchange(), price.symbol(), price.price()));
}
```

This advanced example demonstrates several key reactive patterns:

❶ Sinks provide a bridge between imperative and reactive code, allowing manual emission of items into a stream.

❷ merge combines multiple streams into a single stream, interleaving items as they arrive.

❸ groupBy partitions a stream into multiple substreams based on a key function, enabling parallel processing of different symbols.

❹ window creates time-based chunks of data, perfect for calculating metrics over sliding time windows.

❺ buffer collects items into lists, with sliding windows created by the stride parameter.

❻ Hot streams (created by sinks) allow multiple Subscribers to receive the same events.

❼ Irregular intervals simulate realistic, nonuniform data arrival from different exchanges.

❽ Side effects with doOnNext allow logging without affecting the stream's data flow.

There are helper methods that complete this example.

The `calculateMovingAverage` method computes the average price over a sliding window, which is essential for identifying price trends and smoothing out short-term fluctuations:

```
private static Mono<Double> calculateMovingAverage(Flux<PriceData> window,
                                                    String symbol) {
    return window
        .map(PriceData::price)
        .reduce(new double[]{0, 0}, (acc, price) -> {
          acc[0] += price;  // sum
          acc[1] += 1;      // count
          return acc;
        })
        .map(acc -> acc[1] > 0 ? acc[0] / acc[1] : 0.0)
        .filter(avg -> avg > 0);
}
```

While moving averages help identify trends, we also need to detect sudden price movements. The `detectRapidChange` method compares consecutive price points to alert on significant changes:

```
private static Optional<PriceAlert> detectRapidChange(PriceData prev,
                                                      PriceData current) {
    if (!prev.symbol().equals(current.symbol())) {
      return Optional.empty();
    }

    double changePercent = Math.abs((current.price() - prev.price())
        / prev.price()) * 100;
    if (changePercent > 0.5) { // 0.5% change threshold
      return Optional.of(new PriceAlert(
          current.symbol(),
          String.format("Rapid %.2f%% change: $%.2f → $%.2f",
              changePercent, prev.price(), current.price()),
          AlertType.RAPID_CHANGE
      ));
    }
    return Optional.empty();
}
```

The `getBasePrice` method provides these baseline values for our supported trading pairs:

```
private static double getBasePrice(String symbol) {
  return switch (symbol) {
    case "BTC/USD" -> 50000;
    case "ETH/USD" -> 3000;
    case "SOL/USD" -> 100;
    default -> 1000;
  };
}
```

This is a high-level introduction to reactive streams. This book isn't intended to cover every detail but rather to provide you with a taste of what reactive programming entails. If you wish to learn more, I recommend exploring dedicated books on the subject.

Reactive streams are not the same as Java Streams.

- `java.util.stream.Stream` (*https://oreil.ly/7tgYY*) (Java Streams API) is used to process collections synchronously and in-memory.
- Reactive streams handle asynchronous, event-driven, and non-blocking data processing with support for backpressure.

Backpressure

In reactive programming, backpressure is an integral mechanism that enables a downstream consumer (Subscriber) to signal an upstream producer (Publisher) when it is unable to process data. Essentially, it will allow the consumer to say, "Slow down! I can't process this fast enough."

Let's examine different backpressure strategies using a high-frequency trading scenario:

```
public class BackpressureDemo {
    public static void main(String[] args) throws InterruptedException {
        // Simulate ultra-high-frequency price feed ❶
        Flux<PriceData> extremeFeed = Flux.interval(Duration.ofNanos(100_000))
            .map(i -> new PriceData(
                "HFT-Exchange",
                "BTC/USD",
                50000 + ThreadLocalRandom.current().nextDouble(-100, 100),
                Instant.now()
            ))
            .share(); // Hot stream shared among subscribers

        // Strategy 1: Sampling - Take periodic snapshots ❷
        System.out.println("SAMPLING Strategy:");
```

```java
            extremeFeed
                .sample(Duration.ofMillis(100))
                .take(10)
                .subscribe(price -> System.out.printf(
                    "[SAMPLED] Price: $%.2f at %s%n",
                    price.price(), price.timestamp()));

            Thread.sleep(1500);

            // Strategy 2: Drop - Discard when overwhelmed ❸
            System.out.println("\nDROP Strategy:");
            AtomicInteger dropped = new AtomicInteger(0);
            extremeFeed
                .onBackpressureDrop(price -> {
                    if (dropped.incrementAndGet() % 1000 == 0) {
                        System.out.printf("[DROPPED] %d updates dropped%n",
                                          dropped.get());
                    }
                })
                .publishOn(Schedulers.boundedElastic()) ❹
                .take(Duration.ofSeconds(1))
                .subscribe(price -> {
                    simulateWork(10); // Simulate slow processing
                    System.out.printf("[PROCESSED] Price: $%.2f%n", price.price());
                });

            Thread.sleep(1500);

            // Strategy 3: Latest - Keep only most recent value ❺
            System.out.println("\nLATEST Strategy:");
            extremeFeed
                .onBackpressureLatest()
                .publishOn(Schedulers.boundedElastic())
                .subscribe(price -> {
                    simulateWork(100);   // Very slow processing
                    System.out.printf("[LATEST] Price: $%.2f%n", price.price());
                });

            Thread.sleep(2000);
        }
        private static void simulateWork(int millis) {
          try {
            Thread.sleep(millis);
          } catch (InterruptedException e) {
            Thread.currentThread().interrupt();
            throw new RuntimeException(e);
          }
        }
      }
    }
```

Let's examine each backpressure strategy:

❶ Creates a stream emitting 10,000 items per second, simulating high-frequency trading data.

❷ Sampling takes periodic snapshots, which is ideal when you need regular updates but can't process every item.

❸ `Drop` discards items when the consumer can't keep up; this is suitable when it's acceptable to miss some data.

❹ `publishOn` moves processing to a different thread pool, separating production from consumption.

❺ `Latest` keeps only the most recent unprocessed item, perfect for scenarios where only the current state matters.

Reactor provides different strategies for handling backpressure:

`onBackpressureBuffer()`
Buffers all items until the consumer catches up. Use when no data can be lost, but memory is available.

`onBackpressureBuffer(maxSize)`
Buffers with a limit, failing if exceeded. Provides safety against memory exhaustion.

`onBackpressureDrop()`
Silently drops excess items. Use for real-time data where the latest values matter more than completeness.

`onBackpressureLatest()`
Keeps only the most recent item. Ideal for status updates where intermediate values become obsolete.

`onBackpressureError()`
Fails fast when backpressure occurs. Use when backpressure indicates a system design flaw.

This example illustrates how reactive streams function in a real-world scenario, connecting the concepts of Publishers, operators, Subscribers, and backpressure.

Now, how would our price-monitoring system look if implemented with virtual threads?

Let's compare both approaches using our price-monitoring example:

```
package ca.bazlur.mcj.chap6.virtualthreads;
import ca.bazlur.mcj.chap6.reactive.AlertType;
```

```java
import ca.bazlur.mcj.chap6.reactive.PriceAlert;
import ca.bazlur.mcj.chap6.reactive.PriceData;
import java.time.Instant;
import java.util.*;
import java.util.concurrent.*;
import java.util.concurrent.atomic.AtomicReference;

public class PriceMonitorWithVirtualThreads {
  private static final List<String> SYMBOLS =
      List.of("BTC/USD", "ETH/USD", "SOL/USD");
  private static final List<String> EXCHANGES =
      List.of("Binance", "Coinbase", "Kraken");
  private static final Map<String, AtomicReference<PriceData>> latestPrices =
      new ConcurrentHashMap<>();
  private static final BlockingQueue<PriceAlert> alertQueue =
      new LinkedBlockingQueue<>();

  public static void main(String[] args) throws InterruptedException {
    try (var executor = Executors.newVirtualThreadPerTaskExecutor()) { ❶
      // Start price feeds from each exchange
      for (String exchange : EXCHANGES) {
        executor.submit(() -> generatePriceFeed(exchange));
      }
      // Start processors
      executor.submit(PriceMonitorWithVirtualThreads::processAlerts);
      executor.submit(PriceMonitorWithVirtualThreads::monitorThresholds);
      Thread.sleep(30000);
    }
  }

  private static void generatePriceFeed(String exchange) {
    var random = ThreadLocalRandom.current();
    while (!Thread.currentThread().isInterrupted()) {
      try {
        Thread.sleep(100 + random.nextInt(400)); ❷
        String symbol = SYMBOLS.get(random.nextInt(SYMBOLS.size()));
        double basePrice = getBasePrice(symbol);
        double variation = (random.nextDouble() - 0.5) * 0.01;
        double price = basePrice * (1 + variation);
        PriceData priceData = new PriceData(
          exchange,
          symbol,
          price,
          Instant.now()
        );

        System.out.printf(" %s [%s]: $%.2f%n", exchange, symbol, price);
        // Process this price in a new virtual thread
        Thread.startVirtualThread(() -> processPrice(priceData)); ❸
      } catch (InterruptedException e) {
        Thread.currentThread().interrupt();
        break;
```

Reactive Programming in Java | 289

```
      }
    }
  }

  private static void processPrice(PriceData currentPrice) {
    PriceData previousPrice = latestPrices
        .computeIfAbsent(currentPrice.symbol(), k -> new AtomicReference<>())
        .getAndSet(currentPrice);  ❹
    if (previousPrice != null) {
      detectRapidChange(previousPrice, currentPrice);
    }
    calculateSimpleMovingAverage(currentPrice.symbol(), currentPrice);
  }

  private static void detectRapidChange(PriceData prev, PriceData current) {
    if (!prev.symbol().equals(current.symbol())) return;
    double changePercent = Math.abs((current.price() - prev.price())
                                    / prev.price()) * 100;
    if (changePercent > 0.5) { // 0.5% change threshold
      PriceAlert alert = new PriceAlert(
          current.symbol(),
          String.format("Rapid %.2f%% change: $%.2f → $%.2f",
              changePercent, prev.price(), current.price()),
          AlertType.RAPID_CHANGE
      );
      alertQueue.offer(alert);  ❺
    }
  }

  private static void monitorThresholds() {
    Map<String, Double> thresholds = Map.of(
        "BTC/USD", 51000.0,
        "ETH/USD", 3100.0,
        "SOL/USD", 105.0
    );
    while (!Thread.currentThread().isInterrupted()) {
      try {
        Thread.sleep(2000); //
        thresholds.forEach((symbol, threshold) -> {
          AtomicReference<PriceData> ref = latestPrices.get(symbol);
          if (ref != null) {
            PriceData latest = ref.get();
            if (latest != null && latest.price() > threshold) {
              alertQueue.offer(new PriceAlert(
                  symbol,
                  String.format("Price $%.2f exceeded threshold $%.2f",
                      latest.price(), threshold),
                  AlertType.THRESHOLD_CROSSED
              ));
            }
          }
        });
```

```java
      } catch (InterruptedException e) {
        Thread.currentThread().interrupt();
        break;
      }
    }
  }

  private static final Map<String, LinkedList<Double>> priceWindows =
      new ConcurrentHashMap<>();

  private static void calculateSimpleMovingAverage(String symbol, PriceData price) {
    var window = priceWindows.computeIfAbsent(symbol, k -> new LinkedList<>());
    synchronized (window) { //
      window.add(price.price());
      if (window.size() > 10) {
        window.removeFirst();
      }
      if (window.size() >= 5) {
        double avg = window.stream()
            .mapToDouble(Double::doubleValue)
            .average()
            .orElse(0.0);
        System.out.printf("□□s Moving Avg: $%.2f%n", symbol, avg);
      }
    }
  }

  private static void processAlerts() {
    while (!Thread.currentThread().isInterrupted()) {
      try {
        PriceAlert alert = alertQueue.poll(100, TimeUnit.MILLISECONDS); //
        if (alert != null) {
          System.out.printf(" [%s] %s: %s%n",
              alert.type(), alert.symbol(), alert.message());
        }
      } catch (InterruptedException e) {
        Thread.currentThread().interrupt();
        break;
      }
    }
  }

  private static double getBasePrice(String symbol) {
    return switch (symbol) {
      case "BTC/USD" -> 50000;
      case "ETH/USD" -> 3000;
      case "SOL/USD" -> 100;
      default -> 1000;
    };
  }
}
```

Key differences in the virtual thread approach:

❶ Virtual threads are created implicitly through the executor, making thread creation lightweight and resource-efficient.

❷ Explicit loops with sleep calls replace reactive intervals, requiring manual timing control.

❸ Each price update spawns a new virtual thread for processing, achieving concurrency through thread creation rather than stream operators.

❹ Shared mutable state with atomic references requires careful synchronization, unlike reactive's immutable transformations.

❺ Manual synchronization is needed for shared data structures, whereas reactive streams handle this through operators.

Comparison and trade-offs

Looking at both implementations side by side reveals fundamental differences in each approach. The reactive version utilizes a declarative pipeline where data flows through transformations. For instance, `window(Duration.ofSeconds(5))` creates time-based chunks, `onBackpressureDrop()` elegantly handles overflow, and `groupBy()` enables parallel processing without explicit thread management.

In contrast, the virtual threads version uses imperative code with manual state management—maintaining a `LinkedList` with synchronized blocks for moving averages, using `BlockingQueue` for backpressure, and explicitly creating threads with `Thread.startVirtualThread()`. While reactive code reads like a description of data transformations, virtual thread code reads like a sequence of instructions, making it more familiar to developers used to traditional Java programming but requiring more careful attention to synchronization and state management.

Benefits and Downsides of Reactive Programming

Now that we have a high-level understanding of how reactive systems operate, leveraging non-blocking I/O, adopting an event-driven approach, and utilizing stream-based processing, let's explore the advantages and challenges that accompany this paradigm.

Benefits of reactive programming

First and foremost, reactive programming relies on non-blocking operations and asynchronous execution. This allows applications to handle a large number of concurrent requests while consuming minimal system resources. For I/O-bound workloads, this translates into significantly improved scalability and performance.

Second, reactive programming provides a robust toolkit for writing non-blocking and asynchronous code. It encourages a functional and declarative coding style, which many developers find more intuitive and expressive than traditional imperative programming. When used effectively, reactive code can be more readable and maintainable because it composes data streams and handles events in a structured way.

Moreover, reactive programming seamlessly integrates with modern cloud-native applications, making it particularly well-suited for microservices architectures. It enables efficient data flow and communication between distributed components, reducing bottlenecks and improving responsiveness.

Downsides of reactive programming

Despite its many advantages, reactive programming also presents its own challenges.

First, it introduces a fundamentally different programming paradigm. Developers accustomed to imperative programming may find the learning curve steep. Adapting to reactive patterns, such as composing streams and managing backpressure, requires a shift in mindset and a familiarity with new concepts and techniques.

Debugging reactive code can also be notoriously difficult. The asynchronous nature of execution, coupled with event-driven data flow, makes it challenging to trace errors and understand execution paths. The logical flow we see in the code is completely different from the actual execution, making both mental debugging and IDE debugging challenging.

Consider the following example of reactive code that throws an exception:

```java
import reactor.core.publisher.Flux;

public class ReactiveErrorExample {
    public static void main(String[] args) {
        Flux.just(1, 2, 3, 0, 5)
                .map(number -> 10 / number)
                .subscribe(
                        System.out::println,
                        Throwable::printStackTrace,
                        () -> System.out.println("Done!")
                );
    }
}
```

Running this code results in an exception:

```
java.lang.ArithmeticException: / by zero
    at.ReactiveErrorExample.lambda$main$0(ReactiveErrorExample.java:8)
    at reactor.core.publisher.FluxMapFuseable$MapFuseableSubscriber.onNext(FluxMa
pFuseable.java:113)
    at reactor.core.publisher.FluxArray$ArraySubscription.fastPath(FluxArray.java
```

```
            :171)
        at reactor.core.publisher.FluxArray$ArraySubscription.request(FluxArray.java:
        96)
        at reactor.core.publisher.FluxMapFuseable$MapFuseableSubscriber.request(FluxM
        apFuseable.java:171)
        at reactor.core.publisher.LambdaSubscriber.onSubscribe(LambdaSubscriber.java:
        119)
        at reactor.core.publisher.FluxMapFuseable$MapFuseableSubscriber.onSubscribe(F
        luxMapFuseable.java:96)
        at reactor.core.publisher.FluxArray.subscribe(FluxArray.java:53)
        at reactor.core.publisher.FluxArray.subscribe(FluxArray.java:59)
        at reactor.core.publisher.Flux.subscribe(Flux.java:8836)
        at reactor.core.publisher.Flux.subscribeWith(Flux.java:8957)
        at reactor.core.publisher.Flux.subscribe(Flux.java:8801)
        at reactor.core.publisher.Flux.subscribe(Flux.java:8725)
        at ReactiveErrorExample.main(ReactiveErrorExample.java:9)
```

While the first line correctly identifies `ReactiveErrorExample.java:8` as the source of the issue, the rest of the stack trace consists of internal calls within the Reactor library. The `threaddump` looks like complete gibberish. This makes debugging more complex compared to traditional, synchronous code, where stack traces are usually straightforward.

Another concern is maintainability. While reactive code can be elegant and concise, it may also be harder to understand and modify. The declarative nature of reactive programming, combined with a rich set of operators, often makes it difficult for developers to predict how the code will behave. This can lead to unintentional side effects when making changes.

Finally, while reactive programming excels at managing I/O-bound workloads, it may not be the ideal choice for CPU-bound tasks, much like virtual threads. Traditional multithreading approaches might offer a more intuitive and manageable solution for certain types of applications, but that's not what we are discussing here.

In Closing

Having explored both traditional concurrency models and their shared focus on handling I/O operations, where does that leave us?

This is where I'll share my perspective. Over the years, I've gained experience, and while I have certain biases, I also appreciate the various use cases for different approaches. Every technology has its strengths and trade-offs. Virtual threads offer simplicity and numerous advantages, but one could argue that they lack a straightforward, built-in way to implement backpressure, something that reactive frameworks handle natively. Of course, we can build backpressure mechanisms ourselves, but that responsibility falls squarely on the developer's shoulders.

That said, both paradigms share a common goal: to efficiently manage I/O-bound operations. If I had to choose between them, I would lean toward virtual threads. Reactive programming maintains its relevance, particularly in scenarios that require fine-grained backpressure control, complex data transformations, or event-driven microservices.

Virtual threads shine in high-concurrency, I/O-bound applications. They are particularly useful when handling large numbers of concurrent user requests or working with existing synchronous systems. With virtual threads, we can seamlessly replace traditional OS threads without rewriting code to use non-blocking APIs.

Looking ahead, I believe reactive programming and virtual threads will coexist for the foreseeable future. Over time, we might see some convergence between the two. For example, reactive stream libraries could evolve to leverage virtual threads, enabling developers to write reactive code that is both simpler and more efficient. Similarly, structured concurrency principles may influence reactive programming models, making them more robust and maintainable.

We're already seeing the first signs of this convergence. Vert.x 4.5 (*https://oreil.ly/ Lv3GW*) has begun experimenting with virtual threads, hinting at a future where these two paradigms seamlessly complement each other.

In the long run, virtual threads may become the default choice for many applications due to their simplicity and compatibility with existing synchronous code. The ability to write concurrent programs using familiar imperative programming techniques is a significant advantage; it lowers the barrier to entry and reduces developers' cognitive overhead.

Only time will tell, but one thing is certain: concurrency in Java is evolving, and we, as developers, must evolve with it.

CHAPTER 7
Modern Frameworks Utilizing Virtual Threads

The best way to predict the future is to invent it.
—Alan Kay

With the introduction of virtual threads in JDK 21, the Java ecosystem has witnessed a significant shift in how frameworks handle concurrency. Many modern frameworks have embraced virtual threads to improve performance, scalability, and resource efficiency.

In this chapter, we will explore how leading frameworks, such as Spring Boot, Quarkus, and Jakarta EE, are integrating virtual threads. However, we will not go into the inner workings of these frameworks, as I assume those interested would prefer to explore each one in depth on their own.

Let's begin.

Spring Boot

Spring Boot (*https://oreil.ly/JE9kr*) is one of the de facto frameworks for building enterprise applications in the Java ecosystem.

Historically, Spring Boot web applications have primarily followed a *thread-per-request* model, where a dedicated platform thread handles each incoming client request. While this approach works well under moderate loads, it encounters scalability challenges when dealing with a high volume of concurrent I/O-bound requests, as these requests are always served through platform threads.

To mitigate this, Spring Boot introduced asynchronous programming capabilities with annotations like @Async (*https://oreil.ly/_7x7K*) and abstractions such as

TaskExecutor (*https://oreil.ly/Hkgxi*). However, this approach still relied on limited pools of platform threads, as shown in the following example:

```
@Configuration
public class ThreadPoolConfig {
    @Bean
    public AsyncTaskExecutor applicationTaskExecutor() {

        ThreadPoolTaskExecutor executor = new ThreadPoolTaskExecutor();
        executor.setCorePoolSize(10);
        executor.setMaxPoolSize(100);
        executor.initialize();
        return executor;
    }
}
```

Here, every request or task consumes a thread from a finite pool, potentially leading to performance bottlenecks under heavy loads.

With the release of Spring Boot 3.2, built upon Spring Framework 6.1, in November 2023, official support for Java 21, which finalized virtual threads, was introduced. While Java 17 remains the baseline JDK, Java 21 is now treated as a first-class runtime environment within the framework. A significant aspect of this support is the provision of a simple configuration property to enable virtual threads:

```
# application.properties
spring.threads.virtual.enabled=true .
```

Or in YAML format:

```
# application.yml
spring:
  threads:
    virtual:
      enabled: true
```

Setting this configuration property enables virtual threads throughout the application. Spring Boot automatically configures an `AsyncTaskExecutor` (*https://oreil.ly/8F5jm*) backed by virtual threads (via a `SimpleAsyncTaskExecutor` (*https://oreil.ly/h95RG*)) when no custom executor bean is defined. This configuration applies seamlessly across several concurrency-related features, such as:

- Asynchronous task execution (`@EnableAsync` (*https://oreil.ly/ASk3i*))
- Asynchronous handling of `Callable` (*https://oreil.ly/k5KXf*) return values in Spring
- Spring Web MVC's asynchronous request processing
- Spring WebFlux's support for occasional blocking execution

Let's look at the following example:

```java
import org.slf4j.Logger;
import org.slf4j.LoggerFactory;
import org.springframework.web.bind.annotation.GetMapping;
import org.springframework.web.bind.annotation.RestController;

@RestController
public class GreetingsController {
    private static final Logger LOGGER
            = LoggerFactory.getLogger(GreetingsController.class.getName());

    @GetMapping("/hello")
    public String hello() {
        LOGGER.info("Received request for /hello");
        LOGGER.info("Running on {}", Thread.currentThread());
        return "Hello from Spring Boot";
    }
}
```

While virtual threads are enabled, if we run the Spring Boot application and then send a curl request to the endpoint, we will see the following log in the console:

```
06:11:51.355 [tomcat-handler-0] INFO  c.b.m.c.c.GreetingsController - Received request for /hello
06:11:51.356 [tomcat-handler-0] INFO  c.b.m.c.c.GreetingsController - Running on VirtualThread[#63,tomcat-handler-0]/runnable@ForkJoinPool-1-worker-1
```

Consider a controller method that handles asynchronous requests:

```java
import org.slf4j.Logger;
import org.springframework.web.bind.annotation.GetMapping;
import org.springframework.web.bind.annotation.RestController;
import java.util.concurrent.Callable;

@RestController
public class AsyncController {
    private static final Logger LOGGER
            = LoggerFactory.getLogger(AsyncController.class.getName());
    @GetMapping("/async-call")
    public Callable<String> handleAsyncRequest() {
        return () -> {
            Thread.sleep(500); // Simulate an I/O-bound operation
            LOGGER.info("Running on {}", Thread.currentThread());
            return "Hello from Virtual Thread!";
        };
    }
}
```

If you enable virtual threads, you will see output like this:

```
06:55:01.784 [task-1] INFO  c.b.m.c.controller.AsyncController - Running on VirtualThread[#74,task-1]/runnable@ForkJoinPool-1-worker-1
```

Now, let's explore another practical scenario involving scheduled tasks:

```
import org.slf4j.Logger;
import org.slf4j.LoggerFactory;
import org.springframework.scheduling.annotation.EnableScheduling;
import org.springframework.scheduling.annotation.Scheduled;
import org.springframework.stereotype.Component;

@EnableScheduling
@Component
public class ScheduledTasks {
    private static final Logger LOGGER
            = LoggerFactory.getLogger(ScheduledTasks.class.getName());
    @Scheduled(fixedRate = 1000)
    public void scheduledTask() {
        LOGGER.info("Scheduled task running on:  {}", Thread.currentThread());
    }
}
```

With virtual threads enabled, your scheduled task logs will resemble this:

```
07:01:51.082 [scheduling-36] INFO  c.b.m.c.controller.ScheduledTasks - Scheduled
task running on:  VirtualThread[#105,scheduling-36]/runnable@ForkJoinPool-1-worke
r-5
```

Spring Boot conveniently auto-configures executors and schedulers for task execution. When virtual threads are enabled, it automatically uses `SimpleAsyncTaskExecutor` (*https://oreil.ly/ODEKW*) (named `applicationTaskExecutor`) and `SimpleAsyncTaskScheduler` (*https://oreil.ly/nOpwy*) (named `taskScheduler`). Without virtual threads, it defaults to a `ThreadPoolTaskExecutor` (*https://oreil.ly/rs8sF*) and `ThreadPoolTaskScheduler` (*https://oreil.ly/w769a*) with configurable settings. You can easily customize these defaults or create custom executors and schedulers using Spring Boot's provided builder classes. This seamless configuration helps simplify concurrency management and optimize performance in your applications.

Manual Configuration

If we're using an earlier version of Spring Boot (pre 3.2) or prefer more control over our executor configuration, we can explicitly define a virtual-thread-backed executor.

Let's consider how this customization (`applicationTaskExecutor`) works in practice:

```
import org.springframework.context.annotation.Bean;
import org.springframework.context.annotation.Configuration;
import org.springframework.core.task.AsyncTaskExecutor;
import org.springframework.core.task.support.TaskExecutorAdapter;
import java.util.concurrent.Executors;
```

```
@Configuration
public class VirtualThreadConfig {
  @Bean
  public AsyncTaskExecutor applicationTaskExecutor() {
    return new TaskExecutorAdapter(Executors.newVirtualThreadPerTaskExecutor());
  }
}
```

With this configuration, any use of `@Async` methods in your application will automatically run on virtual threads instead of traditional platform threads, as illustrated here:

```
import org.springframework.scheduling.annotation.Async;
import org.springframework.stereotype.Component;
import java.util.concurrent.CompletableFuture;

@Component
public class RemoteApiService {
  @Async
  public CompletableFuture<String> fetchDataFromRemoteApi() {
    try {
        Thread.sleep(1000); // Simulating an I/O-bound operation
    } catch (InterruptedException e) {
        Thread.currentThread().interrupt();
    }
    return CompletableFuture
        .completedFuture("Data fetched using virtual thread");
  }
}
```

In Spring's asynchronous programming model, methods annotated with `@Async` rely on the configured `applicationTaskExecutor`. If we replace the default executor with a virtual-thread-based executor, our `@Async` methods seamlessly run on lightweight virtual threads.

When configuring a virtual thread executor manually in Spring Boot, it's important to understand the distinction between using `TaskExecutorAdapter` and `Executors.newVirtualThreadPerTaskExecutor()`. While both enable virtual threads, `TaskExecutorAdapter` provides better integration with Spring's lifecycle management for beans. Consider Spring's management capabilities (e.g., initialization, shutdown) when choosing the appropriate approach.

Additionally, you can leverage virtual threads for your embedded web server to enhance scalability and resource utilization. For example, if you're using Apache Tomcat as your embedded web server, you can customize its protocol handler to utilize virtual threads by defining a `TomcatProtocolHandlerCustomizer` (*https://oreil.ly/mDDIk*) bean:

```
import org.springframework.boot.web.embedded.tomcat
    .TomcatProtocolHandlerCustomizer;
import org.springframework.context.annotation.Bean;
import org.springframework.context.annotation.Configuration;

import java.util.concurrent.Executors;

@Configuration
public class TomcatConfig {

  @Bean
  public TomcatProtocolHandlerCustomizer<?> virtualThreadExecutor() {
    return protocolHandler
        -> protocolHandler.setExecutor(
            Executors.newVirtualThreadPerTaskExecutor());
  }
}
```

Quarkus

Quarkus (*https://quarkus.io*) is a modern Java framework designed to emphasize developer productivity, rapid startup times, and efficient performance. It is ideal for building microservices and serverless applications. Built on Vert.x (*https://vertx.io*) with a reactive programming paradigm, Quarkus has deliberately and explicitly integrated support for virtual threads, enhancing its suitability for concurrent applications.

Unlike a global approach, Quarkus introduces a targeted way to adopt virtual threads through specific annotations. Developers can selectively enable virtual threads on specific endpoints or services by annotating methods with `@RunOnVirtualThread` (*https://oreil.ly/p2aCw*). This annotation instructs Quarkus to execute the annotated method on a virtual thread instead of a traditional platform thread. The framework efficiently handles the lifecycle of these virtual threads, including creation, execution, and lifecycle management.

Quarkus integrates virtual threads mainly through its reactive extensions, combining reactive programming with virtual threading. This approach helps Quarkus applications efficiently handle concurrency, making them particularly suitable for microservices and serverless environments, thanks to their quick startup and efficient resource use.

Quarkus leverages Vert.x as its underlying reactive engine. Vert.x's event-loop concurrency model is different from the traditional thread-per-request model. Quarkus's @RunOnVirtualThread annotation allows developers to offload specific tasks from the Vert.x event loop to virtual threads, preventing blocking operations from impacting the event loop's responsiveness. This combination of reactive programming and virtual threads enhances Quarkus's ability to efficiently handle concurrency.

Here's a practical example of how virtual threads are utilized in Quarkus:

```
package ca.bazlur;
import io.smallrye.common.annotation.RunOnVirtualThread;
import jakarta.inject.Inject;
import jakarta.ws.rs.GET;
import jakarta.ws.rs.Path;
import jakarta.ws.rs.Produces;
import jakarta.ws.rs.core.MediaType;
import org.eclipse.microprofile.rest.client.inject.RestClient;
import org.slf4j.Logger;
import org.slf4j.LoggerFactory;

@Path("/greetings")
public class VirtualThreadApp {
    private static final Logger logger
            = LoggerFactory.getLogger(VirtualThreadApp.class);
    @Inject
    @RestClient
    RemoteService remoteService;

    @GET
    @RunOnVirtualThread
    @Produces(MediaType.TEXT_PLAIN)
    public String process() {
        logger.info("Received greetings request");
        var response = remoteService.greetings();
        logger.info("Received response: {}", response);
        logger.info("Running on {}", Thread.currentThread());
        return response.toUpperCase();
    }
}
```

The `process()` method, annotated with `@RunOnVirtualThread`, will be executed on a virtual thread.

If we run the code, we will get the following log in the console:

```
2025-03-16 00:12:31,453 INFO  [ca.baz.VirtualThreadApp] (quarkus-virtual-thread-1) Received greetings request
2025-03-16 00:12:31,458 INFO  [ca.baz.VirtualThreadApp] (quarkus-virtual-thread-1) Received response: Hey!
```

```
2025-03-16 00:12:31,458 INFO  [ca.baz.VirtualThreadApp] (quarkus-virtual-thread-
1) Running on VirtualThread[#219,quarkus-virtual-thread-1]/runnable@ForkJoinPool
-1-worker-2
```

This log demonstrates that the `process` method is indeed running on virtual threads.

To enable this remote service, we have created an interface as follows:

```
import jakarta.ws.rs.GET;
import jakarta.ws.rs.Path;
import jakarta.ws.rs.Produces;
import jakarta.ws.rs.core.MediaType;
import org.eclipse.microprofile.rest.client.inject.RegisterRestClient;

@Path("/remote")
@RegisterRestClient
public interface RemoteService {
    @Path("greetings")
    @GET
    @Produces(MediaType.TEXT_PLAIN)
    String greetings();
}
```

To register this, we need the following item in the *application.properties* file:

```
quarkus.rest-client."ca.bazlur.RemoteService".url=http://localhost:8081
```

We have just created a simple REST endpoint for external services that serves random greeting messages. We can easily create this REST endpoint by using Java's built-in HTTP server capabilities. The JDK includes classes such as `HttpServer` (*https://oreil.ly/fd9lJ*) and `HttpHandler` (*https://oreil.ly/wphhE*), which allow us to quickly set up lightweight HTTP services without additional frameworks or dependencies:

```
import com.sun.net.httpserver.HttpServer;
import com.sun.net.httpserver.HttpHandler;
import com.sun.net.httpserver.HttpExchange;
import java.io.IOException;
import java.io.OutputStream;
import java.net.InetSocketAddress;
import java.util.Random;
import java.util.concurrent.Executors;

public class SimpleHttpServer {
    private static final String[] GREETINGS = {
            "Hello, world!",
            "Hi there!",
            "Greetings!",
            "Good day!",
            "Hey!",
            "Howdy!",
            "Hola!",
            "Bonjour!",
            "Ciao!"
```

```java
    };

    public static void main(String[] args) throws IOException {
        int port = 8081;
        HttpServer server = HttpServer.create(new InetSocketAddress(port), 0);
        server.createContext("/remote/greetings", new GreetingHandler());
        server.setExecutor(Executors.newVirtualThreadPerTaskExecutor());
        System.out.println("Server started on port " + port);
        server.start();
    }

    static class GreetingHandler implements HttpHandler {
        @Override
        public void handle(HttpExchange exchange) throws IOException {
            if ("GET".equalsIgnoreCase(exchange.getRequestMethod())) {
                String response = getRandomGreeting();
                exchange.sendResponseHeaders(200, response.length());
                try (OutputStream os = exchange.getResponseBody()) {
                    os.write(response.getBytes());
                }
            } else {
                exchange.sendResponseHeaders(405, -1); // Method Not Allowed
            }
        }

        private String getRandomGreeting() {
            Random random = new Random();
            return GREETINGS[random.nextInt(GREETINGS.length)];
        }
    }
}
```

We can directly run this server using Java's source-file launching feature, available from Java 11 onward. This allows us to execute single-file Java programs without explicit compilation steps. Simply open your terminal and run the command:

java SimpleHttpServer.java

This command compiles and runs the file in one step, eliminating the need for manually using `javac`. It's ideal for quickly prototyping or running simple standalone Java applications.

We can even integrate Quarkus's reactive programming capabilities with virtual threads. Let's look at the following code:

```java
import jakarta.inject.Inject;
import jakarta.ws.rs.GET;
import jakarta.ws.rs.Path;
import jakarta.ws.rs.Produces;
import jakarta.ws.rs.core.MediaType;
import org.eclipse.microprofile.rest.client.inject.RestClient;
```

```
import io.smallrye.common.annotation.RunOnVirtualThread;
import io.smallrye.mutiny.Uni;
import java.time.Duration;
import jakarta.enterprise.context.ApplicationScoped;

@Path("/reactive")
public class ReactiveResource {
   @Inject
   HelloService helloService;
   @GET
   @Path("/hello")
   @RunOnVirtualThread
   @Produces(MediaType.TEXT_PLAIN)
   public String hello() {
       return helloService.getHello()
               .await()
               .atMost(Duration.ofSeconds(5));
   }
}

@ApplicationScoped
class HelloService {
   @Inject
   @RestClient
   ExternalService externalService;
   Uni<String> getHello() {
       return externalService.hello();
   }
}

@Path("/reactive")
@RegisterRestClient
interface ExternalService {
   @GET
   @Path("/hello")
   Uni<String> hello();
}
```

The `hello()` method in `ReactiveResource` calls an external service using a reactive REST client (`ExternalService`). The `getHello()` method returns a `Uni<String>`, which represents a deferred computation. Within the `hello()` method, `uni.await().atMost(Duration.ofSeconds(5))` is used to block the virtual thread until the result is available or a timeout occurs.

Jakarta EE

Jakarta Concurrency (*https://oreil.ly/JbYoV*) is a standard specification that enables applications to utilize concurrency while maintaining the benefits of running within a Jakarta EE (*https://jakarta.ee*) runtime. The release of Jakarta Concurrency 3.1

(*https://oreil.ly/ffFz_*) introduced support for virtual threads, allowing applications to leverage Java 21's lightweight threading model.

Virtual threads can be enabled in Jakarta Concurrency 3.1 by specifying `virtual = true` in these annotations:

- `@ManagedExecutorDefinition` (*https://oreil.ly/-ip4E*)
- `@ManagedScheduledExecutorDefinition` (*https://oreil.ly/-TVMe*)
- `@ManagedThreadFactory` (*https://oreil.ly/5nQS-*)

When running on Java 21, virtual threads are used; however, if the application runs on Java 17, which doesn't support virtual threads, Jakarta EE runtimes automatically fall back to using platform threads.

The following example demonstrates how to configure and use virtual threads in Jakarta Concurrency 3.1:

```java
import jakarta.enterprise.concurrent.ManagedExecutorDefinition;
import jakarta.enterprise.concurrent.ManagedExecutorService;
import jakarta.inject.Inject;
import jakarta.ws.rs.GET;
import jakarta.ws.rs.Path;
import jakarta.ws.rs.Produces;
import jakarta.ws.rs.core.MediaType;

import java.util.concurrent.ExecutionException;

@ManagedExecutorDefinition(name = "java:module/concurrent/virtual-executor",
    qualifiers = WithVirtualThreads.class,
    virtual = true)
@Path("/virtualThreads")
public class VirtualThreadExampleService {

  @Inject
  @WithVirtualThreads
  ManagedExecutorService virtualManagedExecutor;

  @Inject
  GreetingService greetingService;

  @GET
  @Produces(MediaType.TEXT_PLAIN)
  public String virtualThreads()
        throws InterruptedException, ExecutionException {
    return virtualManagedExecutor.submit(() -> {
        System.out.println("Received request on virtual thread: "
            + Thread.currentThread());
        return greetingService.getRandomGreeting();
    }).get();
  }
}
```

Now, if we run the preceding code using the Open Liberty runtime we will hit the following endpoint:

```
GET http://localhost:9080/api/virtualThreads
```

You will see the part that executes to get the random greetings; it will be on the virtual threads:

```
[INFO] Received request on virtual thread: VirtualThread[#115,application[jakarta
ee-vthrads]/module[jakartaee-vthrads.war]/managedExecutorService[java:module/conc
urrent/virtual-executor]/concurrencyPolicy:1]/runnable@ForkJoinPool-1-worker-1
```

Similarly, if we want to run virtual threads on a `ManagedScheduledExecutorService` that allows periodic or delayed task execution, we would do the following:

```java
import jakarta.annotation.Resource;
import jakarta.enterprise.context.ApplicationScoped;
import jakarta.enterprise.concurrent.ManagedScheduledExecutorService;
import jakarta.enterprise.concurrent.ManagedScheduledExecutorDefinition;

import java.util.concurrent.TimeUnit;

@ApplicationScoped
@ManagedScheduledExecutorDefinition(
    name = "java:module/concurrent/virtual-scheduler",
    virtual = true // Enables Virtual Threads for Scheduled Tasks
)
public class VirtualThreadSchedulerExample {

  @Resource(lookup = "java:module/concurrent/virtual-scheduler")
  private ManagedScheduledExecutorService scheduledExecutor;

  public void scheduleTask() {
    scheduledExecutor.schedule(() -> {
      System.out.println("Scheduled task running in virtual thread: "
          + Thread.currentThread());
    }, 5, TimeUnit.SECONDS); // Delay execution by 5 seconds
  }
}
```

While Jakarta Concurrency 3.1 provides the specifications for using virtual threads, the actual behavior can vary between Jakarta EE runtimes. You should be aware of potential compatibility issues and read the documentation of their specific Jakarta EE runtime (e.g., Open Liberty, Payara, WildFly) for implementation-specific details and best practices. For example, features and configurations might behave differently or might not be present in all Jakarta EE runtimes.

As of the writing of this book, Open Liberty 24.0.0.6-beta is the first Jakarta EE runtime to fully support Jakarta Concurrency 3.1 with virtual threads. However, as Jakarta EE 11 approaches its final release, other Jakarta EE runtimes, such as Payara, WildFly, TomEE, and GlassFish, are expected to incorporate virtual thread support.

In Closing

Besides the major frameworks like Jakarta EE, Spring, and Quarkus, several other frameworks have also embraced virtual threads to enhance concurrency efficiency in modern Java applications.

One such framework is Helidon Níma (*https://helidon.io/nima*), a microservice framework designed from the ground up to leverage virtual threads natively. Unlike traditional frameworks that retrofit virtual thread support, Helidon Níma is built around virtual threads, making it a lightweight and high-performance solution for microservices.

Similarly, the Micronaut (*https://micronaut.io*) framework automatically utilizes virtual threads if the application runs on a JDK version that supports virtual threads (Java 21 or later). This means developers using Micronaut can transparently benefit from the performance improvements of virtual threads without additional configuration.

As Java continues to evolve, virtual threads have become a key feature for building scalable, efficient, and developer-friendly applications. Whether using Jakarta EE 11, Quarkus, Spring Boot 3, Helidon Níma, or Micronaut, developers now have powerful tools to write highly concurrent applications while maintaining a simple, imperative coding style.

With virtual threads now an integral part of the Java ecosystem, the future of Java concurrency looks more efficient, scalable, and developer-friendly than ever before.

CHAPTER 8
Conclusion and Takeaways

Simplicity is the ultimate sophistication.
—Leonardo da Vinci

We've traveled far together in the concurrency world of Java, from the foundational understanding of classic threads to the exciting innovations of virtual threads, structured concurrency, and beyond. But our adventure has not only been technical, it's also been philosophical. Java continues to evolve, shaped by such values as efficiency, scalability, and simplicity, to meet the ever-changing demands of modern computing.

One of the significant milestones we've discussed is virtual threads, a true paradigm shift in Java concurrency. Historically, creating numerous threads was challenging due to the high resource overhead and constraints imposed by the operating system. Virtual threads address this issue by reducing resource consumption by orders of magnitude and practically offering millions of virtual threads. With computing hardware changing and cloud computing becoming more prevalent, virtual threads will be the go-to approach for scalable Java applications. Their convenience and simplicity enable developers to write clearer, easier-to-maintain asynchronous code, boosting productivity and software maintainability.

Of course, even though adding virtual threads is very easy, it's not something we should do overnight, especially for legacy applications, as it requires planning and gradual implementation. I recommend starting by migrating standalone pieces or services to your existing applications. Incremental deployment allows you to observe, learn, and improve your methods without slowing down your team or system. The introduction of structured concurrency will further clarify complex workflows, making concurrent code safer and easier to read. This reassures you that your code will be more manageable and less prone to errors. Monitor resource usage during initial deployments; discovering bottlenecks early on avoids the most frequent errors. And remember, investing in educating your development team on virtual threads, structured concurrency, and scoped values builds a best-practices culture and continuous improvement.

We should be especially careful about the tricky issue of thread pinning, situations where virtual threads involuntarily bind to specific platform threads for an extended duration, significantly reducing their benefits. Although JDK 24 solves pinning problems related to synchronized blocks, it's necessary to note that not every production system will immediately switch from previous versions, such as JDK 21, to JDK 24. Another likely trap is the mismanagement of `ThreadLocal` variables, which may result in subtle bugs and memory leaks in the context of virtual threads. It's essential to understand the difference between virtual threads and platform threads, especially in blocking I/O operations, since traditional blocking calls won't behave as expected. Traditional monitoring tools might also be insufficient for tracing virtual-thread-specific issues. Adopt more sophisticated monitoring techniques and leverage modern tooling such as the Java Flight Recorder.

Despite the challenges, software developers successfully integrating virtual threads report tangible advantages. They're experiencing meaningful improvements in app scalability, low latency, and better resource utilization. Various articles and reports have cited improved responsiveness, simplified concurrency control, and reduced development cycles observed by enterprises, startups, and cloud providers.

With these improvements, choosing the appropriate concurrency model based on the specific requirements of your application is essential. Virtual threads shine in high-throughput, I/O-intensive applications such as web servers, data processing subsystems, or network services where scalability and convenience are essential without the overhead of context switches for traditional threads. Platform threads remain valuable, especially for CPU-bound computations, native method interoperations, or legacy code where widespread pinning is unavoidable. Reactive programming has advantages in those scenarios where explicit asynchronous programming patterns, effective backpressure management, or event-driven architecture are necessary. Understanding these distinctions allows you to make choices that are suited to the demands of your project.

As we conclude this journey, my advice remains simple: stay curious, experiment boldly, and keep learning. Java's concurrency model evolves best through community feedback, practical experience, and continuous improvement. Engage proactively with these new technologies, share your experiences, and join the active Java community. Regularly keep an eye on OpenJDK (*https://openjdk.org*) to stay informed about innovations, improvements, and ongoing efforts to address remaining concurrency challenges. Your experiences and contributions will shape the future of Java concurrency. This continuous learning will keep you motivated and engaged in the ever-evolving world of Java.

Thank you for sharing this journey with me. May your threads always be lightweight, your applications infinitely scalable, and your code clear, concise, and elegant.

Index

A
access control with semaphores, 54-59
adaptive completion, 192-195
allSuccessfulOrThrow() policy, 140, 150-154, 176
allUntil() policy, 140, 163-165
anySuccessfulResultOrThrow() policy, 140, 146-150
asynchronous APIs, 276-278
asynchronous operations, simplifying with virtual threads, 47-50
asynchronous programming
    with CompletableFuture, 23-25
    with reactive programming, 25-28
    threads (see threads)
AtomicReference data structure, 14
awaitAll() policy, 140, 154-163, 177
awaitAllSuccessfulOrThrow() policy, 140, 141-146

B
backpressure, 286-292
benchmarking, 17
blocked threads, 11-12
blocking operations
    non-blocking I/O versus, 249-272
    single-thread blocking behavior, 249-255
    virtual threads and, 29, 46
buffers, 259

C
cache affinity, 21
CachedThreadPool, 99
Callable interface, 101-102
callbacks, 277-278
carrier threads, 33, 46
CAS (compare-and-swap) technique, 110-112
classical threads (see platform threads)
close() method, in structured concurrency, 134
compare-and-swap (CAS) technique, 110-112
CompletableFuture class, 23-25, 278
completing subtasks, 139
concurrency
    challenges of unstructured, 126-132
    history in Java, 1-2
    parallelism versus, 3
    structured (see structured concurrency)
conditional joiners, 199-202
Configuration interface, in structured concurrency, 179-185
    combining options, 183-185
    named threads in, 180
    timeouts in, 181-183
contentions, 108
context switching, 10
continuations, 113-123
    building virtual threads, 117-121
    implementation example, 114-117
coupling, 220
custom exception types, defining in structured concurrency, 171
custom joiners, 185-202
    adaptive completion, 192-195
    collect all results and exceptions, 186-188
    conditional, 199-202
    quorum-based completion, 189-192
    rate-limited, 196-198

313

D

deadlocks, avoiding, 103-108
debugger, threads and, 5
dynamic scope, 230

E

enabling
    ScopedValue interface, 226
    structured concurrency, 136
event buses, 275
event-driven architecture, 272-276
events, in reactive programming, 279
exception handling, in structured concurrency, 166-179
    exception propagation, 172-174
    general exception types, 177-179
    joining policies and, 176-177
    pattern matching, 168-172
    in subtasks, 174-176
    try-catch blocks, 166-167
exception propagation, in structured concurrency, 172-174
exceptions, threads and, 4-5
Executor framework
    challenges of, 19-20
    configuring thread pools, 96-99
    managing thread lifecycle, 18-19
    starting threads, 8
    types of thread pools, 99-101

F

fail-fast scopes, 50
FFM (Foreign Function & Memory) API, 69
FixedThreadPool, 99
Foreign Function & Memory (FFM) API, 69
fork() method, structured concurrency, 138
forking subtasks, 138
ForkJoinPool, 21-23, 101, 103-113
    cache affinity, 21
    deadlocks, avoiding, 103-108
    for virtual threads, 108-113
    work-stealing algorithm, 21
Future interface, 102

H

happens-before relationships, 202-205
Helidon Níma, 309
high-scale application efficiency, 11-20

HotSpotDiagnosticsMXBean, 86, 213

I

I/O (input/output)
    blocking versus non-blocking, 249-272
    in event-driven architecture, 272-276
    NIO (New Input/Output) versus, 257
    polling and virtual threads, 122
    simulating, 119-120
inefficiency, in threads, 11-12
installing JDK 21, 34-35
interruption of threads, 37-38

J

Jakarta Concurrency 3.1, 306-309
Jakarta EE, 306-309
Java 1.0 threads, 6-8
Java Flight Recorder (JFR), 77-81
Java Streams, 286
jcmd utility, 81-82, 209-212
JDK 21, installing, 34-35
JEP 491, 70
JFR (Java Flight Recorder), 77-81
join() method, in structured concurrency, 134
Joiner interface, 139
    allSuccessfulOrThrow() policy, 150-154
    allUntil() policy, 163-165
    anySuccessfulResultOrThrow() policy, 146-150
    awaitAll() policy, 154-163
    awaitAllSuccessfulOrThrow() policy, 141-146
    list of policies, 140
joining policies
    allSuccessfulOrThrow(), 150-154
    allUntil(), 163-165
    anySuccessfulResultOrThrow(), 146-150
    awaitAll(), 154-163
    awaitAllSuccessfulOrThrow(), 141-146
    custom joiners, 185-202
        adaptive completion, 192-195
        collect all results and exceptions, 186-188
        conditional, 199-202
        quorum-based completion, 189-192
        rate-limited, 196-198
    exception handling and, 176-177
    Joiner interface, 139
    list of, 140

JVM flag, 76-77

K
kernel threads, 32

L
lazy copying, 116
lexical scope, 230
lightweight threads (see virtual threads)
Little's Law, 9, 42-46

M
main thread, 3
maximum number of threads, 10
memory consistency, in structured concurrency, 202-205
memory footprint of threads, 10
memory management
    virtual memory systems, 47
    in virtual threads, 46
Micronaut, 309
migrating to scoped values, 237-245
migration tips for virtual threads, 86-87
modifying selection keys, 267
module import declarations, 159
monitoring
    pinning, 76-81
    ThreadLocal variables, 75-76

N
named threads, in structured concurrency, 180
NanoThread class, 117-118
NanoThreadScheduler class, 119
native method invocations, pinning and, 68-70
native threads (see platform threads)
nested scopes, 205-209, 233-234
NIO (New Input/Output), 257-270
non-blocking I/O (input/output)
    blocking I/O versus, 249-272
    in event-driven architecture, 272-276

O
open() method, in structured concurrency, 134
OS threads (see platform threads)

P
parallelism

concurrency versus, 3
    thread execution, 13-18
parameter passing problem, 217-220
park/unpark mechanism, 66
passing context
    difficulties of, 217-220
    with ThreadLocal variables, 220-225
pattern matching, in structured concurrency, 168-172
performance
    contentions and, 108
    ScopedValue interface, 236
pinning, 61-71
    avoiding with ReentrantLock, 64-67
    monitoring, 76-81
    native method invocations and, 68-70
platform threads, 29
    defined, 32
    structured concurrency with, 214
    virtual threads versus, 31, 33-34
pollers, 122
processors, 280
profiler, threads and, 6
Project Loom (see virtual threads)
Project Reactor, 280
propagating exceptions, in structured concurrency, 172-174
publishers, 280

Q
Quarkus, 302-306
quorum-based completion, 189-192

R
rate limiting, 51-61
rate-limited joiners, 196-198
reactive programming, 25-28
    asynchronous APIs, 276-278
    backpressure, 286-292
    benefits of, 292
    blocking versus non-blocking I/O, 249-272
    challenges of, 293-294
    components of, 280
    data flow in, 279
    definition of, 248
    event-driven architecture, 272-276
    Java libraries in, 280
    reactive streams, 279-286
reactive streams, 279-286

backpressure example, 286-288
Java Streams versus, 286
signals emitted, 280
virtual threads versus, 288-292
read pollers, 122
rebinding ScopedValue interface in nested scopes, 233-234
ReentrantLock, 64-67
request/response lifecycle, 9
resilient concurrent servers, 160-163
running ScopedValue interface, 228-233
RxJava, 280

S

scalability of virtual threads, 40-46, 88
ScheduledThreadPoolExecutor, 100
scheduling virtual threads, 31-32
scoped values, migrating to, 237-245
(see also ScopedValue interface)
ScopedValue interface, 225-245
characteristics of, 226
enabling, 226
migrating to scoped values, 237-245
performance, 236
rebinding in nested scopes, 233-234
running, 228-233
structured concurrency and, 235-235
usability benefits of, 236
scopes
lexical versus dynamic, 230
nested, 205-209, 233-234
relationship with subtasks, 138-139
selection keys, modifying, 267
semaphores
access control with, 54-59
limitations of, 60
usage scenarios, 59-60
servlet containers, 9
sharing data
difficulties of, 217-220
with ThreadLocal variables, 220-225
signals from reactive streams, 280
single-thread blocking behavior, 249-255
SingleThreadExecutor, 100
Spring Boot, 297-302
stack frames, 46
starting threads, 8
structured concurrency, 50-51
benefits of, 132-133

Configuration interface, 179-185
combining options, 183-185
named threads in, 180
timeouts in, 181-183
enabling, 136
exception handling, 166-179
exception propagation, 172-174
general exception types, 177-179
joining policies and, 176-177
with pattern matching, 168-172
in subtasks, 174-176
in try-catch blocks, 166-167
joining policies
allSuccessfulOrThrow(), 150-154
allUntil(), 163-165
anySuccessfulResultOrThrow(), 146-150
awaitAll(), 154-163
awaitAllSuccessfulOrThrow(), 141-146
custom joiners, 185-202
Joiner interface, 139
list of, 140
memory consistency in, 202-205
nested scopes in, 205-209
with platform threads, 214
scope and subtask relationship, 138-139
ScopedValue interface and, 235-235
StructuredTaskScope interface, 133-137
thread dumps in, 209-213
structured thread dumps, 209-213
StructuredTaskScope interface, 133-137
(see also structured concurrency)
subscribers, 280
subscriptions, 280
subtasks
completing, 139
exception handling in, 174-176
forking, 138
relationship with scopes, 138-139
synchronous APIs, 276

T

task distribution, cache affinity and, 21
Thread API, changes for virtual threads, 37-40
thread dumps, 81-86, 209-213
thread groups, virtual threads in, 39
thread pools
benefits of, 92, 255-257
building, 92-96
Callable interface, 101-102

configuring in Executor framework, 96-99
definition of, 91
ForkJoinPool, 103-113
Future interface, 102
types of, 99-101
thread-per-request model, 9
ThreadLocal variables, 220-225
    limitations of, 222-225
    monitoring, 75-76
    ScopedValue usability benefits over, 236-237
    virtual threads and, 71, 225
threads
    blocked, 11-12
    carrier, 33, 46
    costs of, 9-11
    debugger and, 5
    exceptions and, 4-5
    Executor framework, 18-20
    ForkJoinPool, 21-23
    high-scale application efficiency, 11-20
    history of Java concurrency, 1-2
    importance in Java, 2-4
    interrupting, 37-38
    in Java 1.0, 6-8
    kernel, 32
    maximum number of, 10
    memory footprint of, 10
    named, 180
    parallel execution strategy, 13-18
    platform (classical), 29
    profiler and, 6
    starting, 8
    virtual (see virtual threads)
throughput, 10, 41
tight coupling, 220
timeouts, in structured concurrency, 181-183
traditional threads (see platform threads)
try-catch blocks, 166-167
type inference, 152

U

unstructured concurrency, challenges of, 126-132
user-mode threads (see virtual threads)

V

var keyword, 152
Vert.x, 272-276, 303
viewing virtual threads in thread dumps, 81-86
virtual memory systems, 47
virtual threads
    asynchronous operations, simplifying, 47-50
    author recommendations, 311-312
    benefits of, 30, 87-89
    blocking operations, 46
    building with continuations, 117-121
    characteristics of, 28-29
    creating, 36-37
    defined, 33
    environment setup, 34-35
    ForkJoinPool for, 108-113
    I/O polling, 122
    in Jakarta EE, 306-309
    memory management, 46
    migration tips, 86-87
    pinning, 61-71, 76-81
    platform threads versus, 31, 33-34
    in Quarkus, 302-306
    rate limiting, 51-61
    reactive streams versus, 288-292
    scalability, 40-46, 88
    scheduling, 31-32
    in Spring Boot, 297-302
    structured concurrency, 50-51
    Thread API changes, 37-40
    in thread groups, 39
    ThreadLocal variables and, 71, 225
    throughput, 41
    viewing in thread dumps, 81-86
    virtual memory systems, comparison with, 47

W

work-stealing algorithm, 21, 109
WorkStealingPool, 100

Z

zero-copy mechanisms, 259

About the Author

A N M Bazlur Rahman is a Java champion and software engineer with over a decade of specialized experience in Java and related technologies. An active speaker at various international conferences and Java user groups, his talks have often focused on specialized topics such as concurrency and virtual threads. He is a Java Champion and an editor for Java Queue at InfoQ and Foojay.io. He is the founder and current moderator of the Java User Group in Bangladesh, where he has organized educational meetups and conferences since 2013.

Colophon

The animal on the cover of *Modern Concurrency in Java* is a bumblebee (genus *Bombus*). There are over 250 known species of bumblebees throughout the world. They are found primarily in the northern hemisphere, though some species are also found in South America and parts of Indonesia. They have also been introduced to Tasmania and New Zealand.

Bumblebees vary in appearance from one species to another, but they are generally large and furry, with a broader, more rounded body than honeybees. Many species are striped, usually with black and another color ranging from white to yellow, orange, red, or pink. Like honeybees, bumblebees are eusocial and form colonies with a single queen, though they may have as few as 50 bees in a nest. Many species nest underground, and their nests tend to be less organized than those of honeybees, with clusters of cells rather than hexagonal combs. The largest known bumblebee species is the moscardón (*Bombus dahlbomii*) of South America, with queens reaching up to 40 mm (1.6 in) in length.

Bumblebees are important pollinators, though their populations are in decline in many parts of the world due to habitat destruction, land use change, and pesticide use. Many of the animals on O'Reilly covers are endangered; all of them are important to the world.

The cover illustration is by José Marzan Jr., based on an antique line engraving from *The Animal Kingdom Illustrated*. The series design is by Edie Freedman, Ellie Volckhausen, and Karen Montgomery. The cover fonts are Gilroy Semibold and Guardian Sans. The text font is Adobe Minion Pro; the heading font is Adobe Myriad Condensed; and the code font is Dalton Maag's Ubuntu Mono.

O'REILLY®

Learn from experts. Become one yourself.

60,000+ titles | Live events with experts | Role-based courses
Interactive learning | Certification preparation

 Try the O'Reilly learning platform free for 10 days.

www.ingramcontent.com/pod-product-compliance
Lightning Source LLC
Jackson TN
JSHW062201180925
91290JS00009B/38